The Whole Family Low Cholesterol Cookbook

The Whole Family Low Cholesterol Cookbook

by
Helen Cassidy Page
and
John Speer Schroeder, M.D.

Phyllis Ullman, R.D.
Nutrition Consultant

Drawings by David Toy

GROSSET & DUNLAP
A Filmways Company
Publishers   New York

Copyright © 1976 by Helen Cassidy Page and John Speer Schroeder, M.D.

All rights reserved
Published simultaneously in Canada

Library of Congress catalog card number: 74–27951
ISBN 0-448-11864-5 (hardbound)
ISBN 0-448-12150-6 (paperback)

First printing

Printed in the United States of America

Dedicated to our children
and all children, that they
may live well and long

Allison Page

John Eric Schroeder

Kristen Lee Schroeder

Dirk Gregory Schroeder

Contents

Acknowledgment 9

Preface 11

1 Why Change Your Diet? 14

2 The Four C's of Low Cholesterol Cooking 19

3 Dietary Recommendations by Age 32

4 A Six-Month Plan for Change 37

5 The Three Spoons Signpost 39

6 Breakfast 47

7 Cooking As an Art 53

8 Equipping Your Kitchen 57

9 What Comes First 63

10 Consider Soups 83

11 Fowl Fare 99

12 Fish for Compliments 116

13 Meaty Subject 135

14 From the Garden 156

15 Greenery 240

16 Saucery 263

17 The Finishing Touch 279

18 The Breadbasket 307

Calories/Cholesterol/Saturated Fat Content Chart 320

Index 325

Acknowledgments

SIMPLY TO NAME the many people who contributed to this cookbook would seem inadequate thanks. Yet their suggestions, encouragement, inspiration, and tolerance meant a great deal to us during the writing of this book. Their criticisms and contributions have helped us to keep the prose lively and informative at times when our spirits were flagging. We thank our many friends who may recognize the recipes they contributed, which enrich this book. We are beholden to all our friends, families, neighbors, and to those who passed through the Breezeway Library at Stanford University Medical Center, and to those who happened by Helen Page's kitchen for serving as official tasters for each and every recipe and for their suggestions and comments.

We are indebted to our children and families who endured our long absences while at the typewriter and in the kitchen, and yet continued to cheer us and love us.

We are particularly grateful to everyone in the divisions of Cardiology and Immunology at Stanford for sustaining us with their good humor and good will. Particularly, we would like to thank Dr. Donald C. Harrison, Chief, Division of Cardiology, and Dr. James F. Fries, Assistant Professor, Division of Immunology for their enthusiastic support and tolerant attitude toward our frequent conferences and stolen time.

Phyllis Ullman's contributions as Nutrition Consultant were invaluable and the many hours she spent meticulously calculating each recipe are gratefully acknowledged. She is largely responsible for the chapter on nutrition and her excellent suggestions kept this cookbook pointed in the right direction.

In addition to David Toy's excellent drawings, we are grateful for his suggestions, his infectious enthusiasm, and delightful humor.

We must thank Bonnie Obrig for the final manuscript preparation and her excellent technical skills and sound critiques during its preparation.

Dr. Schroeder would personally like to thank Pamela Lewis not only for her editorial skills in preparation of the manuscript, but for her continuing cheerful support and suggestions. Pamela conceived the idea for the breakfast chapter and contributed greatly to it. Her faith in him helped the book become a reality.

Mrs. Page is indebted to the late Grace Ryan for introducing her to the joys of the kitchen and to her friend Wendy Wood for being her friend and for her confidence and encouragement.

Lastly, we are grateful to all the friends with whom we have shared pleasant and memorable meals over the years. Those times came back to us during the writing of this book in the form of recipes, memories, and pleasant reminiscences; and we have tried to share the spirit of warmth and love exchanged between people as they break bread together.

Preface

THIS COOKBOOK IS for all America. It is not a weight-reduction diet book, nor is it for the cardiac patient who requires stringent dietary limitations. Instead, it reflects current medical opinion about restricting dietary cholesterol and saturated fat for *everyone* in hopes of preventing heart disease. Most importantly, it demonstrates that this can be accomplished by simple changes in the daily diet, rather than by eliminating favorite foods. Thus, it can be used by all — the new bride experimenting in her first kitchen, the bachelor chef, the busy wife and mother, as well as persons concerned about their own health. Both the gourmet chef and the family meal planner will find exciting recipes and menu combinations. And, at the same time, will be learning how to restrict fat and cholesterol on a daily basis.

Dr. John Speer Schroeder is a faculty member at Stanford University School of Medicine, renowned as one of the leading heart centers in the world. In his work as clinical cardiologist, teacher, and researcher it became apparent to him that the efforts of extremely dedicated physicians and medical personnel were hardly denting the awesome mortality from cardiovascular disease in this country. Although research and biotechnology advances have helped, it was obvious that more must be done to combat this disease which claims one-half million Americans every year and that additional effort must be directed toward prevention of coronary atherosclerosis. The first chapter outlines the overwhelming evidence linking the American diet of high cholesterol and saturated fat to this epidemic and what must be changed. This cookbook reflects our efforts to teach everyone how easy it is to restrict these components of their diet.

To attack this epidemic, Dr. Schroeder enlisted Helen Cassidy Page, Director of the Helen Page School of Cooking in Palo Alto, California. Mrs. Page is dedicated to the concept that you cannot have a good life without good food. Her experience in teaching and cooking French and Continental cuisines and her repertoire of hundreds of recipes, both simple and exotic, enabled her to create and adapt recipes consistent with the philosophy of good food and good health.

Professional dietary consultation was provided by Phyllis Ullman, R.D., Senior Dietitian for the Stanford Heart Disease Prevention Program. Her background in dietary prevention of heart disease and practical knowledge of developing restricted fat and cholesterol recipes for patients were ideal for this cookbook.

This unique collaboration of a clinical cardiologist dedicated to prevention of heart disease, a chef dedicated to the creation of exciting menus, and an experienced dietitian in a heart disease prevention program provides the professional expertise for this cookbook. This collaboration has provided a new look at diets, food practices, and concepts about cholesterol and saturated fat and permitted a rational approach to the application of current recommended dietary restrictions for these substances.

To accomplish our goal of providing a restricted saturated fat and cholesterol cookbook, we recognized several objectives. First of all, this eating plan must be adopted by the whole family. Children must learn to choose proper foods as they learn to brush their teeth and ride a bicycle. Since we are creatures of habit, our food preferences are critically determined in childhood and ultimately this is where prevention of heart disease through dietary change must start. We have, therefore, designed our recommendations for all age groups.

Second, established food preferences of adults must be recognized. This is a food plan for life, not a fad to be embraced enthusiastically for a brief time and then discarded. We have designed a six-month transition plan to incorporate these changes into the family's meal plan. It is not our intention to whisk away favorite dishes or to totally eliminate any food. Rather, we wish to gradually replace or restrict high-fat items in your diet such as eggs, whole milk, butter, and cheese and offer alternatives for substitution. In addition, changing methods of food selection and cooking complete the transition to a better diet.

Third, one must be able to select foods and recipes without the confusion of calculating milligrams and grams of cholesterol and saturated fat. We have designed the Three Spoons as an easy signpost indicating the calories, saturated fat (F), and cholesterol (C) for each recipe. The more C's or F's in the recipe, the more cholesterol and saturated fat. The recipes in this book use a wide variety of ingredients and methods. Used in conjunction with the Three Spoons signpost, you will rapidly be familiarized with the foods containing high and low amounts of saturated fat and cholesterol. With regular use, it will provide fat and cholesterol information that can be applied to all cookbooks and to food choices when dining in restaurants.

The calculations for the Three Spoons include all ingredients in the recipe, generally using a standard 3-ounce serving of *cooked* beef, lamb, pork, veal, or poultry. Seafood is calculated at 4 or 5 ounces of cooked fish or shellfish per serving. Recipes for whole chicken or fish or roast meats may provide more servings than indicated depending upon size of the roast. However, the serving size should not be increased. All the recipes are calculated for average or recommended serving size. Remember that larger or more portions will increase the saturated fat and cholesterol level as well as calories. This calculation is somewhat difficult for recipes that make several cups or pieces. In those cases we have given the total amount of the recipe and calculated fat and cholesterol for average serving. For example, Guacamole makes approximately 1 cup, and we calculated an average serving as 3 tablespoons. That would yield approximately 6 servings and the calculation is for 1 serving of 3 tablespoons. Sauces and dips are for 2 tablespoons per person except where the number of servings is explicit. For example, Green Salad with Basil Dressing serves 6 and the calculation is for one-sixth or 1 serving. Roquefort Dressing is calculated for 2 tablespoons per serving. Three cookies constitute a serving and breads are ½- to ¾-inch slices.

Although calculations for polyunsaturated fat and carbohydrates could properly be included in the signpost, we have chosen to exclude them for the purpose of simplicity. We recommend foods high in polyunsaturated fat, but feel it is more important to identify the cholesterol and saturated fat levels and to limit their use.

Lastly, we know that food that does not taste good will not be accepted no matter how healthful it is. With this in mind all of the recipes in this book have been tested and received gold stars from the official tasters. It is our conviction that life is too short not to eat well — and wisely.

1
Why Change Your Diet?

The Problem of Heart Disease

AMERICANS SEEM TO accept premature death from heart attacks without question. In 1971, more than 675,000 persons died from heart attack, of which more than 200,000 were under the age of 65 years. Of a total population of over 300 million, an estimated 3.87 million Americans have a history of heart attack or angina pectoris. There is now reason to think that the underlying process of coronary atherosclerosis which predisposes one to a heart attack may be prevented by changing "risk factors" which are associated with heart disease. These risk factors include: 1) smoking, 2) high blood pressure (hypertension), and 3) elevated blood cholesterol. We will attempt to describe the process or development of atherosclerosis, the relation of risk factors to its development, and how dietary modification may retard or even prevent its development.

What Is Coronary Atherosclerosis?

Our heart is a pump which beats over 100,000 times a day moving over 4,000 gallons of blood with oxygen and food to our body tissues. Since the heart is made up of working muscle, it too needs this oxygen-rich blood to keep it alive and working. The supply channels for this delivery of blood to the heart muscle are called the *coronary arteries.* Blockage of the artery for any cause results in stoppage of blood flow to part of the heart muscle, resulting in a heart attack (myocardial infarction), i.e., death of heart muscle. This stoppage not only causes chest pain commonly associated with the symptoms of a heart attack, but may result in heart failure which occurs when the heart can no longer pump sufficient blood to the rest of the body. Over one-half of heart attack victims die within twenty-four hours of the coronary blockage due to fatal abnormalities of the heart's rhythm. The blockage which occurs in these coronary arteries is due to a gradual buildup of cholesterol within its walls which gradually slows the blood flow until it stops completely, precipitating a heart attack. (See illustration.)

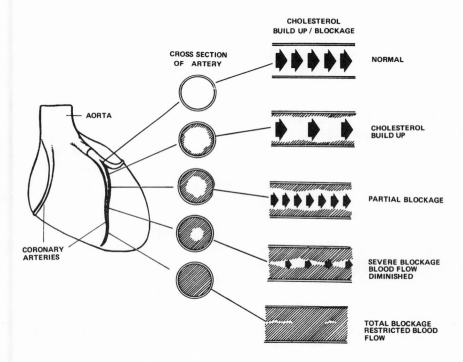

Cholesterol is a waxy substance which the body makes and also occurs in many foods we eat. Studies of the hearts of children who have been killed in accidents, and of young soldiers killed in action during the Korean War have shown the earliest beginnings of cholesterol deposition — some cases quite advanced. Unfortunately, the process usually goes undetected at this phase. Only years later when the narrowing of the artery becomes so critical that it slows or stops blood flow does the disease come to a doctor's attention. At that stage of the disease process, the cholesterol deposition cannot be reversed or removed by any method currently known. Instead, drugs can be administered to decrease the amount of pumping work the heart has to do, but the cholesterol buildup may continue. Heart surgery has been successful in bypassing or detouring the main areas of blockage in the coronary arteries; however, it cannot reverse previous damage due to a heart attack. These facts in addition to increasing knowledge about the type of person most likely to develop a heart attack has led to increased interest in preventing the cholesterol deposition in the coronary arteries (coronary atherosclerosis).

The Cholesterol-Saturated Fat Story

The development of coronary atherosclerosis which results in heart attacks is an insidious process of cholesterol deposition in the wall of the coronary arteries. The deposits build up gradually and slow the blood flow, finally stopping blood delivery to the working, pumping heart muscle. Although the body can make its own cholesterol, it cannot use or excrete more than about 500 mg of cholesterol per day (the equivalent of 2 eggs). Dietary intake over this amount frequently results in elevated blood levels and over a period of time (particularly if associated with other risk factors, such as smoking) leads to cholesterol deposition. Eating saturated fats (usually these animal fats which are solid at room temperature), found primarily in animal meats and dairy products, cause similar elevations in cholesterol. Substituting vegetable oils (polyunsaturates) for animal fats almost always results in a lowering of these fats in the bloodstream because the body does not make cholesterol from them. The many polyunsaturated products now available and almost year-round abundance of fresh fruits and vegetables now permit dietary alteration without significantly affecting palatability, nutrition, or food costs. Chapter 2 outlines the major modifications in food buying and food preparation which will alter significantly a person's intake of cholesterol and saturated fats.

Risk Factors Associated with Heart Disease

Some risk factors cannot really be altered. These include advancing age, the predisposition to atherosclerosis in males, and whether there is a family history of premature heart disease. Other risk factors are not as clearly defined or related to heart disease and are difficult to change. These include the psychological and environmental stresses of living in an organized society, personality factors, and certain diseases such as diabetes mellitus. There are a number of risk factors which are closely related to risk of developing heart disease which can be altered in each individual. These include: smoking, diet, serum cholesterol, and high blood pressure. Other factors which have a less clear-cut relation to heart disease, particularly if none of the above risk factors are present, are being overweight and lack of daily exercise. This book is directed primarily toward dietary modification and its effect on serum cholesterol to decrease the risk of subsequent development of coronary artery heart disease.

Risk Factors Associated with Atherosclerotic Heart Disease	Modification
Age Heredity Sex	Impossible
Urban Living Personality Environment Associated Disease	Difficult
Smoking Diet and Serum Cholesterol High Blood Pressure	Possible by Each Individual
Possible Risk Factors	
Obesity Lack of Daily Exercise	Possible

Medical Evidence Linking Diet and Serum Cholesterol with Heart Disease

Scientists have long suspected that nutrition and dietary habits may be linked to the development of heart disease. One of the most important findings across the world is that no population has significant coronary atherosclerosis if their habitual diet is low in saturated fats and cholesterol. This circumstantial evidence was given further support by findings from the Framingham Study. Study of the inhabitants of this small town in Massachusetts over the past twenty years has shown a strong link between serum cholesterol and risk of coronary heart disease. In fact, a person having a blood cholesterol measurement of 250 mg% (250 milligrams per 100 milliliters of blood) had *twice the risk* of having a heart attack or similar cardiac problems compared to a person with a cholesterol level of 220 mg%. Additionally, it appears that there is no "normal level" beneath which one is entirely protected from atherosclerosis. The lower the cholesterol, the lower one's chance of a heart attack.

Acceptable Serum Cholesterol Levels

age	1–10	less than	170 mg%.
age	10–20	less than	200 mg%.
age	20–40	less than	220 mg%.
age	40–60	less than	220 mg%.
over age 60		less than	240 mg%.

Although studies are continuing, the circumstantial evidence relating high fats in the bloodstream and heart disease is so significant that a recent joint statement by the special advisory committee to the National Heart and Lung Institute states "Pending confirmation by appropriate diet or drug trial, it, therefore, would appear prudent for the American people to follow a diet aimed at lowering serum lipid concentrations. For most individuals, this can be achieved by lowering intake of calories, cholesterol, and saturated fats."

There is now considerable scientific medical evidence that dietary modifications can reduce these abnormally high serum fats and hopefully, the development or progression of cholesterol deposition in the heart's coronary arteries. Several studies have now definitely shown that even minor changes in daily intake of cholesterol and saturated fat will lower blood cholesterol in the average person. The time has come for all of us to modify our diet. This book provides the methods for these modifications without interfering with one's nutrition or dietary enjoyment.

Who Needs a Modified Daily Diet?

The reports of coronary atherosclerosis in children and young adults suggest we all must start young if the cholesterol deposition is to be actually prevented. Chapter 3 will give guidelines for various age groups and particularly for children and teen-agers that modify fat intake but which allow normal growth and development. If the entire family eats a regular diet which is restricted in saturated fats and cholesterol, children growing up within the family unit will most likely follow suit.

2
The Four C's
of Low Cholesterol Cooking

THE FOUR C's of low cholesterol cooking boil down to that one magical word **change**:

1. **Change** the kind of fat
   — Use liquid polyunsaturated oils in place of solid shortenings.
   — Use margarine in place of butter.

2. **Change** the foods
   — Choose those with less fat and sugar.
   — Select lean cuts of meat and trim off visible fat. Eat fish, poultry, and veal more often than beef, lamb, and pork.
   — Eat less bacon and sausage, frankfurters, cold cuts. Substitute low-fat milk for whole milk and cream. Avoid, or use sparingly, butter rolls, commercial biscuits, muffins, doughnuts, sweet rolls, cake, crackers, egg bread, cheese bread, commercial mixes containing whole eggs and whole milk. Limit egg yolks to 3 or 4 per week.

3. **Change** the method of food preparation
   — Cook with margarine and vegetable oils.
   — Bake, broil, roast, and panfry.
   — Skim excess fat from cooked foods.

4. **Change** the source of calories
   — Use more fresh vegetables and fruits, grains, and nuts. Decrease fatty foods and refined sugars and starches.

In changing your diet to restrict cholesterol and saturated fat, it is important to continue to choose a well-balanced diet and to *modify* the quantities and kinds of foods. Choose foods that will supply the necessary amounts of calories, protein, carbohydrates, and fats.

General sources of protein and carbohydrates are known to all of us. Animal products, such as meat, fish, poultry, eggs, cheese, and milk, provide most of the protein. Carbohydrates are obtained from vegetable sources, for example, breads, cereals, starches, fruits, vegetables, and sugars. Fats deserve a more detailed examination. We shall discuss the kinds of fat to use and to avoid; the kinds of foods which are high in cholesterol and saturated fats; the kinds of cooking methods which will restrict saturated fat; and the sources of calories.

Change the Kinds of Fat

These oily substances in our diet add flavor and enhance the appearance of our food. Fats are the largest single source of calories in the diet since they provide over twice as many calories per weight as protein and carbohydrate. For example, 1 teaspoon of oil or butter will supply 4 to 5 grams of fat and 35 to 45 calories, while 1 teaspoon of sugar supplies 18 calories.

Since there is such a high concentration of cholesterol and saturated fat as well as calories in animal sources of fat, we will suggest numerous changes in the quantity and types of fat used. Generally, we have decreased the amount of saturated fat and increased the unsaturated fat.

Fats are either animal or vegetable in origin. Butter, cream, lard, and meat fats are from animals and are called saturated. They are usually solid at room temperature and when eaten contribute to the production of cholesterol in the human body. There are a few vegetable sources of saturated fats, notably coconut and palm oils and chocolate. Unsaturated fats are those which are usually liquid at room temperature and are obtained from seeds and grains. Vegetable fats or oils are processed from a liquid to a solid form by the addition of hydrogen. This hydrogenation makes solid shortenings and spreads more saturated even though they are derived from vegetable oils. Some products are only *partially hydrogenated* such as peanut butter and most margarines, and are, therefore, less saturated than *hydrogenated* products.

The ideal diet would use only unsaturated fats in their liquid form, but this is not always satisfactory. For more variety and satisfaction at mealtime, a few partially hydrogenated products can be used and still maintain a low saturated fat intake.

The basic rules for changing the kinds of fats are:
1. Using vegetable oil instead of lard or hydrogenated shortenings.
2. Using margarine instead of butter.

Vegetable Oils

Vegetable oils are the recommended sources of fat, since most are polyunsaturated. This means that they may help the body balance out excess saturated fats from other sources.

The best oils to use are listed in order of the greatest polyunsaturation to the least: safflower, sunflower, corn, soybean, cottonseed, sesame, peanut, and olive. Some nut oils, such as walnut and almond, are also highly unsaturated and can be used when available. Olive and peanut oils should be used less often since they are the least unsaturated of the oils.

Coconut and palm oils are used frequently in food processing and many commercial products such as nondairy creamers may contain these. These vegetable oils are unusual in that they are saturated. We do not recommend the use of coconut and palm oils or the foods that contain them.

Hydrogenated or partially hardened vegetable oils and shortenings are those which have been changed from the unsaturated (liquid) form to the saturated (solid) form through the process of hydrogenation. Food processors change vegetable oils to make them firmer and easier to use or to preserve them. Because hydrogenated fats are **saturated,** and contribute to the body's production of cholesterol they are used in this cookbook as little as possible.

An easy rule to follow is: If it is liquid at room temperature it is most likely unsaturated; if it is solid at room temperature, it is saturated fat.

Margarines

Butter is an animal fat and contains both cholesterol and saturated fat. Substitute margarine for butter *at all times.* All margarines made of safflower, corn, soybean, and cottonseed oils are recommended for their unsaturated fat.

Read the labels for the list of ingredients. Ingredients are listed in order of predominance in the product. Choose margarines that list *liquid oil* as the first ingredient, such as "liquid corn oil." If a label lists partially hardened oil, hydrogenated vegetable oil, animal fat, or coconut oil as one of the first ingredients, it will contain more saturated fat and should not be used. If a choice is necessary, however, choose partially hydrogenated or hardened, rather than fully hydrogenated oil.

Diet margarines have added water and "whipped in" air. They have about half the calories and are as unsaturated as their counterparts. Read the label to determine the ingredients.

Change the Kinds of Foods

We all need variety in our diet. A combination of foods furnishes the daily nutritional needs, but a diversity of foods provides enjoyment. It is not necessary to eliminate completely any favorite foods when modifying your cholesterol and saturated fat intake. You must, however, be aware of the high fat and cholesterol-containing foods, and limit their quantity, substituting whenever you can with lower fat foods. Cholesterol comes primarily from animal products, such as eggs, red meats, and liver. Controlling the sources of cholesterol in the diet and the frequency with which they appear on the menu is the key to lowering cholesterol in the body. Well-marbled steaks, liver paté, or mushroom omelette can still be enjoyed, but should be limited to occasional treats. Cultivate a taste for a wide variety of vegetables and make them a more dominant part of your menus. If your market has a special section for regional products, experiment with vegetables such as Mexican jicama, Chinese bok choy, okra, rice noodles, and the numerous different dried beans. Poultry and fish can be served often in their many international variations without tiring the palate. Investigate regional and national cuisines which use distinctive flavorings and cooking styles which use less meat and dairy products. Serve salads daily, both as entrées and accompaniments, they can be a major part of the menu with planning and imagination. Reserve rich desserts for birthday celebrations. Finish meals with fresh fruit or sherbet. Even breakfasts can be diverse and imaginative without resorting to the eggs and bacon routine.

In summary, menus can be rich in variety and satisfaction without jeopardizing your heart. This section will guide you in choosing foods which provide the best and easiest way to restrict cholesterol and saturated fat intake without restricting your food enjoyment.

Red or Muscle Meats

Meats contain a high proportion of cholesterol and saturated fat. Therefore, changes must be made if red meats constitute a major portion of your dinner menu. We suggest not more than 4 to 5 servings of red meats *of any kind* per week. Red meats include beef, lamb, and pork. Veal has a lower fat content and may be used more frequently than beef. *We recommend a serving size of 3 ounces of cooked meat* which provides plenty of protein without excessive fat.

Grades of Meat

Prime is the highest grade but also contains the most fat, usually 40 to 45 percent. This grade is most frequently reserved for restaurants, and is usually more expensive than the other grades.

Choice is lower in fat content, 25 to 35 percent, but still rates high in flavor and tenderness. This grade is most frequently found in supermarkets.

Good is lower in fat, 20 to 25 percent but tenderness and moistness are sacrificed unless cooked properly.

Other grades, although lower in fat content, are not usually available in regular markets.

Take advantage of the lower fat content and lower priced grades of meat by using them in recipes that call for long, slow cooking in a flavorful stock or sauce.

Cured and smoked meats tend to be high in fat content, about 30 percent. Visible fat should be removed if possible, and the pan drippings of all cooked meats should be discarded.

Canned meats may or may not be high in fat since animal fat or hydrogenated shortenings are sometimes added in the processing. The label will state if extra fat has been added.

Sausages and luncheon meats are generally high in animal fat. These meats contain 30 to 50 percent fat and should be restricted to no more than 1 or 2 servings a week.

Poultry

Chicken and turkey are excellent, inexpensive sources of protein. Although about equal to red meat in cholesterol, they are low in saturated fat. Most of the fat in poultry is located in and under the skin which can be removed before cooking.

Chicken is an ideal replacement for red meats, is easily available, and lends itself to many interesting dishes.

Game hens, wild birds, and game such as duck, pheasant, venison, and rabbit are very low in fat and may be enjoyed frequently. Domestic duck and goose are much higher in fat than wild ones and should be reserved for special occasions. *We recommend a serving size of 3 ounces of cooked poultry or game.*

Fish

Fish, both fresh and salt water types, is another easily available and delicious source of protein. Although fish contains almost the same amount of cholesterol as red meat, it contains little or no saturated fat. Therefore, include fish of all kinds in your menus several times a week. *We recommend a serving size of 4 to 6 ounces of cooked fish.*

Shellfish

Although relatively low in fat, shellfish has more cholesterol than red meat. Shrimps and lobsters are highest of the shellfish in cholesterol and we recommend they not be eaten more than once a week. Cholesterol content of other shellfish such as crabs, oysters, mussels, clams, and scallops is similar to poultry and may be eaten once or twice a week, with *a recommended serving size of 4 to 6 ounces cooked shellfish.*

Dairy Products

All dairy products are high in cholesterol and saturated fat. In fact, this category of foods requires the most alterations. This includes whole milk, cream, butter, cheese, sour cream, churned buttermilk, and ice cream.

Some of these items, such as whole milk, butter, and ice cream, can be eliminated almost completely from your shopping list. For others, substitutions can be made easily for both eating and cooking. Low-fat and nonfat milk can replace whole milk. Skim milk includes low- and nonfat varieties. Nonfat is fat free, while low-fat contains approximately 2 percent fat. A quick check of the contents on the container will tell you which you are buying because the brand name may be confusing. Nonfat dry milk and skimmed evaporated milk, which contains just a trace of fat, are also available. The important food values are retained while saturated fat is eliminated. Low-fat milk can be substituted for whole milk in all recipes. Nonfat milk can be used in many recipes and served freely for drinking.

Ice milk and sherbet have less fat than ice cream. Some imitation ice creams are made with saturated fat such as coconut oil, so read the labels carefully to select those which have been made with safflower or soybean oils. Pass up those containing animal fat, cream, butter, hydrogenated fat, and/or coconut oil.

Other items on the dairy list can be used in small quantities from time to time. A spoonful of sour cream, or half-and-half, can be used to add a nice finish to a dish, but low-fat yogurt or cultured buttermilk can be used in place of sour cream in dips and sauces. Choose cultured buttermilk rather than churned buttermilk to add a creamy texture to sauces and dressings.

Cheese

Cheese is one of the more common sources of saturated fat and cholesterol, which must be limited. A few cheeses are lower in fat such as low-fat cottage cheese, Farmer's cheese, Sap Sago, low-fat ricotta and some partially skimmed milk cheeses, such as mozzarella, Lappi (partially skimmed), Tybo, and others. These cheeses have approximately 15 to 20 percent fat. Other hard cheeses and creamed cheeses can contain as much as 50 percent fat. *Limit your intake of these cheeses to 4 to 6 ounces per week.*

Eggs

Although eggs are a good and relatively inexpensive source of protein, they contain an extremely high proportion of cholesterol for their size. Cholesterol is in the fat part of the egg, the egg yolk, whereas the white contains the protein. We recommend not more than 3 to 4 egg yolks be eaten during the week, either as whole eggs or in cooking. Egg whites may be used as often as desired. Many of our recipes are adapted to use less whole eggs than usual, and some recipes will use extra egg whites.

Several egg equivalents, modified to eliminate the egg yolks are available in powdered, liquid, or frozen forms. They are satisfactory replacements for the egg ingredients in certain recipes, particularly for souffés, scrambled eggs, and baked goods.

Prepared Foods

Commercially prepared foods frequently contain unnoticed sources of saturated fat and cholesterol and must be carefully selected. Dehydrated, canned, or frozen foods, sauces, puddings, cake mixes, cookies, biscuit and pastry mixes may be convenient kitchen helpers but generally contain hydrogenated and saturated fat. They are also usually more expensive than making a dish from scratch, which insures the quality of the ingredients. If you do use commercial products, check the labels and avoid those with added butter, eggs, cream, and hydrogenated shortenings. Canned creamed soups are another hidden source of cream and animal fat and should not be used. Soups made with bouillon or stock bases, however, will contribute little or no fat.

Commercial Substitutes

Whether to use commercial substitutes for high cholesterol and saturated fat products is a matter of personal preference. We have tested many commercial substitutes and found some to be quite satisfactory in taste and cooking adaptability. Coating agents, which keep foods from sticking to cooking surfaces, are made from vegetable products and can be helpful in food preparation. They have little nutritional value and do not impart any flavor to the food. They can be used as a substitute for oil in sautéing and for coating pans and baking dishes to prevent sticking. The commercial egg substitutes, which come in refrigerated or frozen containers, contain only egg white and substitute oil for the yolk. Recipes usually containing eggs, ranging from Hollandaise Sauce, breads, puddings, Mayonnaise, and batters, can be made with the substitutes with varying degrees of success. Puddings suffer the most in our testing, both in flavor and texture. The sauces, Hollandaise and Mayonnaise, were surprisingly good and the egg mixtures work extremely well in cake batters. Egg substitutes are also excellent for coating foods to be fried.

Nondairy creamers have varying degrees of acceptability. There are many available in frozen, liquid, or powdered form. These products can be used as coffee creams, or to add smoothness to sauces and soups. Check the label for ingredients. Some of the popular brands may contain coconut oil and should not be used.

Sugar

Sugar does not contain cholesterol or saturated fat, but excessive amounts may contribute to heart disease by raising the tryglyceride level in the blood. Sugar is present in the American diet in many ways, and we get more than we realize. For calorie control, dental health, and heart health, we recommend decreasing and eliminating highly sugared foods such as sweet desserts, candies, sweetened cereals, and sweetened beverages. Substitute more fresh fruit and fruit juices with little or no added sugar. Sugar substitutes may be used if calorie control is needed.

Alcohol

Alcohol may contribute to elevated triglyceride levels, particularly in the overweight person. We recommend moderation in the use of alcohol and the substitution of fruit and vegetable juices or unsugared beverages. We do use wine in some recipes, however, since the alcohol evaporates in the cooking process while the flavor remains.

Breads and Cereals

Breads, cereals, and starches are fillers in our diet. They contain little or no fat but they do provide energy-giving carbohydrate as well as protein, minerals, and vitamins, particularly vitamin B complex.

The only restrictions we suggest are to use those breadstuffs which do *not* have *added* eggs, butter, or shortening in their preparation. Forgo fancy butter-flavored breakfast or sweet rolls, rich cakes, and fried items, such as doughnuts.

Fruits and Vegetables

These foods are primarily carbohydrate with little protein and almost no fat, even the unsaturated type. We encourage generous use of all kinds of fruits and vegetables. The infinite variety available in our markets makes this group of foods the easiest and most interesting to prepare and serve.

Nuts, Seeds, and Beans

Look to this group of foods for other sources of protein. Nuts and seeds contain unsaturated fat and need be limited only if you are watching your weight. Dried beans are also good sources of protein and are useful as "protein extenders."

Peanut butter is a popular source of protein. Look for the "oily" or "old fashioned" kind, which is unsaturated.

Change the Cooking Methods

Changing the fats and foods in your diet is the first step to dietary prevention of coronary heart disease. Changing the cooking methods will complete the transition.

Of course the most important change will be in your choice of cooking fats. In all recipes calling for butter, substitute margarine. In all other recipes, lard, solid shortening, and other saturated fats, such as bacon and pork fat, can be replaced by vegetable oil. This includes recipes for baking, sautéing, frying, and sauces.

Each vegetable oil has special qualities. You may want to experiment to see which type of oil best suits your needs and particular tastes. Safflower oil is highest in polyunsaturates but used alone may not be the most flavorful. Corn oil has a tendency to stick and foods sautéed with this type of oil must be stirred frequently. A combination of soybean and cottonseed oils has been most satisfactory in our recipes. Some popular brand name vegetable oils combine these two. Olive oil is not as unsaturated as other oils, but its flavor is distinctive and desirable, particularly in salad dressings, and some Mediterranean dishes. The essence of olive oil can be retained and the unsaturation increased by mixing two-thirds olive oil with one-third polyunsaturated oil in those recipes. When selecting a liquid oil, check the source of the oil on the label.

The type of cooking can affect the amount of saturated fat ultimately contained in the dish. Broiling, roasting, barbecuing, panfrying and any other method that causes loss of fat in the meat are preferred. These methods do not require the additon of any fat to the recipe. Many recipes call for searing or browning the meat before adding it to a mixed dish or casserole. This seals in the moisture and flavor. A minute amount of oil in the pan or a quick spray with a coating agent before cooking over a high heat is all that is necessary for searing. Choose recipes that call for meats with a lower fat content and then give them a long, slow simmering in fragrant sauces, such as casseroles and ragouts. They are delightful alternatives to fried foods. A wide range of flavors can be enjoyed in casserole cooking by using foods and ideas from different national cuisines. Many delicious and unusual combinations can be created with meat, poultry, fish, wine, sauces, stocks, vegetables, herbs, and spices.

Do not serve any of the fat that accumulates on the surface of a dish during long cooking periods. Remove and discard this fat either by refrigeration, which allows the fat to congeal making removal easy, or by carefully skimming the surface of the dish with a metal spoon. Do not stir while skimming or the fat will be mixed back into the dish. If possible, let the dish stand for fifteen minutes or so to allow the fat to rise to the surface.

When you are baking choose recipes that require few eggs or just egg whites. We tend to forget about eggs in cakes and breads because they are not visible.

Deep-fat frying need not be eliminated from your diet if vegetable oil is used, but be aware that these dishes are highly caloric. Repeated heating of vegetable oil by deep-oil frying, particularly in commercial establishments, does increase the saturation by 5 to 10 percent. This is not a serious problem in most home cooking if the oil is reused less than two or three times before discarding. When deep-oil frying or stir-frying, pay careful attention to the temperatures of the oil. If the temperature of the oil falls below 375° the oil is too cool and more fat will be absorbed by the food.

These recommendations are based on sound cooking techniques which will enhance the flavor of your food as well as protect your heart.

Change the Source of Calories

The last area to be considered in this transition is the source of calories. If weight control is a problem you will want to decrease the number of calories. As we have stated previously, fat contributes the greatest portion of calories in our diet. Selecting more fresh fruit and vegetables, grains and nuts, instead of meat, reduces the total amount of calories as well as the amount of saturated fat. Refined sugars and starches contribute to the calorie intake and also to high triglyceride levels, another factor in heart disease.

It is helpful, however, to be generally aware of the calorie content of foods and food groups in your menu planning. The middle spoon of the signpost approximates the number of calories for an average serving in a recipe, and for the entire meal where menus are listed. The tables below indicate what your ideal weight should be and the range of calories needed to maintain that weight for varying levels of activity and body size.

When you are selecting your foods, give thought to where you are getting your calories, even though you may not have to consider the number.

Modify Your Buying Habits

1. Don't grocery shop when hungry or before mealtime.
2. Make a shopping list and don't get swayed from your planned needs.
3. Don't buy those irresistible snack items next to the check-out stand.
4. Substitute low calorie for high calorie food items at least once daily.
5. Don't buy foods to have on hand for other people (i.e., cookies for the children). Face up to who is really eating most of the extras.

Modify Your Eating Habits

1. Don't be taken in by miracle weight-reduction programs. Any weight

Ideal Weight*

Men — age 25 and over		Women — age 25 and over	
Height	Weight	Height	Weight
5'2"	124	4'10"	102
5'3"	127	4'11"	104
5'4"	130	5'0"	107
5'5"	133	5'1"	110
5'6"	137	5'2"	113
5'7"	141	5'3"	116
5'8"	145	5'4"	120
5'9"	149	5'5"	123
5'10"	153	5'6"	128
5'11"	158	5'7"	132
6'0"	162	5'8"	136
6'1"	165	5'9"	140
6'2"	171	5'10"	144
6'3"	177	5'11"	148
6'4"	181	6'0"	152

*Average desirable weight including indoor clothing and shoes.

lost tends to come back rapidly. It takes time and extra food to gain weight. It will take time and less food to take it off.
2. Write down everything you eat for 1 week. Decide which obviously fattening items (particularly desserts and snacks) you can live without and don't purchase them. Allow yourself "goodies" less frequently.
3. Eat smaller portions; don't take seconds. Use smaller serving dishes.
4. Learn to eat slower and chew your food more thoroughly.
5. Learn to enjoy flavors and textures rather than quantities.

How to Achieve Your Ideal Weight
1. Calculate your ideal weight from the table above.
2. Determine to lose gradually over months.
3. Modify your eating habits to cut out and cut down on the foods that make you gain weight.
4. Be more active; however, the next table shows that increased activity alone can't possibly burn very many excess calories. Calculate the time it would take you to run off yesterday's intake at 20 calories per minute.

Daily Caloric Needs for Maintaining Ideal Body Weights at Varying Levels of Physical Activity*

IDEAL WEIGHT

Activity Level	Examples	100–120 lbs.	120–140 lbs.	140–160 lbs.	160–180 lbs.
inactive	housebound	1400 cal.	1500 cal.	1700 cal.	1900 cal.
light activity	student salesperson office worker bus or truck driver	1700 cal.	2100 cal.	2500 cal.	2800 cal.
moderate activity	homemaker with children automechanic mail deliverer (foot)	1900 cal.	2500 cal.	2900 cal.	3300 cal.
hard activity	carpenter gardener heavy construction worker	2500 cal.	2900 cal.	3300 cal.	3800 cal.

*Actual caloric need will depend on other minor factors for each individual.

Energy Required to Burn Up Common Food Items
(for average 170-pound man)

Food Item	Serving	Calories	ACTIVITY (Approximate Minutes Required)		
			Walking	Running	Lying Down
Whole Milk	8 oz.	165	32	9	128
Nonfat Milk	8 oz.	80	16	4	62
Ice Cream	½ cup	165	31	9	128
Beer	8 oz.	115	22	6	88
Peach	1 medium	35	7	3	27
Pancake	1 4-in. dia.	60	11	3	46
Waffle	1 square	210	40	11	161
Beef	3-oz. piece	245	47	13	188
Fish	3-oz. piece	145	28	7	111
Peas	1 cup	55	11	3	43
Potato	1 medium	90	18	5	70
Potato, French Fried	10 pieces	155	30	8	119
Potato Chips	10	115	21	6	88
Hamburger	1	350	67	18	269
Doughnut	1	150	29	8	116
Fruit Pie	1	375	73	19	268

3
Dietary Recommendations by Age

Diet for the Growing Years

A GREAT DEAL is known about nutritional needs for growth. However, the specific needs regarding cholesterol, saturated fat, and unsaturated fat for the growing child have not been fully determined. It is well established that there are parts of the world where children grow normally both physically and intellectually on foods very low in saturated fat and cholesterol.

In the following pages we have outlined general guidelines for the selection of foods for different age groups which will furnish all the essential nutrients for growth and development. The suggestions made will change or limit the saturated fats and cholesterol.

Eating habits established during the growing period, where there is the greatest need for more calories in proportion to body size, sometimes carry over into adulthood. As a result, the intake of calories is frequently greater than the body requires as physical growth slows down and stops.

Overweight is one probable risk factor in heart disease. Learning to control weight, to lose weight if necessary, and to maintain ideal weight is of prime importance in decreasing this risk factor.

Although this book is not primarily a reduction diet book we have tried to select and identify foods and recipes which will help keep calorie intake under control, as well as saturated fat and cholesterol intake.

It is important that the diet be good for the whole family and that the child eat the same food as the rest of the family in order to acquire ideal, lifelong dietary habits.

Age 0 to 1 Year

This is the most rapid growth phase in a person's life. A baby usually will triple his body weight in the first year. Breast and/or bottle feedings and the gradual addition of solid foods provide varying amounts of fats. Although lower fat intake should be a lifelong habit, we do *not* recommend any dietary alterations until more is known about nutritional requirements during this phase.

Age 1 to 5 Years

Children are given solid foods usually by the sixth month and they begin to acquire food tastes according to what they are fed. If the child is given a variety of foods in an amiable setting, he learns to choose and enjoy most foods that will be available to him for a good many years to come. It is during this formative period that some dietary alterations can be instituted, different from those that were previously accepted, which will hopefully affect food habits and likes and dislikes. These include:

1) Drinking low-fat milk in place of whole milk and the use of lower and nonfat milks in food preparation.
2) Having fewer high carbohydrate desserts and snacks — that is, those with less sugar. Replace with fruits and less highly sweetened cookies and beverages.
3) Using vegetable oils, particularly safflower, corn, cottonseed, and soybean, in food preparation.
4) Using margarine in place of butter as a table spread and in food preparation.
5) Having not more than 3 servings per week of smoked meats such as bacon, ham, sausage, luncheon meats, and wieners.
6) Having more vegetables and fruits, raw and cooked, in place of commercially prepared mixed dishes.
7) Having all foods prepared without large amounts of added sugars, fats, and sauces.

Age 5 to 12 Years

The grade school and preteen period may be characterized by both predictable and unpredictable ups and downs in appetite and dietary likes. The young person is widening his social sphere and learning about what other people eat. He is susceptible to the enticements and overwhelming advertising claims of the hundreds of different competing food items available. Since most of the meals are eaten at home, a fair amount of control can still be exercised, and the family diet of low-fat milk, margarines, few fried and sugared foods is still the greatest influence on his nutritional state. The occasional eating out with peers or in eating places where ice cream, french fries, and other high-fat or sugared foods are served will do little or no harm. A healthy attitude toward "sometimes" foods can be established without making them into desirable forbidden fruits or bringing on confrontations in the family over food preferences.

In addition to the recommendations listed for 1- to 5-year age group, we recommend:

1) The use of nonfat milk exclusively. Most schools now offer nonfat milk as well as whole milk.
2) Emphasizing fruit and nuts for snacks rather than sugared foods such as cookies and candies or soft drinks.
3) Serving fish and poultry 3 to 4 times per week on a regular basis.
4) Keeping naturally sweetened juices or beverages on hand.
5) Helping keep good weight control by having fewer highly sugared desserts or fried foods.

Age 12 to 21 Years

This is a period of rapid growth and development in all areas, not only physically but intellectually and socially. It can be characterized by extremes in dietary choices varying from trials of fad weight-reducing diets to long sieges of endless hamburgers and soft drinks with the gang. Many poor eating habits are started during this time, which may require considerable effort to change later in life. If a variety of healthful foods has been introduced consistently during the growing period and enjoyed in the family setting, young people will have good nutritional foundations, to which they will return. Although, as with life styles, the teen-ager may experiment now and then with different food patterns which may seem more exciting and exotic than the fare at home.

Although there is little control over eating and food choices outside the home, this is a particularly critical time to emphasize learning to get along without foods high in cholesterol and saturated fat. This can be most easily accomplished by controlling what food is available in the home, that is, nonfat milk will be drunk by the thirsty teen-ager if he has been brought up on it and especially if nothing else is available. By this time children tend to prefer low-fat products if they have been raised on them.

The current interest young people have in natural foods and a less commercialized diet has led to great interest in proper nutrition. With boys taking food preparation classes in school, there may be increasing interest in home food preparation and less dependency on convenience foods or those prepared with saturated fats. Restricted intake of saturated fats and cholesterol at home will at least balance out the hot dogs, hamburgers, and french fries. Those treats should be discouraged but not fought against vigorously.

Diet for the Adult Years

Age 21 to 65

This is a critical period during which not only the dietary patterns, but attention to other risk factors, such as hypertension, will affect the health picture and chance of developing heart disease in the fifty's and sixty's.

During adulthood, the most difficult feature seems to be calorie control, particularly in America. Since only about 20 percent of the income is spent on food, it is easy to buy more than is required. An extra 80 calories a day (1 6-oz. bottle of soft drink or 1 extra ounce of meat) will result in a 15-pound gain over a period of 5 years.

Although exercise is important in maintaining general health and a sense of well-being, by itself, it is a difficult way to lose weight. We suggest a weekly weighing and an attempt to decrease the quantity of food eaten to about one-half the normal whenever present weight exceeds the ideal weight. (See weight chart on page 29.) During this period, we believe it is mandatory to restrict dietary cholesterol and saturated fat as previously outlined. There is no doubt that diet influences the level of blood fats which has been so closely linked to development of premature heart disease.

We recommend strict adherence to dietary restriction of saturated fat and cholesterol for the person himself and as an example for his children.

Many adults must dine out frequently, which can jeopardize their reduced fat and cholesterol diet. Use of this book will enable one to become familiar with the primary foods to avoid in restaurants.

The Adult over 65 Years

There is little evidence or reason to think that dietary alterations *begun* at this age will significantly affect one's life expectancy. However, being overweight is detrimental to one's health and feeling of well-being at any age. Weight can be effectively reduced with attention to the kinds and quantities of foods eaten. It is very difficult to change long-standing food habits unless the motivation to do so is stimulated by serious need, such as an illness or a desire to improve one's health status.

Recent studies of long-lived persons in all parts of the world showed that their daily caloric intake was approximately 600 calories less than that in the average American diet. It is unusual to see an overweight elderly person, particularly a man, who does not have coronary heart disease. The leaner person appears to be not only healthier, but more active and with less debilitating problems.

We suggest moderate changes in food intake, designed to keep total fat and calorie intake at a lower level. Eating more fresh fruits and vegetables, smaller portions of meats, cereals, and starches; being very careful of added sugars and fats, even saturated types; using fewer sauces and fried foods; and serving desserts and sweetened breadstuffs less frequently will do more to help weight control than endless counting of calories.

4
A Six-Month Plan for Change

PEOPLE TEND TO be very protective of their right to enjoy a good meal. Most of us enjoy experimenting with new dishes and tastes from time to time but we don't want to change our entire eating pattern overnight. It is unreasonable to expect one to discard all the old favorites and make substitutions all at once.

Furthermore, unless a person has a serious heart condition for which he would need to follow a decidedly more rigid and therapeutic plan than this one, it is not necessary to abruptly change the family meals. A transition period of six months is adequate to acquaint the family with this modified-fat-and-cholesterol food plan. Objections to change can be overcome when your family is reassured that food habits and preferences will be respected.

The following six-month plan is designed to acquaint your family with a lower cholesterol, lower saturated fat menu plan, which will gradually replace those potentially harmful high-fat and cholesterol items with healthful ones without drastically affecting lifelong food likes, dislikes, and biases.

First Month

- Change from whole milk to low-fat milk.
- Use vegetable oil for all fried food preparation and dressings.
- Select lean cuts of all meats and trim off visible fat before cooking.
- Bake, broil, grill, panbroil more frequently than fry.

Second Month

- Buy margarine, particularly the soft types in place of butter for a table spread and when needed in cooking.
- Limit eggs to not more than 3 or 4 per week.
- Try various cereals for the morning meal in place of the usual egg.
- Increase the use of fish and poultry for main meals; have meat not more than once a day.

Third Month

- Cut down on high-sugar desserts — iced cakes, cookies, and the like.
- Substitute more fruits and low-fat milk desserts.
- Cut down on fancy breads, sweet rolls, pastries.
- Emphasize more fruits and vegetables in meals and between meals.

Fourth Month

- Start using nonfat milk.
- Use lower fat cheeses.
- Do more baking, broiling, grilling, or stewing.
- Limit bacon, sausage, luncheon meats, and wieners to not more than 3 servings per week.

Fifth Month

- Use more peanut butter, dried peas, beans in place of eggs, cheese, and meat.
- Use more whole grain cereals and breads.
- Use more fibrous or raw vegetables.
- Substitute sherbet or ice milk for ice cream.

Sixth Month

- Maintain good weight control by decreasing quantities of all foods eaten.
- Serve red meats no more than 5 times per week.
- Limit hard cheeses to not more than 4 ounces per week.
- Serve more meatless meals during the week.

5

The Three Spoons Signpost

ALTHOUGH EXPERTS MAY disagree, considerable medical evidence points to the wisdom of limiting the daily intake of cholesterol to 250–350 milligrams and saturated fat to 30–35 grams. The Three Spoons signpost, designed to eliminate the necessity of counting these milligrams and grams, shows clearly and quickly the amount of cholesterol and saturated fat in a single portion of any given recipe. The signpost C's and F's are based on the following figures:

Three Spoons Guide

	Cholesterol		Saturated Fat
–	0–20 mg.	–	0–2 g.
C	21–75 mg.	F	2–4 g.
CC	76–100 mg.	FF	4–7 g.
CCC	101–150 mg.	FFF	7–10 g.
CCCC	over 150 mg.	FFFF	over 10 g.

Now, to answer the query "What's for dinner?" the family cook can consider the season, the occasion, and the Three Spoons. Whether planning an elaborate holiday menu, complete with a beautifully roasted bird, candied yams, and mince pie, or a simple Sunday supper, let the Three Spoons guide you to choosing dishes and menus that will please your families' hearts and palates. This easy-to-read signpost is located at the corner of each recipe and specifies the calories, cholesterol, and saturated fat for each portion. The sign-post-marked sample menus in this chapter indicate the amounts for the total menu, calculated for 1 person. The menus are generally calculated for 4 servings so if you stretch a menu to 6 people the amounts consumed will be less. Rather than having to worry about computing grams and milligrams of saturated fat and cholesterol, simply follow the scale as designated by the number of C's for cholesterol, F's for saturated fat, and actual calories per serving. By using this indicator you will be able to tell at a glance whether the recipe you have chosen is low in cholesterol and saturated fats. If, at dinner, you find yourself under the recommended amounts of cholesterol and saturated fats for the day, you may decide to splurge on dessert.

As you plan menus, remember that the Three Spoons reflect the amount of calories, cholesterol, and saturated fat in 1 serving, and that these all increase as you add other parts of your meal. In general, try not to eat more than 4 C's or 4 F's at any one meal. Shrimp, cauliflower pudding, and beef steak with Madeira sauce could all be eaten separately but are well over the recommended amounts if they appear on the same menu. If your total weekly intake of saturated fat and cholesterol has been low, you can splurge on chopped liver or a wedge of cheese with your fruit. Interesting menu planning is a fringe benefit of the Three Spoons system. Menus containing too many sauces or several rich dishes tend to mask the flavors of the individual dishes, and subtle flavors in each are lost. The Three Spoons guide prevents overloading meals with too many rich dishes and a tastefully balanced menu will result. After trying just a few recipes you will become familiar with the foods and types of dishes that contain cholesterol and saturated fat and those recipes that can be enjoyed limitlessly. The following menus give a sampling of the various ways dishes can be combined to create healthful, exciting meals.

Three Spoons Signpost Menus

Lamb Curry
Rice
Condiments
Pear Chutney
Pomegranate Salad
Banana Flambé

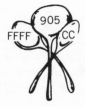

Fisherman's Stew
Twice-Baked Potatoes
Green Salad with Roquefort Dressing
Banana Bread

Flank Steak Teriyaki
Baked Carrots and Apples
Mushroom and Zucchini Salad with Shallot Dressing
Angel Food Cake with Raspberry Sauce

Duck with Olives
Red Cabbage with Apples
Puréed Carrots and Turnips
Iced Lemon Meringue with Raspberry Purée

Mushroom Soup
Mexican Chicken Salad
Gazpacho Salad Mold
Pear Tart

Beef Esterhazy
Caraway Noodles
Sliced Tomatoes with Basil Dressing
Stewed Apples with Vanilla Sauce

Chinese Almond Chicken
Green Beans, Mushrooms, and Onions
Steamed Rice
Green Salad
Fresh Pineapple

French Onion Soup
Sole Apollo
Garlicky Carrots
Spinach Salad
Apple Tart

Chicken Breasts with Mushroom Sauce
Peas and Lettuce
Salad with White Wine Dressing
Ice Milk with Apricot Sauce

Baked Red Snapper
Spinach Timbale
Orange and Onion Salad
Persimmon Pudding with Lemon Sauce

Beef Carbonnade
Boiled Potatoes
Green Salad with Basil Dressing
Pears Poached with Red Wine

Stir-Fried Beef and Broccoli
Rice
Pickled Apple Salad
Plum Ice Milk

Brittany Beef
Noodles with Poppy Seeds
Tomatoes à la Schroeder
Green Salad
Spice Cake

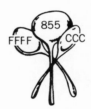

Tomato Bisque
Chicken Teriyaki
Pilaf
Marinated Cucumbers on Lettuce
Baked Apples

Cream of Potato Soup
Hamburger with Mushroom Sauce
Cauliflower Pudding
Green Bean Salad
Raspberry Sherbet

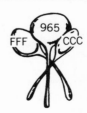

Swiss Steak
Baked Beets
Vegetable Salad
Water Ice

Trout with Almond Sauce
Lemon Potatoes
Tomatoes Stuffed with Spinach
Poached Pear with Apricot Sauce

Chicken Soufflé
Vegetable Carousel
Green Salad
Chocolate Pound Cake

Spinach-Stuffed Snapper
Gracie's Baked Acorn Squash
Carrot Mold
Chocolate Cheese Cake

Cold Broccoli with Warm Hollandaise Sauce
Curried Halibut
Rice and Condiments
Fruit Platter

Lamb Shanks
Steamed New Potatoes
Green Beans and Mushrooms
Fruit Ambrosia

Borscht
Dilled Halibut
Zucchini and Mushrooms
Steamed Rice
Apple Crisp

Trout Stuffed with Mushrooms
Steamed New Potatoes
Green Beans Ravigote
Wilted Spinach Salad
Rita's Rice Pudding

Cioppino
French Bread
Green Salad
Caraway Tea Loaf and Fresh Fruit

Mushroom Consommé
Hot Chinese Chicken Salad
Burnt-Leather Cake with Burnt-Leather Icing

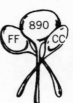

Breakfast

BREAKFAST IS ONE of the most controversial food subjects. "To eat or not to eat," that is the question; "The best meal of the day," or "Black coffee, please." The storm has raged for some time and has many proponents on both sides.

The true meaning of the term breakfast is to "break the fast" imposed by an 8-hour rest. Eating breakfast is firmly established as a good health practice. Most bodies do seem to need some sustenance to get daily activities going. Even busy morning schedules can include a habit of some quick nourishment.

The familiar breakfast foods of eggs, bacon, sausage, sweet rolls, or other breakfast breads with butter contain a larger percent of cholesterol and saturated fats than any other meal for the calories eaten. We advocate eating breakfast (in case this has NOT been your pattern) but recommend changes in the kinds of food for a more heart-healthy breakfast. Between one-third to one-fifth of the nutrients needed for optimum health should be taken in the first meal or eating period of the day.

Listed below are 5 light, 5 medium, and 5 moderately high calorie breakfasts which will provide the necessary calories and nutrients without large amounts of cholesterol and saturated fat.

Low Calorie (150 to 200 calories)
1. ½ grapefruit or 4 ounces unsweetened grapefruit juice
   1 slice whole wheat toast
   1 pat margarine

2. milk shake with 8 ounces nonfat milk, ½ cup berries, 1 teaspoon sugar
   2 bread sticks
3. 1 whole orange, peeled and sliced
   8 ounces nonfat milk
4. ½ canteloupe
   4 ounces chicken and rice soup
   1 rye crisp
   coffee or tea
5. ½ cup fresh fruit
   1 teaspoon sugar
   ½ cup plain, low-fat yogurt

Medium Calories (300 to 500 calories)
1. 8 ounces orange juice
   4 tablespoons low-fat cottage cheese, mixed with 1 teaspoon sugar and
      vanilla extract on 1 slice dark bread. Broil under broiler for 3 to 5
      minutes until hot and bubbly.
2. 8 ounces nonfat milk
   ½ papaya
   1 bagel, toasted
   1 tablespoon peanut butter
   2 teaspoons jelly
3. 1 slice pineapple, broiled
   3 tablespoons low-fat cream cheese, mixed with ¼ cup chopped black
      olives on 1 slice whole wheat toast
   4 ounces nonfat milk
4. baked apple with cinnamon and raisins
   ¾ cup cooked cereal
   1 tablespoon sugar
   4 ounces nonfat milk
   coffee or tea
5. 1 slice dark bread, toasted, spread with banana slices and peanut butter
   1 ounce cheese cubes
   hot spiced tea

High Calories (500 to 800 calories)
1. ½ melon, any kind
   1 cup cooked cereal
   1 English muffin
   2 pats margarine

2 teaspoons jam
4 ounces low-fat milk
2. ½ cup hot spiced-fruit compote
   2 blueberry or bran muffins
   2 pats margarine
   2 ounces broiled ground meat or turkey patty
   coffee or tea
3. 4 ounces cranberry juice
   3 6-inch pancakes
   1 tablespoon margarine
   2 tablespoons syrup
   8 ounces nonfat milk
4. 4 ounces apricot nectar
   1 cup dry cereal
   ½ banana, sliced, or ½ cup fresh fruit
   1 English muffin, toasted
   2 slices mozzarella cheese
   4 ounces nonfat milk
5. ½ grapefruit, broiled and drizzled with 1 tablespoon honey
   ½ cup cottage cheese, mixed with ½ cup applesauce
   1 slice banana bread
   1 pat margarine
   8 ounces hot cocoa, made with low-fat milk

New Ideas for Breakfasts

Breakfast can be the most stereotyped meal of the day. The word breakfast may be distasteful to many people. Brunch implies a later hour, but is frequently a more interesting meal because a wider variety of food is usually served. Breakfast should and can have as much variety as brunch or lunch, at the very least. To avoid stereotyped breakfasts one may include his or her own unusual or personal food preferences.

The basic criteria for any meal also apply to breakfast: nutrition, visual appeal, taste, calories, and convenience.

In selecting your breakfast menu, remember that teen-agers as well as adults may respond more favorably to seasoned foods, than to the usual breakfast fare. Teen-agers may enjoy a hamburger even at breakfast time. Serve teen-agers leftovers (from any meal), if this idea appeals to them. The dinner that is nutritionally correct will still be nutritionally correct at breakfast time. A nutritionally balanced cold breakfast supplies the same vitamins as a nutritionally balanced hot breakfast. A bowl of fresh fruit (available now year round) may bring sunshine to a breakfast on a cloudy day. A collection of breakfast snacks may appeal to light breakfast eaters. Snack packs, prepared ahead of time, of raisins, sliced apples, dried fruit, walnuts, and dry crispy cereal are convenient for children and adults during the early morning rush for school and work. Use your own preferences for early morning snack packs to be served with juice and a glass of skim or low-fat milk. The variety of suggestions below should fire everyone's imagination and appeal to a wide variety of tastes.

Suggestions:

1. Broiled cottage cheese on toast. Spread toasted bread with layer of cottage cheese, sprinkle with brown sugar and cinnamon, and broil for 2 to 3 minutes. Try cut-up fresh fruit, mixed with cottage cheese, as a change.
2. Toasted English muffin with peanut butter and honey or marmalade.
3. Leftover, cold, cooked vegetables: asparagus, broccoli, artichoke, or carrots with lemon-flavored mayonnaise or yogurt.
4. Broiled Canadian bacon on whole wheat toast.
5. Broiled open-face cheese and sliced tomato on dark rye toast.
6. Sliced oranges with low-fat, plain yogurt or Cottage Cream (see Saucery) and brown sugar; any sliced fresh fruit with low-fat yogurt and maple or brown sugar.
7. Fresh fruit and cottage cheese drizzled with honey.
8. Mashed fresh or canned fruit with mozzarella cheese on crackers.
9. Broiled fish cubes and mushrooms on toasted English muffins.
10. Mashed, cooked fish or chicken and mayonnaise and lemon on toast rounds, lightly broiled.
11. Whole wheat toast with low-fat cream cheese served with broiled grapefruit half, sprinkled with brown sugar and few drops of sherry.
12. Fresh or canned fruit topped with plain or flavored yogurt and wheat germ.
13. Toasted bran or fruit muffins with cheese spread.
14. Cinnamon toast, fruit juice, and cheese wedges.
15. Hard-boiled egg whites stuffed with tuna or chicken salad.
16. Soups — hot or cold — tomato, split pea, black bean, minestrone, potato, corn or clam chowder or other cream style made with low-fat milk; served with toast strips or bread sticks.
17. Broiled baked beans on brown bread served with chilled fruit cup.
18. Toasted tortilla with sliced tomato, sliced olives, and grated cheese.

19. Chipped beef heated in melted margarine and served on toast triangles.
20. Creamed chipped beef or shredded chicken on toasted English muffin.
21. Broiled sliced pineapple with cottage cheese on toast rounds.
22. Fruit sherbet topped with fresh or canned fruit and wheat germ or sesame seeds.
23. Toast topped with applesauce, cinnamon, and brown sugar and a few raisins or chopped nuts.
24. Homemade granola: rolled oats, sesame seeds, shredded nuts, wheat germ, served with nonfat or low-fat milk.
25. Rice pudding made with skim or low-fat milk, sugar, cinnamon, raisins, or other dried fruits.
26. Cottage cheese with chopped dates or stewed prunes.
27. Jello with fruit and mashed cottage cheese or low-fat yogurt topping.
28. Instant cereal breakfast with skim or low-fat milk.
29. French toast made with orange juice, cooked in margarine, and sprinkled with powdered sugar and Cottage Cream.
30. Panfried fish cakes in margarine (shredded fish-salmon, tuna, or any suitable fish), mixed with cracker crumbs and canned evaporated skim milk, seasonings.
31. Panfried corned beef hash, garnished with broiled fresh fruit (peach half, apricot, apple or pear or pineapple slices).
32. Hot spiced fruit compote.
33. Sardines.
34. Fried mush.
35. Broiled, crisp Canadian bacon and peanut butter on toast.
36. Fried apples with brown sugar and cinnamon.
37. French toast made with stale bread dipped in egg white, milk, cinnamon, nutmeg, and served with fresh fruit or syrup.

Calories at Breakfast

If calories are a problem for you, some may be slipping in at breakfast time without your being aware of it. For example, an English muffin has twice as many calories as a slice of toast. If you have jam and margarine on the muffin, you will be adding 250 to 300 more calories. Danish pastries are 250 calories and doughnuts are 200. If you have 2 doughnuts, an 8-ounce glass of orange juice, and coffee with cream (instead of low-fat milk) and sugar, 500 calories of your day are already eaten. So think through your breakfast carefully; are there ways you can substitute or switch without affecting your breakfast enjoyment?

Here are calorie ranges for the most popular acceptable breakfast foods:

toast, 1 slice	65 calories
English muffin	140 calories
toasted fruit pastry	200+ calories
margarine	110 calories per tablespoon
jam	50–60 calories per tablespoon
dry cereal, 1 cup, with low-fat milk	150 calories

7

Cooking As an Art

OF ALL THE arts, cooking has the longest and richest heritage. It began with man himself and reflects his evolution from caveman to a member of a highly mechanized and sophisticated society. We no longer tear meat apart with our hands and teeth, or dig for roots and berries. Nor are we dependent upon our immediate environment for variety in our diet. Whole economies are based on the harvesting and production of foodstuffs. Modern refrigeration and transportation make seasonal and regional delicacies available to everyone all year round. We have intricate heating and freezing systems for the preparation of food. Finely crafted silver, china, and crystal are collected for the proper presentation and enhancement of exotic dishes. The cuisine of a nation is a mark of its culture and traditions. Our own cuisine is a rich blending of many countries and cultures. The melting pot of the world has benefited greatly from the influence of Europe and the Orient. You can pinpoint the origin of people not only by the sound of the voice but also by the way they lay a table. Food has evolved from the simple necessity of daily subsistence to an integral part of our culture. All the various ceremonies of life are celebrated by feasting. Weddings, births, victories, meetings of heads of nations are all marked by great dinners. Man no longer satisfies merely his hunger when he eats but also his sensory appetites. The enjoyment of food is a thoroughly sensuous and deeply satisfying experience. Jean A. Brillat-Savarin aptly described the "pleasures of the table" in his treatise, *The Physiology of Taste.* His formula for a memorable meal including the right combination of food, wine, music, and witty and amiable companions holds true to today even though we may dispute his choices of food. Altering the menu to eliminate the Frenchman's love of eggs, butter, cream, and cheese does not interfere with the "pleasures of the table."

Since food is such an important part of our daily life, it is fitting that its preparation be considered an art. And art it surely is. If it were not for the transient quality of the completed work, I daresay there would be museums devoted to the celebration of the perfect soufflé or a superbly poached fish masked in a delicate sauce. The art of the kitchen is sensuous in the true meaning of the word — delighting us with rich colors, fragrances, textures, and tastes. It is creative and individual, demanding imagination, innovation, and flair. It draws upon many different talents. A feel for color comes first to mind. A beautifully balanced menu reflects an artist's use of a palette as well as flavors and textures to complement and contrast the different dishes. Every color of the spectrum is to be found in the garden to inspire us. Plump red tomatoes, lush green peppers, golden orange carrots, and shiny deep purple eggplants are as luscious to look at as refreshing to taste. There is a tactile pleasure in cooking. The many varieties of textures provide interest in our meals. Crunchy, smooth, creamy, soft, tender, crisp — these adjectives conjure up thoughts of many enticing dishes. The feel of food during preparation is uniquely satisfying. Kneading bread is good for the soul. Just ask anyone who has had the experience of feeling flour, water, and yeast come alive under their hands to form a smooth, elastic, resilient mass. The sense of smell becomes an instrument of pleasure in the kitchen. The perfumes of Paris have yet to duplicate the fragrance of freshly baked bread or a casserole heady with the aroma of garlic, onions, and wine. And of course, taste. There are few pleasures as deeply satisfying as that first bite of a favorite morsel; perhaps a chicken sautéed with onion and delicately flavored with wine, or a rich savory soup flavored with a lovely marriage of vegetables and herbs. One may break into a spontaneous smile and some have even been known to purr as the delicious mouthful is savored.

The presentation of a meal can be a dramatic performance when care is given to the details of mood and setting. Whether you are serving a leisurely Sunday breakfast or a festive holiday feast, special touches set the stage for your creations; artful garnishes of fresh parsley or condiments in contrasting colors; fresh flowers, candles, a pretty table setting all add to the mood. These things, too, call upon your creative talents.

The creation of fine food requires not a born talent but a sensitivity to the needs and requirements of each dish. Love, patience, and understanding are the ingredients of success in the kitchen. Love of good food and the enjoyment of sharing your creations with family and friends can give your meals a stamp of your own unique ability. This, perhaps, is the talent necessary to be a good cook. It is assumed you appreciate good food, and you are encouraged to acquire the patience in the kitchen. Do not force things to happen. Let foods take their own time to develop their full flavor and texture. Take the time to perform the extra steps that will ensure a better dish. Strain a sauce that is lumpy, skim *all* the fat from a gravy. The quality of your dish, in terms of appearance, taste, and health, will be a reward for your effort. Understanding the rules is the basis for the technical ability that ensures quality. This information, in addition to guidelines on limiting cholesterol and saturated fat intake, has been thoroughly outlined in the preceding chapters. This book will be a guide to preparing meals that are deliciously satisfying as well as healthful. It is not necessary to feel deprived to ensure a healthful diet. Perhaps medicine should taste bad to be good for you but that axiom does not carry over into the kitchen. This knowledge then, of the tools, rules, and foods of the kitchen, will give you the confidence to attempt new dishes and unusual combinations of food without fear of failure. Fear of the kitchen has surely stifled the talent of many potentially good chefs. It amazes me that creative, talented people are afraid of assembling a few ingredients in a bowl or stirring a sauce on the stove, yet they can build bridges, fly planes, run offices and homes without a hitch.

Once the fear of the kitchen has been overcome, or perhaps the boredom developed through years of prepackaged, prepared, predigested, sterile, uninteresting meals, a whole new world opens up. The senses become more finely honed. You learn to cook with your whole body. You listen for the sound of a sauce going from a barely audible gurgling to the soft pop of a boil. The gentle bubbling of a hearty soup is soft background music to the sharp staccato of crisp vegetables being finely diced. The sense of touch is essential in cooking. Your hands are your best tools, there isn't a gadget in the world that can replace them. You use them to pat, spank, pinch, measure, knead, poke, and prod. My finger tips tell me when chicken breasts have baked just enough without becoming dry and tough, when flour and shortening have been worked together just enough to ensure a perfect pastry crust, when bread has been kneaded to the proper elasticity. My sense of smell is an essential tool in the kitchen. I can detect a sauce that has been cooked over high heat too long and will impart a scorched flavor to the dish, and of course my nose summons me very quickly when I am called to the phone and have left something on the stove. These techniques become second nature in time and you will find that the more you rely on your senses and your hands, the more comfortable you will be in the kitchen.

Now you are equipped to practice your art. We will detail the methods and ingredients. When you have learned them well use them as a starting point. Do not be afraid to experiment. Trust your judgment that an addition or subtraction will enhance the dish. Invent your own combinations. In a word — create.

8
Equipping Your Kitchen

Gadgets

MOST MEALS CAN be prepared with a minimum of equipment. There are, however, a multitude of implements available which can be invaluable in the kitchen. Your tools, whether gadgets or appliances, should be chosen carefully with consideration given to the size of your family, the kind of cooking you enjoy and the amount of cooking you do. You can spend a fortune in little thingamajigs that are attractive but add little to the kitchen armamentarium. There are a variety of oyster shuckers, cherry pitters, and corn scrapers on the market but if you are allergic to shellfish, can't stand cherries, and won't eat corn unless it is on the cob you will only succeed in cluttering kitchen drawers at the expense of having a perfectly appointed kitchen. Think carefully about the gadget you are considering; do you really need it, and if so, will it do the job? You will find your own favorites but these are some of my preferences and prejudices.

I can't live without:

Timer: An accurate one with a loud bell, or better yet two accurate timers. You will frequently have two dishes going at once.

Strainers: Several grades of mesh and various sizes and shapes are available. Use for draining vegetables, straining berries, removing lumps from sauces, rinsing pasta, etc.

Whisks: I have a passion for them, all sizes and shapes from a tiny slim whisk that is 2 inches long to a huge antique balloon whisk that is used exclusively for beating egg whites. They are excellent for stirring sauces to a smooth consistency but have two drawbacks: Some foods get caught in the wires, notably spinach, and can be a nuisance to clean and when used in pans with straight sides the round bottom of the whisk will not get in the "corners." Otherwise they are indispensable.

Wooden spoons: As many as will fit in your kitchen. The handles will not burn your fingers, the wood does not interact with metal or food, and they are **quiet** as you scrape and stir. Some of the hard plastic spoons are handy but they have the disadvantage of melting near heat.

Colander: Excellent for draining.

Potato ricer: A must for smooth mashed potatoes, and puréeing.

Skimmer: Metal spoon with a round, slotted bowl that is set at an angle. This is a multipurpose tool to be used for anything from skimming the bay leaf out of the soup to serving the stew.

Tongs: Like wooden spoons, you can't have too many. For picking up awkward food like corn on the cob, turning chicken and meats without piercing the flesh and drying them out, etc.

Kitchen shears: Good ones are worth the investment. Use for cutting poultry, trimming artichoke leaves, cutting cheesecloth, etc.

Peelers: Necessary for trimming all stalk and root vegetables.

Rubber spatulas: Used for getting that last little bit out and avoiding waste.

Lemon squeezers: Prevent seeds from falling into food and drinks. Small, individual ones are inexpensive and can be served at the table for fish and vegetable dishes.

Round pastry cutter: They come in various sizes; I like one about 1½ inches in diameter for cutting bread rounds for croutons and canapés.

Measuring cups and spoons: Liquid measuring cups are graduated and come in 1- to 4-cup sizes. Dry measuring cups come in sets from ⅛ cup to 1 cup. Dry ingredients are leveled off at the top for accuracy. Measuring spoons can be found in sets from ⅛ teaspoon to 1 tablespoon.

Slotted spoon: Very useful for draining, skimming, and serving.

Spatula: Many sizes and shapes are available. Good for turning food, loosening and serving food.

Cheese grater: I prefer the kind with a fitted box attached. Freshly grated cheese is superior to the packaged kind even though it is used sparingly. It is also used for grating lemon and orange rind, and various vegetables.

I do not recommend:

Garlic press: Squeezes bitter oils into your dish and leaves flavorful pulp in the press to be discarded. Instead mince the garlic bud with a chef's knife.

Shrimp deveiner: A paring knife does a better job.

Mushroom brush and slicer: Awkward and time-consuming. Instead, soak mushrooms in vinegar water for 30 seconds and rub 2 or 3 together briskly between the palms of your hands under cold running water. A chef's knife is the best tool for slicing anything.

Banana slicer: I have never found slicing a banana difficult.

Basting bulb: Usually squirts basting juices across the room. Difficult to manipulate and to clean. A 2-inch paint brush with white bristles is better.

Cookware

I have often been consulted by my students when they decide to invest in cookware. My advice is again, consider need as well as your purse. Kitchen tools should be given more thought than gadgets, the investment is so much greater. It is better to have a few multipurpose pieces of cookware of good quality than a whole set of inexpensive pots and pans that will not hold up. Most of us will be cooking for many years and it does pay to opt for quality rather than quantity. You must also consider the utility of the equipment. A fish poacher is a good investment if you plan to poach a whole fish frequently. However, if this is something you will do rarely, you can improvise with a roasting pan and foil and spend the money instead on a good heavy Dutch oven.

I would unequivocally recommend cast iron coated with porcelain enamel as my first choice for all around kitchen use. Cheaper grades chip easily so buy one of the better known brands. This cookware gives even heat and can be used for surface cooking as well as in the oven.

Copper pans are a luxury unless you cook a great deal. But if you do you will not regret the investment. Copper is one of the best conductors of heat but it does take a little time to get used to its properties. Copper is lined with either steel or tin and depending upon the lining, has even greater heating properties. Tin heats best but stainless steel is easier to clean so it is a matter of personal choice. Both are very good. Copperware gets very hot so things will burn easily if not watched. Be cautious until you are used to it. All copperware has metal handles, probably because they are ovenproof and therefore more versatile, so keep potholders handy to prevent scorched fingers. Quality is determined by the thickness of the copper layer and Swiss, French, and American brands are the best in that order. Beware of Portuguese- and Italian-made pans. The copper wears out quickly. Most copper should be relined at some point but you will get better service if you start out with good quality. I find the American brand which is lined with stainless steel easy to maintain and cooks extremely well.

Stainless steel would be my next choice. This ware is made by any number of companies and there is quite a good selection. Stainless steel has the advantage of being easy to clean but it can develop hot spots and therefore cook unevenly.

Aluminum has the disadvantage of interacting unfavorably with some foods and metals. Acid foods in particular suffer and you may find sauces turning gray. It is a soft metal and constant scraping with a metal spoon or fork over the years will result in small chips of aluminum in your dish. It also has a tendency to develop hot spots.

Cast-iron skillets and pots have a great deal of charm as well as being quite functional. They are good for dishes requiring long slow simmers. Iron does rust, however, so a coating of vegetable oil after each washing will protect the surface. This is especially important if you live in a damp climate.

In selecting any cookware look for thickness and weight. You are safer with reputable companies rather than off brands, generally speaking. Teflon, in my opinion, has limited use. I like it on cookie sheets and some baking dishes but if used on skillets and saucepans it frequently peels off.

Cutlery

Proper selection of cutlery will save hours of struggling with chopping and slicing chores over the years. Knives that take a good sharp edge and have proper balance and shape take the drudgery from mincing and dicing. It is so much easier to slice an onion with a blade that glides through due to its sharp edge. Not all steel will do this for you however. German and French factories produce the best cutlery. Carbon steel will hold an edge longer but stainless steel is easier to clean. Carbon also discolors, especially on contact with onion and it also is subject to rust. The test of a good knife is not how long it will hold an edge but how well it takes one. Even the best of steel will be dulled with frequent use but a good knife will be razor sharp when given a few strokes with a steel. Knives should be sharpened before each use with a steel, and sharpened with a carborundum or whetstone once a month. Use knives on a chopping board only. Metal and tile surfaces ruin blades. Do *not* use roller or electric sharpeners which may nick the blade. Do not let knives stand in water nor be washed in a dishwasher. Wipe off immediately and store after use. A good knife will last a lifetime if chosen and cared for properly. A steel and carborundum should be purchased with your knives. If a restaurant supply house is available in your area you will find a greater selection of equipment and will undoubtedly receive some instruction in sharpening your knives.

Appliances

Appliances are a boon to modern kitchens. They take so much drudgery and hard work out of cooking. There are a few appliances I would consider necessities and some luxuries depending upon your needs.

A blender is definitely a necessity. A good one will blend, purée, chop, pulverize, mix, combine several steps, and save washing bowls. They are not all alike and do not choose one according to the number of buttons. There is little difference in speed when you get over 10 buttons but the price does go up proportionately. A good blender with 6 to 8 speeds will serve most needs. A cycle button is nice for unclogging food lodged in the bottom. I would recommend a model with a removable bottom for easy cleaning. Extra jars can be purchased with some makes and that is a convenience.

Electric mixers also save a great deal of time. Whether choosing a table model or a hand mixer select a model with sufficient speeds. Low, medium, and high may not be enough to handle heavy batters or doughs. Choose a portable model that fits your hand and is not too heavy.

You can find appliances to perform almost every kitchen chore. You can open cans, perk coffee, squeeze juice, grind coffee beans, and peel potatoes electrically. The question again is how much would you use it. Would you be better off with a 59-cent can opener and a good chef's knife instead of an electric toy?

Utensils

A collection of kitchen utensils such as cutting boards, cookie sheets, pie tins, cake pans, soufflé dishes, and ramekins will reflect your tastes in cooking. If you enjoy baking you will find your cupboards overflowing with a variety of Bundt pans, spring form pans, muffin tins, and pie plates. However, if you do like to serve casseroles, you will supply yourself with an assortment of ovenproof dishes and ramekins. There are a few basic utensils which are necessary in any kitchen. Bowls in all sizes are important. Try to find ones with spouts to make pouring easier. At least one cookie sheet should be in your cupboard. A cookie sheet makes a handy tray when putting a rack of ramekins under the broiler and is a drip catcher for dishes that might splatter in the oven. Pie plates and cake pans do double duty for such dishes as broiled mushrooms, baked tomatoes, and baked squash.

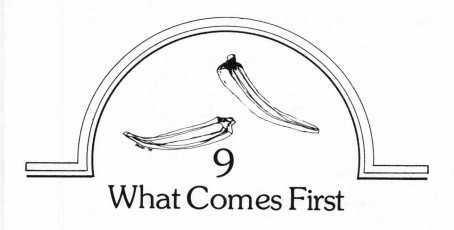

9
What Comes First

INTRODUCING A MEAL with a tantalizing morsel whets the appetite. Served with a cocktail or glass of wine, this pleasant custom sets the tone for the meal. Chips and dips are fine cocktail party fare but the first course of appetizers should be an interesting prelude to dinner and should be planned to complement the meal. If soup is the first course, it need not be served at the table but can instead be passed in attractive mugs to guests seated comfortably in the living room. Cold, cooked vegetables served with a vinaigrette or hollandaise sauce always make an appealing appetizer. If the first course is to be more elaborate, such as eggs in aspic, eliminate fancy hors d'oeuvres, substituting perhaps some dry roasted nuts or a bowl of fresh strawberries. Whatever your choice, keep it light and simple; avoid dulling the senses for the meal to follow.

When serving canapés to a cocktail crowd or preparing trays of finger foods for a tea, you can choose from many dips and spreads to be served with sticks of raw vegetables, toast rounds, fancy crackers, or biscuits. A dot of avocado spread on a cherry tomato, a sliver of cucumber dressed with dill dip or blue cheese spread offer a refreshing change from the familiar onion dip. This is the time to experiment with some unusual combinations, witness our peanut butter and chutney mixture, or take your cue from another part of the menu, for example a thick vegetable purée to serve as a dunk for raw carrots, rather than a vegetable course. Go a little wild and let your friends rave about your flair with food.

Avocado Dip
Makes 1⅓ cups

¾ cup avocado, peeled and mashed
1   cup low-fat cottage cheese
2   teaspoons onion, grated
1   teaspoon lemon juice
1   teaspoon Worcestershire sauce
1   level teaspoon salt

1. Place the avocado in a blender. Gently rinse the cottage cheese under running water. Drain thoroughly and place in the blender with the remaining ingredients. Purée until smooth. Taste for seasoning.
2. Serve with crackers or chips. If not to be served immediately, cover with plastic wrap, placing the wrap directly on the dip to prevent it from discoloring.

Dill Dip
Serves 6

½ cup buttermilk
½ cup mayonnaise
1   teaspoon dill weed
1   teaspoon Beau Monde seasoning (optional)
1   tablespoon fresh parsley, minced, or ½ tablespoon dried paprika

1. Blend all ingredients thoroughly. Garnish with a dash of paprika.
2. Chill thoroughly before serving as a dip for cold, cooked, or raw vegetables or crackers.

Guacamole
Makes 1 cup

Cool and velvety smooth, this makes a tangy dip for raw vegetables or crackers.

¾   cup avocado, peeled and mashed
2   tablespoons mayonnaise or yogurt
2   tablespoons canned green chili peppers, diced
1   tablespoon lemon juice
2½ teaspoons onion, finely grated
salt and pepper to taste
paprika

1. Blend all the ingredients until smooth. Garnish with a dash of paprika.
2. If not to be served immediately, cover with plastic wrap, making sure the wrap touches the surface of the dip, preventing the air from getting to it and discoloring it.

Hoummus
Serves 8

Try this different dip with sesame crackers or tortilla chips.

1   *15-ounce can garbanzo beans*
2   *tablespoons sesame seed, toasted*
2   *tablespoons sesame oil*
3   *tablespoons lemon juice*
1   *large clove garlic*
¼ *teaspoon ground cumin (optional)*
dash of Tabasco sauce

1. Drain the garbanzo beans and reserve the liquid. Place in a blender or food mill. Add the remaining ingredients. Add about ¼ cup of the reserved liquid and blend until smooth, adding more liquid as necessary. Taste for seasoning and serve.

Salsa
Serves 6 to 8

This is an excellent dip for tortilla or poquita chips.

3   *tomatoes, peeled, seeded, and finely chopped*
½ *cup onion, finely chopped*
½ *cup green or red pepper, finely chopped*
½ *cup celery, finely chopped*
4   *ounces chili peppers, diced*
¼ *cup salad oil*
3   *tablespoons red wine vinegar*
½ *teaspoon celery seed*
1   *teaspoon coriander seed, crushed*
1½ *teaspoons salt*
dash of Tabasco sauce

1. Combine the tomatoes, onion, green pepper, celery, and chili peppers.
2. Add the oil, vinegar, and seasonings and refrigerate overnight.
3. Serve with tortilla or corn chips.

Asparagus Foldovers
Serves 12

Fresh or frozen asparagus makes an appearance in this unusual appetizer.

> 12 *slices bread*
> ½ *cup Blue Cheese Sauce (see Saucery)*
> ¼ *cup Parmesan cheese, grated*
> 12 *spears asparagus*
> 4 *tablespoons margarine, melted*

1. Trim the crusts from the bread. Spread with the Blue Cheese Sauce and sprinkle with the Parmesan cheese.
2. Cut the asparagus spears in half and place them diagonally on the bread slices. Fold over and secure with a toothpick.
3. Brush the foldovers with margarine and bake in a 400° oven for 10 to 12 minutes or until lightly browned. Serve hot.

Sweet and Sour Chicken Wings
Serves 6

This appetizer is particularly appealing because it can be prepared ahead of time.

> 24 *chicken wings*
> 1 *cup water*
> ¾ *cup brown sugar*
> ½ *cup soy sauce*
> ¼ *cup vinegar*
> ⅛ *cup vegetable oil*
> 1 *clove garlic, diced*
> 1 *teaspoon ground ginger, or Chinese Five Spices*
> ½ *cup cornstarch or flour*

1. Disjoint wings and reserve tips for soup stocks. Cut each wing in half at the joint and place in bowl.
2. Mix water, sugar, soy sauce, vinegar, vegetable oil, garlic, and spices.
3. Marinate in refrigerator at least 3 hours, preferably overnight.
4. Coat wings with cornstarch or flour by shaking in a paper bag, 2 or 3 at a time. Redip gently in marinade.
5. Place on a lightly oiled cookie sheet or pan. Bake for 45 to 50 minutes at 350°.
6. Can be refrigerated at this point and warmed prior to serving.

Tuna Cream
Serves 12

This is a lovely spread for crackers, thin slices of French bread or melba toast.

1   *3-ounce can tuna*
¼ *cup nondairy creamer*
¼ *cup mayonnaise*
½ *teaspoon celery salt*
½ *teaspoon garlic salt*
½ *teaspoon lemon peel*
3   *tablespoons fresh parsley, minced, or 1½ tablespoons dried*

1. Place the tuna and nondairy creamer in a blender. Blend until smooth. Add the remaining ingredients and beat until creamy. Serve chilled.

Vegetable Dip
Serves 10

5   *green onions, finely minced*
2   *beef bouillon cubes, crushed*
⅛ *teaspoon Beau Monde seasoning*
1   *cup buttermilk*
1   *cup mayonnaise*

1. Combine the onions, bouillon cubes, and Beau Monde. The bouillon cubes should be crushed to a fine grainy texture. Stir in the buttermilk and blend thoroughly.
2. Add the mayonnaise and blend until smooth. Serve well chilled with cold, cooked, or raw vegetables or crackers.

Peanut Butter Chutney Spread
Serves 6

This unusual combination is delicious on thin wheat crackers.

½ *cup chunky-type peanut butter*
3   *tablespoons chutney, chopped*
1   *tablespoon nondairy creamer*
dash Worcestershire sauce
¼ *teaspoon garlic salt*
2   *tablespoons red wine*

1. Blend all ingredients thoroughly, adding just enough wine for a smooth consistency.

Cocktail Chicken Wings
Serves 8

These delectable appetizers can be made ahead and reheated before serving.

16 chicken wings
⅔ cup soy sauce
½ cup brown sugar
¼ teaspoon salt
¼ teaspoon garlic salt
¼ cup sherry
¼ cup green onions, diced

1. Remove tips from the chicken wings and reserve for making soups. Cut the wings in two pieces at the joint.
2. Place the remaining ingredients in a shallow baking dish or skillet. Stir until sugar and salt have dissolved.
3. Add the chicken pieces and simmer 45 minutes or until done. Turn pieces occasionally while cooking.

Oysters Rockefeller
Serves 6

2   dozen oysters in their shells
Puréed Spinach (see From the Garden)
2   tablespoons nondairy creamer
2   tablespoons margarine
4   tablespoons shallots or green onions, finely minced
salt and pepper to taste
¼ cup fresh parsley, minced
1   tablespoon Pernod (optional)
2   tablespoons Parmesan cheese, grated
rock salt (optional)

1. Shuck the oysters and place half the shell on a baking sheet covered with ½ to ¾ inch of rock salt. Place an oyster on each shell.
2. Heat the Puréed Spinach and stir in the nondairy creamer.
3. Melt the margarine and add the shallots. Sauté until soft and stir into the spinach mixture. Season to taste with salt and pepper.
4. Place a tablespoon of the spinach on each oyster. Sprinkle with the parsley, Pernod, and grated cheese.
5. Place in a 450° oven until the oysters are plump, about 10 minutes. Run under the broiler to brown and serve immediately.

Pot Stickers

Makes about 15 pieces

A shopping trip for sesame oil will be justified when you taste these succulent Chinese morsels.

FILLING:

1 pound ground beef, or mixture of beef, lamb, and pork
½ cup onion, finely minced
2 egg whites
2 teaspoons cornstarch
1 teaspoon sesame oil
1 tablespoon sherry
¾ teaspoon soy sauce
½ teaspoon sugar
freshly ground pepper
1 clove garlic, finely minced
1 sliver fresh ginger or ¼ teaspoon ground

WRAPPING:

Wonton skins (bought in oriental food store)
2 scant tablespoons vegetable or sesame oil, if available

SAUCE:

1 teaspoon soy sauce
1 teaspoon dry mustard
¼ cup hot catsup
dash of red pepper oil (optional)

1. Place filling ingredients in a bowl and blend thoroughly.
2. Spoon a small amount of mixture onto a Wonton skin and fold diagonally over filling. Moisten edges and pinch together tightly.
3. Put the pot stickers on a plate and place on a rack in a steamer. (A wok, steamer, or foil-covered roasting pan may be used.) Steam for 20 minutes.
4. Heat oil in a skillet and when hot (but not smoking) add the steamed pot stickers. Cook on one side only until bottom is lightly browned. Remove to a serving dish.
5. Blend sauce ingredients and serve as a dip for hot pot stickers.

Seviche
Serves 6

While not cooked in the conventional manner, this is definitely not raw fish. The acid in the lime juice "cooks" the fish while it is marinating. The result is a marvelous tangy fish salad, or first course.

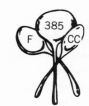

2 *pounds firm, white fish (sole, halibut) or scallops*
¾ *cup lime juice*
¾ *cup lemon juice*
1 *medium red onion, sliced*
1 *clove garlic, quartered*
½ *teaspoon chili powder*
1 *avocado, peeled, seeded, and chopped*
2 *large tomatoes, peeled, seeded, and chopped*
4 *tablespoons vegetable oil*
2 *tablespoons coriander, chopped (optional)*

1. Cut the fish fillets into bite-sized pieces but don't cut them too small or they will disintegrate. Place them in a single layer in a glass or ceramic dish. (Do not use metal.)
2. Blend juices and pour over the fish. Layer the onion slices on top. Cover and refrigerate for at least 6 hours. Turn the fish occasionally.
3. Add the remaining ingredients. Again, cover and chill 6 more hours or overnight. This will keep in the refrigerator for 3 days. Serve very cold on lettuce leaves or mound on melba toast.

Onion Rounds
Makes 24

24 *bread rounds*
½ *cup mayonnaise*
3 *tablespoons onion, grated*
½ *teaspoon Worcestershire sauce*
¼ *teaspoon garlic salt*
paprika

1. Cut bread rounds from slices of bread using a crouton cutter or small juice glass.
2. Blend the mayonnaise, onion, Worcestershire sauce, and garlic salt. Taste for seasoning. Spread each bread round with about 1 teaspoon of the mixture and sprinkle with a dash of paprika.

3. Place the rounds on a cookie sheet and place under the broiler for about 3 minutes or until golden. Serve hot.

Sweet and Sour Meatballs
Serves 12

These tempting appetizers are perfect dipped in Polynesian sauce.

1½ *pounds very lean ground beef*
¾   *cup quick-cooking or old fashioned oats*
1   *5-ounce can water chestnuts, drained and finely diced*
¼   *cup onion, grated*
½   *teaspoon garlic salt*
1   *tablespoon soy sauce*
¼   *teaspoon chili powder*
1   *whole egg*
½   *cup low-fat milk*
1   *tablespoon vegetable oil*
1   *8-ounce can crushed pineapple*
1   *cup brown sugar, firmly packed*
2   *tablespoons cornstarch*
1   *cup beef bouillon*
2   *teaspoons soy sauce*
½   *teaspoon ginger, powdered, or 1 tablespoon fresh ginger, grated*
¼   *cup green pepper, chopped*

1. Blend the ground beef, oats, diced water chestnuts, grated onion, garlic salt, soy sauce, chili powder, whole egg, and milk. Mix thoroughly and form into round shapes about 1 teaspoon each. Heat the vegetable oil and brown the beef balls on all sides. Do not overcook. Drain.
2. Drain the pineapple and reserve the juice. Blend the sugar, cornstarch, bouillon, soy sauce, and ginger in a saucepan. Bring to a boil and stir until thickened and clear.
3. Stir in the pineapple, green pepper, and meatballs and simmer 10 to 15 minutes or until meatballs are cooked through. Serve hot in the sauce with toothpicks.

Blue Cheese Wonders
Makes 18 to 20 slices

We found the blue cheese seasoning on the spice rack to make these tangy morsels.

> 1 *cucumber, peeled and thinly sliced*
> 1 *3-ounce package of Neufchâtel cheese, softened*
> 1 *tablespoon blue cheese seasoning*

1. Prepare cucumber and set aside.
2. Blend the cheese and seasoning thoroughly. Taste for seasoning, adding more blue cheese flavoring if desired. Spread on the cucumber rounds.

Stuffed Eggs
Serves 12

> 12 *eggs*
> 2 *tablespoons vinegar*
> *Yankee Chicken Salad* (see *Greenery*)
> *paprika*

1. Place the eggs in a pan of cold water and add the vinegar. Bring to a simmer and cook for 12 minutes. Do not let them boil or overcook. Drain and hold under running cold water. Cool and shell. Slice in half and discard the yolks.
2. Dice the Yankee Chicken Salad very finely for a smooth consistency. Spoon the salad into the egg white, garnish with a dash of paprika, and serve as an appetizer.

Quesadillas
Serves 4

This Mexican version of a grilled cheese sandwich can be served as an entrée, a luncheon dish, or cut in squares and served as an appetizer.

> 6 *ounces jack or Lappi cheese*
> 2 *egg equivalents*
> 1 *tablespoon canned green chili peppers, diced*
> 3 *tablespoons margarine*
> 8 *flour tortillas*

1. Combine cheese, eggs, and chili peppers in a bowl. Place a small amount in the center of each tortilla. Fold in half.
2. Melt margarine in a skillet and add the tortillas. Cook until golden about 2 minutes and flip and brown on the other side. Cooking more than two at a time is tricky. Add more margarine for browning if necessary. Serve immediately.

Eggs in Aspic
Serves 6

This classic makes a shimmering appearance as a first course or luncheon dish.

> 6   *eggs, hard-boiled*
> 1   *envelope gelatin*
> ¼ *cup cold water*
> 2   *cups chicken stock*
> 2   *tablespoons Madeira wine*
> *fresh tarragon leaves or sprig of parsley*
> *cooked asparagus tips or broccoli flowerettes*
> 6   *thin slices cooked chicken*

1. Slice the eggs in half lengthwise and discard the yolks.
2. Dissolve the gelatin in the cold water.
3. Heat the chicken stock, stir in the dissolved gelatin, add the Madeira wine, and chill until slightly thickened but still runny.
4. Place two tarragon leaves crisscrossed or a sprig of parsley in the bottom of a ramekin. Spoon ¼ inch of gelatin over the bottom.
5. Place two asparagus tips or a broccoli flowerette in each egg. Place in the ramekin, vegetable side down. Cover with gelatin. Place a slice of chicken over the egg and cover it with gelatin. Chill thoroughly.
6. Unmold just before serving by running a knife around edge and placing the ramekin in a bowl of hot water for 10 seconds. Place serving dish over the ramekin, invert, and shake gently until the aspic loosens. Garnish with parsley and serve immediately.

Stuffed Celery

An excellent appetizer or snack, celery can be stuffed with any number of combinations. Some favorites are:

1. Chop ¼ cup black olives and mix with 2 ounces Neufchâtel cheese. Spread on crisp, chilled celery stalks.
2. Guacamole.
3. Chicken salad.
4. Neufchâtel, pimientos, and bacon bits.
5. Blue Cheese Dressing (see Saucery)

Antipasto
Serves 24

This is best if made several days before serving. It keeps for weeks.

1   cup wine vinegar
⅔   cup vegetable oil
12 ounces tomato paste
1   teaspoon salt
1   teaspoon pepper
1   small jar pickled onions
6   small onions, peeled and sliced
2   cups green beans, cooked
½   cup green olives
1   pound carrots, cooked and sliced
½   cup mushrooms, quartered
1   cup dill pickles, sliced
1   6-ounce can tuna
1   cup black olives

1. Heat the vinegar, vegetable oil, tomato paste, salt, and pepper in a saucepan. Place in a large glass or ceramic bowl.
2. Add the remaining ingredients, using the juice from the pickled onions,

green olives, and pickles. Other vegetables may be added if desired such as peppers, celery, or cauliflower. Cover and refrigerate 4 days before serving.

Deviled Clams
Serves 6

1½ *dozen clams*
2 *tablespoons vegetable oil*
2 *tablespoons green onions or shallots, finely diced*
1 *slice Canadian bacon*
1½ *tablespoons fresh chives, minced*
1 *teaspoon fresh minced or dried parsley*
1 *teaspoon sherry*
dash of Worcestershire sauce
dash of Tabasco sauce
½ *teaspoon mustard*
salt and pepper to taste
2 *tablespoons bread crumbs*
3 *tablespoons margarine*

1. Scrub the clams well to remove any sand. Place in a large pot with 1 cup of water or just enough to cover the bottom. Cover and steam until the shells open. Discard any clams that open before cooking or any that remain closed after steaming.
2. Remove the meat from the shells. Discard the rubbery neck and finely dice the clams. Heat the oil and sauté the onion or shallots until soft. Sauté the Canadian bacon until slightly crisp and mince. You should have about 3 tablespoons of minced bacon.
3. Combine the clams, onions, Canadian bacon, and remaining ingredients, using just enough bread crumbs to make a firm mixture.
4. Fill each clam shell with the mixture and sprinkle the tops lightly with bread crumbs. Place ½ teaspoon of margarine on each one.
5. The clams may be prepared ahead to this point and refrigerated. Before serving, place the clam shells on a baking sheet and heat under the broiler until browned. Serve hot.

Stuffed Cucumbers
Makes about 30 slices

> 2   *cucumbers, 6 to 8 inches long*
> ½   *cup boiled ham, finely diced*
> 1   *tablespoon onion, grated*
> 2   *tablespoons dill pickle, minced*
> 1   *hard cooked egg white, finely diced*
> 2   *tablespoons celery, minced*
> ½   *teaspoon mustard (optional)*
> ¼   *cup mayonnaise*

1. Peel the cucumbers and, with a narrow spoon or melon baller, scoop out the seeds so that you have a tube.
2. Combine the remaining ingredients and taste for seasoning. Stuff this mixture into the cucumber and chill thoroughly.
3. To serve, slice diagonally in ½-inch pieces.

Eggplant Caviar
Serves 12

This vegetable purée is scrumptious anytime but the flavor improves with age. If possible, prepare 24 hours ahead.

> 1   *large eggplant*
> 3   *tablespoons olive oil*
> 3   *tablespoons vegetable oil*
> 1   *cup onion, finely chopped*
> ½   *cup green pepper, diced*
> 2   *cloves garlic, minced*
> ½   *cup zucchini, diced*
> 2   *large tomatoes, peeled, seeded, and chopped*
> ½   *teaspoon sugar*
> 2   *teaspoons salt*
> *freshly ground pepper*
> 2   *tablespoons lemon juice*

1. Bake the unpeeled eggplant at 425° for about 1 hour until soft and wrinkled. The skin may blister.
2. Heat the oils in a skillet and sauté onion until soft but not brown. Add green pepper, garlic, and zucchini and cook over medium heat for 5 minutes. Set aside.
3. Peel the eggplant and fully dice the pulp. Add to the onion mixture. Add

tomatoes, sugar, salt, and pepper and blend well. The mixture should be a coarse purée.

4. Place over high heat and bring to a boil, stirring. Reduce heat and cover. Simmer for 45 minutes, then uncover and continue cooking until liquid has evaporated and the mixture is thick. Stir from time to time. Taste for seasoning. Add more garlic if necessary. Continue cooking for at least 10 minutes. Add lemon juice and taste again. Chill. Serve on crackers, thinly sliced pumpernickel, or rye bread.

Marinated Carrots
Serves 8

3 tablespoons vegetable oil
3 cloves garlic, minced
1 tablespoon onion, chopped
¼ cup vinegar
½ teaspoon salt
freshly ground pepper
1½ teaspoons mustard
1 tablespoon whole pickling spices
1 pound carrots, cut into ¼-inch slices
1 onion, sliced

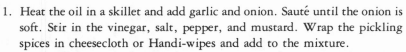

1. Heat the oil in a skillet and add garlic and onion. Sauté until the onion is soft. Stir in the vinegar, salt, pepper, and mustard. Wrap the pickling spices in cheesecloth or Handi-wipes and add to the mixture.
2. Add the carrots and simmer for 10 minutes or until tender when pierced with a fork. Remove the cheesecloth-wrapped spices, and transfer carrots to a shallow dish. Cover with the liquid and onion slices.
3. Marinate, refrigerated, for 24 hours. Baste occasionally. Serve chilled.

Herbed Olives Antipasto
Serves 8

2 8-ounce cans black pitted olives
2 tablespoons vegetable oil
⅛ cup olive oil
3 tablespoons red wine vinegar
1 clove garlic, crushed
1 teaspoon dried oregano, or 2 teaspoons fresh oregano

1. Combine all ingredients in a shallow dish.
2. Marinate for 24 hours in the refrigerator, stirring occasionally.

Mushroom Caviar
Serves 6

This is a nice canapé when served on toast squares.

3   *tablespoons margarine*
1   *cup green onions, chopped*
2   *cups mushrooms, chopped*
1   *tablespoon lemon juice*
salt and pepper
1   *tablespoon dill weed*
⅔   *cup Sour Topping (see Saucery)*
8   *thin slices rye or wheat bread*

1. Melt the margarine in a saucepan and add the onions. Sauté until soft. Add the mushrooms, lemon juice, and salt and pepper to taste. Sauté until the mushrooms are soft. Raise the heat to evaporate any liquid.
2. Stir in the dill and Sour Topping. Taste for seasoning.
3. Remove the crusts from the bread and cut in quarters. Toast and serve with the Mushroom Caviar.

Mushroom Pâté
Makes approximately 2 cups

¾   *pound mushrooms, washed and coarsely chopped*
¾   *cup shallots, minced*
6   *tablespoons margarine*
salt and pepper
¼   *cup brandy*
1 to 2 *tablespoons lemon juice*

1. Melt the margarine in a skillet and add the shallots and sauté over low to medium heat until soft but not brown, at least five minutes.
2. Add the mushrooms, season lightly with salt and pepper, and stir quickly over high heat for two minutes. The heat must be high or the mushrooms will render a large amount of liquid and the pate will be runny. Add the brandy and ignite, then stir with a long-handled spoon until the flames die out.
3. Put the mixture in a blender and purée until smooth. Add the lemon juice to taste and check for seasoning. Chill thoroughly. This is best served the following day.

Mushrooms à la Grecque
Serves 6

Marinating for several days improves the flavor of these morsels.

1   *pound small button mushrooms*
1   *tablespoon vinegar*
½   *cup vegetable or olive oil*
½   *cup water*
2   *tablespoons wine vinegar*
1   *clove garlic, chopped*
½   *teaspoon salt*
8   *whole black peppercorns*
1   *bay leaf*
½   *teaspoon pepper*

1. Place the mushrooms in water to cover, add tablespoon of vinegar. Wash, rinse and drain mushrooms, then place in a saucepan. Add the remaining ingredients and simmer until tender. Store in the refrigerator for several days before serving.
2. Serve with toothpicks.

Roast Peppers
Serves 4

Simple, but delicious. These may also be served in salads or as antipasto.

1 *green or red pepper per person*
Sauce Vinaigrette (see Saucery)
black pepper, finely ground

1. Preheat oven to 400°.
2. Place whole peppers on a cookie sheet and place in oven until the skin bursts and the pepper is tender. Do not scorch.
3. Slice and remove seeds. Cover with the vinaigrette dressing and a sprinkle of freshly ground pepper. Serve chilled. May also be served with just vegetable oil and salt and pepper.

Breaded Vegetable Medley
Serves 8

These delicious morsels can be served as appetizers or a vegetable course. A quick version of this recipe uses a good brand of seasoned croutons or poultry stuffing. Or, make your own bread crumbs and add a combination of oregano, sage, garlic, and onion salt. Use a variety of vegetables, choosing from eggplant, zucchini, peeled and seeded tomato slices, onion rings, scallions, carrot and potato slivers, celery sticks, cauliflower, artichoke hearts, and green beans.

> 3   cups mixed, prepared vegetables
> ½ cup flour
> 2   egg whites
> ½ teaspoon salt
> dash of pepper
> ½ teaspoon Worcestershire sauce
> ½ cup seasoned poultry stuffing, bread crumbs, or seasoned croutons
> oil for frying

1. Peel and slice the vegetables. Shake with the flour in a paper bag. Beat the egg whites slightly. Add salt, pepper, and Worcestershire sauce. Dip floured pieces into this mixture and then into crumbs.
2. Heat the oil to 375° in a skillet and add the breaded vegetables, a few at a time. Add just enough oil to liberally coat the bottom of the pan.
3. Turn the vegetables once or twice and when they have browned nicely, remove to a crumpled paper towel to drain. Serve hot.

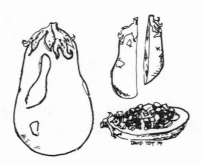

Stuffed Mushrooms
Serves 4

These may be prepared ahead. Expect them to be devoured immediately.

12 *large fresh mushroom caps, stems removed*
salt and pepper
3 *tablespoons shallots or green onions, finely minced*
2 *tablespoons margarine*
1 *tablespoon oil*
stems from the mushroom caps, finely minced
¼ *cup Madeira wine (optional)*
3 *tablespoons fine, white, dry bread crumbs*
¼ *cup Swiss cheese, grated*
¼ *cup Parmesan cheese, grated*
4 *tablespoons fresh parsley, minced, or 2 tablespoons dried*
½ *teaspoon fresh tarragon, or ¼ teaspoon dried*
salt and pepper
2 to 3 *tablespoons nondairy creamer*
3 *tablespoons Swiss cheese, grated*
2 *tablespoons melted margarine*

1. Sprinkle the mushroom caps lightly with salt and pepper. Place them hollow-side up in baking dish.
2. Sauté the shallots or green onions in margarine and oil for 3 to 4 minutes without browning. Add mushroom stems and sauté 5 to 6 minutes until the mushroom pieces begin to separate from each other and are lightly browned. Add Madeira wine, if desired, and boil it down rapidly until almost entirely evaporated.
3. Remove from heat and mix in the bread crumbs, cheeses, parsley, tarragon, and seasonings. Blend in creamer, a spoonful at a time, using just enough to moisten the mixture but keep it sufficiently stiff to hold its shape in a spoon. Correct seasoning.
4. Fill the caps with the stuffing. Top each with a pinch of the remaining Swiss cheese and a few drops of melted margarine. (The mushrooms may be done ahead to this point and refrigerated until ready to serve.)
5. Before serving, bake in upper third of a preheated, 375° oven for 15 to 20 minutes until caps are tender and stuffing has browned lightly on top. Serve hot.

Frito Misto
Serves 8

This dish is a combination of fresh vegetables dipped in a batter and deep fried. You can choose zucchini, turnips, eggplant, onion rings, cauliflower, green onions, celery strips, thin slivers of carrots or potatoes, french cut green beans, tomato slices which have been peeled and seeded, parsley sprigs, or any favorite vegetable. Slice the vegetables into small pieces or strips. Follow the instructions for deep-oil frying and remember to skim any excess batter from the fat or it will burn and impair the flavor of the oil.

BASIC DEEP-OIL FRYING BATTER:

- ½ *cup light beer*
- ¾ *cup flour*
- 1   *teaspoon salt*
- 1   *beaten egg white*
- 4   *cups vegetables, cut in sticks or strips*

1. Pour the beer into a bowl and sift the flour into it, stirring to make a smooth batter. Add the salt and stir.
2. Beat the egg white until it forms stiff peaks and then stir gently into the batter until it is smooth.
3. Seasonings can be added to the batter to enhance the flavor. For example, garlic salt and oregano give a definite Italian flavor to zucchini, eggplant, and tomatoes.
4. Unused batter can be refrigerated for several days. Add another beaten egg white before using.
5. Dip the vegetables into the batter and then into the hot oil. When puffy and golden on both sides remove to a crumpled paper towel to drain. Serve hot, lightly salted.

10
Consider Soups

PICTURE A COLD winter evening, a fire in the hearth, and a tureen of steaming onion soup. Or perhaps Sunday brunch — a mixture of interesting people and a leisurely meal started off with mushroom consommé; or take a hot summer evening, a light supper outdoors, beginning with a bowl of iced cucumber soup to take the edge off a busy, hot day. These settings are perfect for soups. Soups find their place on any menu, any time of the year. While some soups require hours of simmering to bring out the full flavor of rich stocks and succulent vegetables, many can be whipped together in minutes. Elegant creamed soups, one expects only to find on the menus of the best restaurants, can be put together in no time at all, thanks to electric blenders. Take a seasonal vegetable, simmer it to tendernesss in a good homemade chicken stock (see page 87), add a complementary herb or two, whirl in the blender, and cream with nondairy creamer or low-fat milk, and presto: you have a tantalizing first course. Present your diners with a large tureen of hearty potato chowder, a crisp salad, and a bowl of fresh fruit; and you have a simple, nourishing, and delicious supper. Consider soups for breakfast, as well as dinner. What better way to escape the high cholesterol and fat routine of bacon and eggs. How about fruit soups as an interesting beginning to a meal? They particularly complement pork, game, and fowl. Served first thing in the morning, or for a midnight supper, soups belong in your day.

Cold Apricot Soup
Serves 6

This is an unusual first course but excellent with fowl, pork, or game.

    1 *pound dried apricots*
    cold water to cover
    ½ *cup dry white wine*
    1 *cup nondairy creamer*
    4 *teaspoons sour cream*

1. Place the apricots in a bowl and cover with cold water. Use about 1½ cups but make sure it covers the fruit. Let soak and soften for 1 hour.
2. Purée the apricots and water in a blender until smooth. Add wine and stir.
3. Add the nondairy creamer and blend thoroughly. Chill and serve with a dab of sour cream.

Cold Cucumber Soup
Serves 4

Delicious on a hot summer day.

    1 *large cucumber, peeled, seeded, and chopped*
    2 *cups chicken stock*
    1 *teaspoon dill*
    ½ *cup buttermilk or yogurt*

1. Simmer the cucumber in the chicken stock until tender, approximately 10 minutes.
2. Whirl in a blender until smooth.
3. Add the dill and buttermilk or yogurt and taste for seasoning. Stir until smooth.
4. Chill thoroughly. Serve very cold.

Mushroom Consommé
Serves 4

This is best made from scratch. But, if you do not have time to make your own beef stock, canned beef bouillon makes an adequate substitute.

    3 *cups beef stock or bouillon*
    2 *tablespoons onion, diced*
    2 *tablespoons carrots, diced*

2   *tablespoons celery, diced*
2   *tablespoons vermouth*
¾ *cup mushrooms, sliced*
2   *tablespoons dry sherry*

1. Place the beef broth in a saucepan and add the onion, carrots, celery, and vermouth. Bring to a boil, then reduce heat to a simmer for 20 minutes. Strain.
2. Add the mushrooms to the strained broth. Simmer for 5 minutes.
3. Add the sherry just before serving.

Gazpacho
Serves 8

Cold and spicy, this soup revives the spirit on a hot summer day.

3   *cups tomatoes, peeled, seeded, and chopped*
2   *large cucumbers, peeled, seeded, and diced*
½ *cup celery, diced*
½ *cup green pepper, diced*
½ *cup onion, diced*
1   *clove garlic*
2   *cups tomato or tomato-vegetable juice*
2   *teaspoons lemon juice*
4   *tablespoons wine vinegar*
¼ *cup vegetable oil*
dash of Tabasco sauce
salt and pepper to taste
¼ *cup cucumbers, minced*
¼ *cup celery, minced*
¼ *cup green pepper, minced*

1. Chop the tomato pulp finely. Try to reserve as much of the juice as possible.
2. Place the diced cucumber, celery, green pepper, onion, and the garlic in a blender and purée or mince until very, very fine. Add this to the tomatoes and blend well.
3. Stir in the juices, wine vinegar, and vegetable oil and mix thoroughly. Season with Tabasco sauce and salt and pepper. If a spicier soup is desired add more onion and garlic. Chill thoroughly and serve with the minced cucumber, celery, and green pepper sprinkled on top.

Senegalese Soup
Serves 4

As with all curried dishes, add this pungent spice carefully, taste frequently.

    1 *tablespoon margarine*
    1 *tablespoon flour*
    ½ *teaspoon curry powder*
    2 *cups chicken stock*
    1 *green apple, grated*
    salt and pepper to taste
    ½ *cup nondairy creamer or low-fat milk*
    slivers of cooked white chicken
    coconut, chopped
    chives, chopped

1. Melt the margarine in a saucepan over low heat. Add the flour and curry powder and stir for at least 2 minutes.
2. Heat the chicken stock and gradually add it to the flour mixture. Bring to a boil and stir until slightly thickened. Add the grated apple and simmer for 15 minutes. Season to taste with salt and pepper.
3. Stir in the nondairy creamer and chill thoroughly. This soup may also be served hot. Garnish with slivers of cooked white chicken, a few shreds of coconut, and chopped chives.

Tomato Bisque
Serves 8

    2 *cups leeks*
    vegetable spray or 2 tablespoons vegetable oil
    3 *tablespoons margarine*
    3 *tablespoons flour*
    1 *cup low-fat milk, hot*
    1 *large can whole tomatoes, drained*
    ½ *tablespoon basil, fresh or dried*
    2 *cups chicken stock*
    1 *cup nondairy creamer*

1. Trim the leeks and slice in ¼-inch pieces.
2. Spray the saucepan with vegetable spray and place the leeks in the sauce-

pan. Cook covered, over low to moderate heat, until the leeks are soft.

3. While the leeks are cooking, melt the margarine in a saucepan over low heat. Add the flour and stir well, continue cooking over low heat for 2 minutes.

4. Remove from heat and slowly and gradually add the hot milk, stirring constantly.

5. Bring to a boil and then reduce the heat and simmer for 5 minutes or until the sauce has thickened and is smooth. If there are any lumps at this point, pass through a sieve and return to the saucepan.

6. When the leeks are done add the tomatoes and basil and pour in the chicken stock and then the white sauce.

7. Whirl through a blender until puréed and smooth and add the nondairy creamer. Reheat gently and serve.

Easy Chicken Stock
Makes 2 quarts

Chicken stock, both easy to make and delicious, is the basis for most soups and can be flavored to suit individual tastes. Bones, necks, and backs should be stored in a plastic bag in the freezer and reserved for making soup. The only caution in this recipe is to be sure the stock does not boil. The material that floats to the surface must be skimmed off from time to time for if the soup boils this will return to the stock, make it cloudy, and impair the flavor.

1 *whole stewing chicken or 3 pounds of bones and parts*
1 *teaspoon salt*
1 *onion, chopped*
1 *sprig thyme*
2 *quarts water*
1 *clove garlic*

1. Place the chicken in a large pot and cover with water. Bring to a simmer. Do not let it boil vigorously. Add remaining ingredients.

2. Skim foamy, gray material from the surface from time to time with a metal spoon.

3. Simmer for 40 minutes for chicken parts, or until stewing chicken is tender. Remove chicken and strain. Chill and remove congealed fat.

4. Chicken stock may be frozen for future use.

Avocado Bisque
Serves 8

    2   tablespoons margarine
    ½   cup onion, chopped
    2   tablespoons flour
    3   cups chicken stock
    1   tablespoon lemon juice
    1   clove garlic, minced
    1   teaspoon salt
    freshly ground pepper
    ½   teaspoon curry powder
    1   large ripe avocado
    1   cup low-fat milk
    ½   cup buttermilk

1. Melt the margarine in a skillet. Add the onion and sauté until soft, but not brown.
2. Add the flour and cook for at least 2 minutes. Stir in the chicken stock and bring to a boil and stir until the mixture thickens.
3. Add the lemon juice, garlic, salt, pepper, and curry powder. Simmer for 10 minutes. Add the avocado and pureé in a blender until smooth.
4. Add the milk and buttermilk, season for taste. May be served hot or cold.

Carrot and Leek Soup
Serves 8

    1   pound carrots, peeled and sliced
    1½ cups leeks, white part only, sliced
    bay leaf
    5   cups chicken stock
    salt and pepper to taste
    1   cup nondairy creamer
    chopped parsley, fresh or dried

1. Combine carrots, leeks (thoroughly washed to remove sand), bay leaf, and chicken stock in a saucepan. Bring to a boil and reduce heat. Cook gently for 20 minutes or until carrots are tender.
2. Remove the bay leaf and discard. Pureé the soup mixture in a blender or press vegetables through a sieve.
3. Add the nondairy creamer and reheat. Season to taste with salt and pepper and garnish with a sprinkle of chopped parsley.

Cream of Mushroom Soup
Serves 6

The touch of lemon is a surprise in this smooth, wonderful soup.

½ *pound mushrooms*
½ *lemon*
2 *tablespoons margarine, melted*
1 *cup onion, chopped*
2 *tablespoons flour*
4 *cups chicken stock*
2 *cups water*
salt and pepper
3 *tablespoons nondairy creamer*

1. Chop the mushrooms and sprinkle with the juice of ½ lemon.
2. Melt the margarine and add the mushrooms and onion. Cook slowly until the onions are soft. Add the flour and cook 2 minutes stirring constantly.
3. Add the chicken stock and water, season with salt and pepper, and cook at a *slow* boil for 20 minutes.
4. Whirl the soup in a blender and strain if still lumpy.
5. Season to taste. More lemon juice may be added. Reheat and add the nondairy creamer. Serve.

Cream of Potato Soup
Serves 6

Served cold, this becomes vichyssoise.

2 *tablespoons margarine*
1½ *cups leeks, mainly white part, sliced*
2 *cups boiling potatoes, peeled and sliced*
2½ *cups chicken stock*
salt and pepper
1 *cup low-fat milk*
chopped chives

1. Melt the margarine in a skillet. Add leeks and sauté until soft but not brown. This should take approximately 15 minutes. **Do not brown.**
2. Add potatoes, stock, and salt and pepper and bring to a boil. Reduce heat and simmer for 30 minutes or until the potatoes are tender.
3. Whirl the soup through a blender or force through a food mill.
4. Check seasoning. Add milk and stir thoroughly. Serve with sprinkle of chopped chives for garnish.

Curried Carrot Soup
Serves 4

> 1   tablespoon vegetable oil
> 1   cup onion, diced
> 2   cups carrots, diced
> 2   cups chicken stock
> ¾   cup low-fat milk
> 1   teaspoon curry powder, or to taste

1. Heat the vegetable oil in a skillet and add the diced onion. Sauté until soft.
2. Add the carrots and chicken broth and cook over a moderately high heat until the carrots are quite tender and the stock has reduced to 1 cup.
3. Whirl in a blender until smooth.
4. Add the milk and curry to taste, blend until smooth, and reheat. Serve hot.

Cream of Celery Soup
Serves 6

> 1   tablespoon margarine
> ½   cup onion, chopped
> 2   cups celery, diced
> 1   teaspoon thyme, dried
> 2   cups chicken stock
> salt and pepper
> ¾   cup low-fat milk

1. Melt the margarine in a skillet. Add onion and sauté until soft. Do not brown.
2. Add celery, thyme, chicken stock, and salt and pepper. Bring to a boil and reduce heat to a simmer. Continue cooking until celery is quite tender.
3. Whirl the soup in a blender until puréed and add the milk until the desired consistency. Reheat and serve.

Winter Squash Bisque
Serves 8

> 1   butternut squash, seeded and quartered
> 2   green apples, peeled, seeded, and quartered

1 *large onion, peeled and chopped*
¼ *teaspoon rosemary*
¼ *teaspoon marjoram*
3 *cups chicken stock*
2 *cups water*
salt and pepper to taste
½ *cup low-fat milk*

1. Add the squash, apples, onion, herbs, chicken stock, and water to a large pot.
2. Bring to a boil and reduce heat to a simmer. Continue cooking until the vegetables are tender, about 45 minutes.
3. Remove the skin from the squash and purée the soup in a blender until smooth. Season with salt and pepper.
4. Add the milk, stir until smooth, and serve hot.

Cream of Spinach Soup
Serves 8

2 *cups of leeks, mainly white part, washed thoroughly and chopped*
2 *tablespoons water*
2 *bunches of fresh spinach, or 2 packages frozen spinach*
2 *cups chicken stock*
½ *teaspoon salt*
dash of freshly ground pepper
½ *cup low-fat milk*
juice of ½ lemon

1. Place leeks in a saucepan with the water and cover. Cook until soft, about 20 minutes.
2. For frozen spinach, thaw completely and squeeze thoroughly between your hands to remove **all** the moisture. For fresh spinach, wash in a vinegar bath and rinse. Place spinach in a saucepan. **Do not add any water.** The water clinging to the leaves is sufficient. Stir over moderately high heat until the spinach has completely wilted. Drain thoroughly and cool slightly. Squeeze to remove any additional water.
3. When leeks are soft, add the spinach and chicken stock and cook for 10 minutes. Add salt and pepper and check for seasoning.
4. Whirl through a blender until smooth.
5. Add the low-fat milk and lemon juice. Test for seasoning; add more lemon juice if desired. Reheat for 3 minutes and serve.

Borscht
Serves 6

He.e is one version of this justly famous Russian soup.

½ cup carrots, diced
1 cup onion, diced
2 cups fresh beets, shredded
2 cups beef stock
2 cups water
¼ cup cabbage, shredded
1 tablespoon wine vinegar
4 teaspoons sour cream
4 teaspoons cucumber, shredded

1. Simmer carrots, onion, and beets in the beef stock and water for about 20 minutes.
2. Add the cabbage and vinegar and cook another 15 minutes.
3. Chill thoroughly.
4. Combine sour cream and cucumber and serve soup with a dollop of this mixture. This soup can also be served hot.

Italian Soup
Serves 6

2 tablespoons olive oil
1 cup onion, chopped
3 cloves garlic, minced
1 large green pepper, diced
2 cups zucchini, sliced
1 cup celery, diced
2 large cans tomatoes
1 teaspoon salt
6 cups chicken stock
1 teaspoon fresh oregano, minced
1 teaspoon basil, fresh or dried
½ cup alphabet macaroni
salt and pepper to taste
⅓ cup Parmesan cheese, grated

1. Heat the olive oil in a Dutch oven or large skillet. Add onion, garlic, and green pepper and sauté until soft.

2. Add zucchini, celery, tomatoes, salt, stock, herbs, and macaroni. Bring to a boil and reduce heat to a simmer.
3. Simmer for ½ hour. Test for seasoning.
4. Serve hot with a sprinkling of Parmesan cheese.

Lobscouse
Serves 6

This is for the Cassidy family, Sunday dinners, and Tuesday leftovers.

1 *leftover leg of lamb bone*
8 *cups cold water*
2 *teaspoons salt*
2 *onions, quartered*
1 *carrot, diced*

1. Place the lamb bone, water, salt, onions, and carrot in a Dutch oven or large stock pot. Simmer for 1½ hours and check for seasoning.
2. Serve with boiled potatoes.

French Onion Soup
Serves 6

3 *tablespoons margarine*
1 *tablespoon olive oil*
6 *red onions, cut into ¼-inch slices*
salt and pepper to taste
1 *tablespoon sugar*
4 *cups beef stock*
2 *tablespoons brandy (optional)*
1 *tablespoon Parmesan cheese, freshly grated*
French bread

1. Melt the margarine in a heavy skillet and add the olive oil. Add the sliced onions and sauté over medium heat until soft but not brown. This will take 10 to 15 minutes. Stir occasionally until they are transparent.
2. Add salt, pepper, and sugar. Cook further until the onions are very limp.
3. Add the beef stock and let simmer for 30 minutes. Just before serving, stir in the brandy.
4. Cover with the cheese and place in a 350° oven for 8 minutes.
5. Remove from oven, place a slice of French bread in each soup bowl and cover with soup. Serve.

Minestrone
Serves 8

> 1   cup white beans
> 1   quart water
> 1   tablespoon olive oil
> 4   cloves garlic, minced
> 3   pieces Canadian bacon, diced
> 2   cups onion, chopped
> 8   cups chicken stock
> 1   cup celery, chopped
> 1   cup potatoes, diced
> ½   cup zucchini, diced
> ½   cup carrots, diced
> 2   cups canned tomatoes, drained and chopped
> 2   tablespoons fresh parsley, chopped, or 1 tablespoon dried
> 2   tablespoons fresh oregano, or 1 tablespoon dried
> 2   tablespoons fresh basil, or 1 tablespoon dried
> ½   cup elbow macaroni
> salt and pepper to taste
> ¼   cup Parmesan cheese, grated

1. Soak the beans for at least 6 hours in 1 quart cold water.
2. Heat the olive oil in a skillet or Dutch oven and add the garlic and Canadian bacon. Sauté until the bacon begins to brown. Add the onion and sauté until soft. Add the beans and water and cook until the beans are tender.
3. Add the chicken stock, vegetables, herbs, and macaroni and simmer until the vegetables are tender, about 30 minutes, but do not overcook.
4. Season to taste with salt and pepper and serve with a sprinkling of Parmesan cheese.

Oriental Goodness Soup
Serves 6

This soup is simple, fast, and delicious. The vegetables can be varied to suit individual tastes. Important: do not overcook!

> ¼   cup peanut oil
> 3   small cloves garlic, minced
> 2   teaspoons fresh parsley, minced
> ½   cup cauliflower, diced
> ½   cup celery, diced

½ *cup mushrooms, diced*
½ *cup asparagus, diced*
½ *cup onion, diced*
½ *cup tomatoes, diced*
½ *cup zucchini, diced*
4   *cups water*
2   *bouillon cubes*
¼ *cup soy sauce*
¼ *cup sesame or sunflower seeds*

1. Heat the peanut oil in a Dutch oven or large skillet. Add garlic and parsley and sauté for 2 minutes.
2. Add vegetables, water, and bouillon cubes. Bring to a boil and cover; reduce heat and cook for 8 minutes.
3. Add soy sauce to taste. Add sesame or sunflower seeds and cook for another 2 minutes. Serve.

Chicken Gumbo
Serves 8

This soup is hearty enough to serve as a main course.

1   *stewing chicken, cut up*
8   *cups water*
1   *teaspoon salt*
1   *clove garlic, minced*
1   *large can tomatoes, drained, or 2 cups fresh, chopped*
½ *cup corn niblets*
1   *cup okra, sliced*
½ *cup onion, diced*
1   *green pepper, diced*
¼ *cup rice*
2   *cups water*
salt and pepper to taste

1. Add the chicken, water, salt, and garlic to a large pot. Simmer as for stock (see page 87) until the chicken is very tender, about 2½ to 3 hours. Skim the fat, remove the chicken, and dice the meat.
2. Add the vegetables, rice, water, and chicken to the stock and season with salt and pepper.
3. Simmer for 30 to 35 minutes, or until vegetables are tender.
4. Correct seasoning and serve hot.

Barley Soup
Serves 8

1   stewing chicken, disjointed
1   cup onion, chopped
2   teaspoons salt
8   cups water
½   cup barley
½   cup celery, diced
½   cup carrots, diced
1   teaspoon thyme
1   bay leaf

1. Disjoint the chicken and place in a Dutch oven or stock pot.
2. Add onion, salt, and water. Simmer for 1 hour. Do not let it boil or the stock will become cloudy. Skim the top from time to time to remove the frothy residue.
3. Add barley, vegetables, and herbs, and simmer for 1 hour or until chicken is tender.
4. Remove bay leaf and discard. Remove the skin and bones from the chicken, dice the meat, and return it to the soup.
5. Taste for seasoning and serve.

Chinese Soup
Serves 6

This soup can be a meal in itself, particularly if served with a Chinese bun called Bou Tze (a soft bun stuffed with sweet pork).

¼   ounce dried seaweed (optional but adds a distinctive oriental flavor)
4 to 6 large dried mushrooms
4   cups chicken stock
1   teaspoon salt
½   cup Chinese noodles
¼   cup water chestnuts, sliced
1   cup greens, sliced (spinach, swiss chard,
    or bok choy, including stalks and leaves)
2 to 3 sprigs Chinese parsley (cilantro)
2   tablespoons sherry
1   tablespoon soy sauce
3   green onions, sliced thinly, lengthwise

1. Cover dried seaweed and mushrooms with cool water and soak for 1 to 2 hours. Drain thoroughly, reserving the liquid.
2. Combine chicken stock, salt, and water from mushrooms and seaweed.
3. Bring to boil and add noodles, water chestnuts, sliced greens, Chinese parsley, sherry, soy sauce, mushrooms, and seaweed. Simmer for 5 minutes only, stirring occasionally.
4. Garnish with sliced green onions and serve immediately. This soup is best if the vegetables have not been overcooked and are still crunchy.

Corn Chowder
Serves 8

2	*tablespoons margarine*
1½	*cups raw potatoes, diced*
1	*cup onion, diced*
	salt and pepper to taste
½	*cup green pepper, diced*
2	*tablespoons flour*
2	*cups chicken stock*
2	*cups corn niblets*
1	*cup nondairy creamer*

1. Melt the margarine in a skillet, add potatoes and onions and cook for about 1 minute. Add salt, pepper, and green pepper and cook until tender or about 5 minutes.
2. Add the flour and stir thoroughly forming a smooth paste. Cook for 2 minutes, stirring continuously.
3. Add the chicken stock and corn. Bring to a low boil and add the nondairy creamer. Simmer for 5 minutes and serve.

Far East Soup
Serves 4

2	*cups chicken broth*
2	*cups water*
3	*water chestnuts, sliced*
¼	*cup cooked chicken, diced*
4	*large leaves lettuce or spinach*
2	*tablespoons soy sauce*
¼	*cup green onions, chopped*

1. Heat chicken broth and add the remaining ingredients.
2. Simmer 10 minutes or until onion is tender. Season to taste. Serve hot.

Pea Soup
Serves 8

    2 *cups dried split peas*
    6 *cups cold water*
    2 *bay leaves*
    1 *ham bone*
    1 *teaspoon salt*
    1 *cup onion, diced*
    1 *cup carrots, diced*

1. Wash and cover peas with cold water. Soak for 2 hours. Drain.
2. Add 6 cups cold water, bay leaves, ham bone, and salt. Bring to a boil, and reduce heat to a simmer. Cook covered for 1½ hours.
3. Add onion and carrots and simmer for another 1 to 1½ hours.
4. Remove bone and bay leaves. Any meat left on the bone can be removed and diced.
5. Chill and then remove the fat.
6. The soup can be strained and served as a purée or served with the onion and carrots. Add any leftover diced ham as a garnish.

Potato Chowder
Serves 8

    2½ *cups potatoes, diced*
    1   *cup onion, chopped.*
    4   *cups chicken stock*
    ½   *cup celery, chopped*
    ½   *cup carrots, diced*
    ¼   *cup green pepper, diced*
    1   *cup low-fat milk*
    1   *cup corn niblets*
    ¼   *cup Candian bacon, diced and sautéed*
    salt and pepper to taste

1. Add the potatoes and onion to 2 cups of the chicken stock. Simmer for 10 minutes or until the potatoes are tender. Purée.
2. Add the celery, carrots, and green pepper to the remaining chicken stock and simmer for 10 minutes.
3. Add the potato purée, milk, and corn niblets to the vegetables. Stir in and heat thoroughly. Add the Canadian bacon, and season with salt and pepper. Serve hot.

11
Fowl Fare

IF ALL THE recipes for cooking chicken were collected they would fill volumes. This is surely the most versatile of entrées, for nothing else is suited to so many different dishes. Chicken suits every national cuisine and just about every taste. Do you like roast bird? Choose walnut stuffing or Chicken à la Niçoise or surround it with Spring Vegetables for plain but hearty fare. You can take poultry into the backyard and barbecue it, serve it with the most elegant of sauces, or toss it into a salad and you still haven't exhausted the uses of chicken. There are times when the leftovers taste better than the original, as in Chicken Soufflé. Need an hors d'oeuvre? Try Sweet and Sour Chicken Wings. Stuck for a new soup? Let Chinese Chicken Soup begin your meal.

Chicken can be baked, broiled, barbecued, poached, or steamed. Braised chicken, such as Coq au Vin, always tastes better when done a day ahead, so it is a perfect entrée for entertaining.

Turkey, on the other hand, has been neglected in the kitchen. Roast turkey with all the trimmings may be one of the nicest ways to serve turkey but it is certainly not the only one. Turkey legs and wings can be adapted to most chicken recipes with a slightly longer cooking time. Barbecued turkey is not only economical but delicious as well. When roasting turkey, forego the stuffing and fill the cavity instead with oranges and onions for an incredibly moist bird. The traditional dressing can be cooked and served separately, if you like.

Domestic poultry, except for duckling, is lower in fat than meat and you are encouraged to partake of it frequently. When fowl is on the table, your heart and tastebuds will thank you.

Roast Chicken with Almond Dressing
Serves 4 to 6

    ¼ *cup almonds*
    6 *tablespoons margarine*
    3 *tablespoons onion, finely chopped*
    6 *tablespoons mushrooms, finely chopped*
    4 *cups bread crumbs, freshly made, which have been dried overnight*
    1 *cup cucumber, minced*
    ¼ *teaspoon powdered clove*
    1 *teaspoon sage*
    ½ *teaspoon salt*
    ¼ *teaspoon pepper, freshly ground*
    4 *tablespoons white wine*
    1 *5-pound roasting chicken*

1. Preheat oven to 350°.
2. Chop the almonds and place on a cookie sheet in a 350° oven for 10 minutes or until light brown.
3. Melt the margarine in a small skillet and sauté the onion and mushrooms until soft but not browned.
4. Combine almonds, onion, and mushrooms with the remaining ingredients in a bowl and toss well. Lightly stuff the cavity of the chicken with the dressing.
5. Place on a rack in a roasting pan and cover with foil. Cook in a 325° oven for 1½ hours. Remove foil and baste with the juices in the bottom of the pan until browned, about another 15 minutes.

Roast Chicken Niçoise
Serves 6

Hot, crusty, French bread completes this one-dish meal.

    1 *roasting chicken*
salt and pepper
  1½ *cups chicken stock*
    ½ *cup vermouth or white wine*
    ½ *pound eggplant, peeled and sliced*
    3 *medium tomatoes, peeled and quartered*
    2 *medium onions, peeled and sliced*
    1 *green pepper, seeded and sliced*
    1 *small clove garlic, halved*
salt and pepper

1. Lightly salt and pepper the inside of the chicken. Place the chicken on a rack.
2. Place the chicken stock and vermouth in the bottom of a roasting pan. Arrange the vegetables and garlic over the liquid, and lightly salt and pepper. Place the rack with chicken over the vegetables and cook in a 325° oven at 15 minutes per pound or until the juices run clear when poked with a fork. Baste chicken every 30 minutes to brown.
3. When done remove the chicken to a serving platter. Skim all the fat from the vegetables and arrange them around the chicken. Carve and serve.

Cashew Chicken
Serves 4

This recipe was graciously given to us by Ming's restaurant in Palo Alto, California.

2   *chicken breasts, boned and skinned*
5   *tablespoons peanut oil*
1   *teaspoon cornstarch*
½   *teaspoon salt*
¾   *cup cashew nuts, unsalted*
½   *cup chicken stock*
½   *cup mushrooms, sliced*
¾   *cup bamboo shoots, sliced thinly*
1   *cup snow peas*
dash of pepper
½   *teaspoon sugar*
2   *teaspoons soy sauce*
2   *teaspoons cornstarch mixed with 2 teaspoons water*

1. Cut the chicken into wafer thin slices and mix with 1 tablespoon of the peanut oil and 1 teaspoon cornstarch. Turn the chicken to coat thoroughly.
2. Place 1 tablespoon of peanut oil in a very hot skillet and add the salt. Sauté the nuts until slightly brown. Remove to a separate dish.
3. Add the remaining oil and when very hot but not smoking add the chicken. Turn frequently until the chicken meat turns white.
4. Add the stock, mushrooms, bamboo shoots, and snow peas. Cover and cook for 1 minute.
5. Add the pepper, sugar, soy sauce, and cornstarch mixture. Stir over heat until the sauce thickens. Add the cashews and when hot, serve with rice.

Roast Chicken with Spring Vegetables
Serves 6

Colorful vegetables cut in attractive shapes lend themselves to an artful presentation when arranged around the beautifully roasted chicken. Three Cornish game hens can be used in place of the chicken.

1   *roasting chicken*
1   *pound potatoes, peeled*
1   *pound turnips, peeled*
1   *pound asparagus, peeled*
1   *pound green beans*
1   *pound carrots, peeled*
¼   *cup vegetable oil*
salt and pepper
¼   *cup vermouth or dry white wine*
¼   *cup water or stock*
4   *tablespoons margarine*
1   *teaspoon sugar*

1. Place the chicken on a rack in a 325° oven and roast 15 minutes per pound or until the juices run clear when pierced with a knife. Baste occasionally with the pan juices. While the chicken is cooking, soak the potatoes in a bowl of ice water for 1 hour. Drain thoroughly.
2. Cut the turnips into small 2-inch strips. Slice the asparagus stalks in half, the beans into 2-inch strips, the carrots into 2-inch strips and then quarters. With a melon baller cut small rounds of the potatoes. Steam all the vegetables except the potatoes until tender.
3. Heat the vegetable oil and sauté the potatoes until golden. Lightly salt and pepper them. Set aside.
4. When the chicken is done remove it to a serving platter and skim off all the fat. Add the wine and water or stock to the juices and bring to a boil. Reduce heat slightly and cook vigorously until the liquid has reduced to half. Strain.
5. Melt the margarine in a skillet, add the sugar and cook for 1 to 2 minutes until golden. Add the cooked vegetables and toss briefly until reheated and nicely glazed.
6. Place the vegetables and potatoes around the chicken and pour the sauce over them. Carve and serve.

Chinese Almond Chicken
Serves 4

As with all Chinese dishes, have all ingredients prepared and ready next to the stove before you begin.

BASIC CHINESE MARINADE:

1   *teaspoon cornstarch*
1   *teaspoon light soy sauce*
2   *teaspoons sherry*
¼   *teaspoon sugar*
½   *teaspoon vegetable oil*

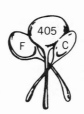

2   *cups chicken, uncooked and diced*
½   *cup slivered almonds, toasted*
1   *cup celery, diced*
½   *cup green onions, finely sliced*
½   *cup water chestnuts, sliced*
1   *cup fresh mushrooms, sliced*
1   *cup snow or sugar peas*
3   *tablespoons vegetable oil*
1   *cup chicken stock*
2   *tablespoons cornstarch*
2   *tablespoons water*
1   *teaspoon soy sauce*

1. Combine the ingredients for the marinade.
2. Add the chicken to the marinade and coat completely. Let stand while you prepare the vegetables.
3. Toast the almonds in a 350° oven 8 minutes or until light brown.
4. Prepare the celery, onions, chestnuts, and mushrooms. Wash snow peas if fresh.
5. Heat the vegetable oil in a wok or a large skillet. The oil must be *very* hot.
6. Add the chicken and stir-fry. If the chicken sticks to the bottom of the pan, the oil is not hot enough.
7. Add vegetables and chestnuts and stir-fry another minute. Add chicken stock, cover, and simmer for 5 minutes. Meanwhile mix the cornstarch, water, and soy sauce into a paste and after simmering, remove the cover and stir the cornstarch mixture into the chicken and vegetables.
8. Add almonds and simmer, stirring until it thickens, about 1 minute. Serve over rice.

Chicken Teriyaki
Serves 4

Marvelous hot or cold, barbecued or broiled.

> *1 frying chicken, cut up*
> *Teriyaki Sauce (see Saucery)*
> *1 orange, peeled and thinly sliced*
> *fresh parsley sprigs*

1. Place the chicken in a shallow dish and cover with Teriyaki Sauce. Marinate for 2 to 4 hours, turning the chicken twice.
2. Broil or barbecue the chicken, brushing frequently with the sauce. Remove to a serving platter. Brush the orange slices with the sauce and broil for 1 minute. Arrange them around the chicken. Garnish with parsley and serve.

Hawaiian Chicken
Serves 8

> *⅓ cup cornstarch*
> *2 frying chickens, cut up*
> *½ cup vegetable oil*
> *1 #2½ can pineapple chunks, drained*
> *3 large white onions, sliced*
> *1 cup celery, diced*
> *3 green peppers, sliced*
> *¼ cup dark brown sugar*
> *¼ cup soy sauce*
> *2 tablespoons fresh ginger, sliced, or 1 teaspoon powdered ginger*

1. Put the cornstarch in a paper bag and shake the chicken in it until coated.
2. Heat the oil and sauté the chicken until well browned, about 20 minutes.
3. Remove the chicken. Place the pineapple chunks, onions, celery, and green peppers in a deep Dutch oven or roasting pan.
4. Add the brown sugar, soy sauce, and ginger to the skillet and when heated, pour over the vegetables.
5. Add chicken, cover, and cook over low heat for 30 minutes or until the chicken is tender and the sauce has thickened. Stir occasionally, turning the chicken pieces. Serve with rice.

Honey-Glazed Barbecued Soy Chicken
Serves 4

If a barbecue is not available this succulent chicken can also be done under the broiler.

1   *frying chicken, cut into serving pieces*
¼   *cup vegetable oil*
¼   *cup wine vinegar*
2   *teaspoons soy sauce*
2   *teaspoons dry mustard, or 3 tablespoons prepared mustard*
¼   *teaspoon pepper*
1   *teaspoon salt*
2   *tablespoons brown sugar*
¼   *cup honey*

1. Combine all the ingredients except the honey. Pour over the chicken pieces and marinate for 2 hours or overnight in refrigerator.
2. Barbecue until done, turning frequently and brush with the marinade.
3. Blend the honey into approximately ¼ cup of the remaining marinade. Brush on the chicken and continue cooking until nicely glazed. Serve.

Chicken Breast Citron
Serves 6

2   *cups sour cream substitute, or Sour Topping (see Saucery)*
¼   *cup lemon juice*
4   *teaspoons Worcestershire sauce*
3   *tablespoons seasoned salt*
6   *chicken breasts, boned and skinned*
1½   *cups* fine *bread crumbs*
⅓   *cup melted margarine*
paprika

1. Combine the sour cream substitute, lemon juice, Worcestershire sauce, and seasoned salt. Place the chicken breasts in a shallow dish and cover with this mixture. Marinate 4 to 6 hours or overnight.
2. Remove the chicken from the marinade 1 hour before serving and roll in the bread crumbs. Place in a single layer on a rack in a lightly oiled pan. Drizzle the melted margarine over the chicken and sprinkle lightly with paprika.
3. Bake at 350° for 40 to 50 minutes until the chicken is tender. Serve hot.

Chicken Breasts with Mushroom Sauce
Serves 4

> piece of wax paper, cut to fit a covered casserole
> 4   chicken breasts, boned
> 3   tablespoons melted margarine
> juice of ½ lemon, about 1 teaspoon
> salt and pepper to taste
> ¼   pound mushrooms, sliced
> ¼   cup green onions, chopped
> 3   tablespoons flour
> 1⅓ cups hot chicken stock
> 3   tablespoons sherry

1. Cut a piece of wax paper to fit the cooking dish. This intensifies cooking and keeps chicken moist. Preheat oven to 400°.
2. Melt the margarine in an ovenproof, covered dish, add lemon juice and the chicken breasts. Add the chicken pieces, turning them until coated with the margarine and juice.
3. Place in casserole, add salt and pepper, and cover with the wax paper, pressing it around the chicken. Cover the casserole and place in a preheated 400° oven for 7 minutes. Chicken is done when the meat has turned white and is springy to the touch. If not quite done return to the oven. Do not overcook lest they become dry.
4. Remove chicken to a separate dish and keep warm. Add mushrooms and onions to the margarine in the casserole and sauté until soft. Add flour, and stirring constantly over low to medium heat, cook for at least 2 minutes.
5. Remove from the heat and add the hot stock in a slow steady stream stirring vigorously. Return to the heat and bring to a boil, stirring constantly. Reduce the heat slightly and boil gently for 1 minute, then simmer 5 minutes.
6. Add the sherry and simmer for another 5 minutes. Arrange the chicken on a serving platter and cover with the sauce.

Chicken Jerusalem
Serves 6

> 1   frying chicken, cut up
> salt and pepper
> 3   tablespoons margarine
> 3   tablespoons oil

¾ *pound mushrooms, sliced*
2 *packages cooked, frozen artichoke hearts*
3 *tablespoons flour*
1 *cup chicken stock, heated*
6 *tablespoons sherry*

1. Remove any excess fat and skin from the chicken pieces. Lightly salt and pepper.
2. Melt the margarine in a large skillet and add the oil. Brown the chicken slowly, about 20 minutes. Remove the chicken to an ovenproof casserole.
3. Sauté the mushrooms in the skillet and then add the artichoke hearts and stir in the flour. Stir over medium heat for at least 2 minutes. Add the chicken stock, bring to a boil, reduce the heat and add the sherry. Cook at least 2 minutes over medium heat, stirring occasionally. This step is crucial in flavoring the mushrooms and artichokes.
4. Pour the sauce over the chicken and bake in a 375° oven for 35 to 40 minutes or until the chicken is done. Arrange the chicken on a serving dish, surround with the mushrooms and artichokes and spoon the sauce over all. Serve hot.

Chicken à la King
Serves 4

1 *tablespoon margarine*
¼ *cup celery, diced*
½ *cup mushrooms, diced*
1½ *cups White Sauce made with chicken stock (see Saucery)*
¼ *teaspoon garlic salt*
dash of Worcestershire sauce
1 *cup cooked chicken, diced*
½ *cup cooked peas*
¼ *cup slivered almonds, lightly toasted in a 350° oven*
4 *tablespoons chopped pimiento-stuffed green olives*
salt and pepper to taste
3 *tablespoons nondairy creamer*
1 *tablespoon sherry*

1. Melt the margarine in a skillet and add the celery. Sauté until tender and add the mushrooms. Stirring continuously, cook for 4 minutes.
2. Add the white sauce and blend in thoroughly. Stir in the remaining ingredients except creamer and sherry. Taste for seasoning.
3. Add the nondairy creamer and sherry. Taste again, and serve over toast points, noodles, or steamed rice.

Chicken Soufflé
Serves 4

This recipe is an excellent cover-up for leftover chicken.

1   *tablespoon Parmesan cheese, grated*
3   *tablespoons margarine*
3   *tablespoons flour*
1½ *cups low-fat milk, heated*
salt and pepper
3   *egg substitutes*
1   *cup chicken, cooked and diced*
4   *egg whites*
pinch of cream of tartar

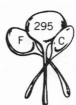

1. Preheat the oven to 325°. Lightly oil a soufflé dish or round ovenproof baking dish and sprinkle the cheese on bottom and sides. If the dish is shallower than 3 inches, make a collar by placing foil around the outside and securing it with a safety pin or tying with string.
2. Melt the margarine in a skillet over low heat and add the flour. Stir until blended and cook for 2 minutes. Remove from the heat and stir in the milk. Bring to a boil, reduce the heat, and stir until thickened. Season to taste with salt and pepper.
3. Remove from the heat and add the egg substitute by large spoonfuls, stirring quickly after each addition. The eggs will curdle in the hot sauce unless mixed quickly. Fold in the chicken. You can make ahead to this point. Place a piece of plastic wrap on the surface of the sauce, sealing the edges to prevent a film from forming. Chill if made more than 30 minutes ahead. Warm slightly when ready to continue.
4. Beat the egg whites, gradually increasing the speed until foamy. Add the cream of tartar and beat until stiff peaks form. Do not overbeat. Stop as soon as they hold their own shape.
5. Add ¼ of the egg white to the sauce base and stir gently. Fold in the remaining egg whites; do not overfold or the egg whites will deflate. Don't worry if a few small clumps of egg whites are visible. Place in a *preheated* oven for 35 minutes or until puffy and golden. Serve immediately, as it rapidly deflates.

Coq au Vin
Serves 4

A chicken in every pot is a good idea, especially if it's coq au vin.

24 *white onions*
24 *mushrooms*
2 *tablespoons olive oil*
¼ *pound Canadian bacon*
1 *large chicken, cut up*
1 *teaspoon sugar*
1 *clove garlic, minced*
¼ *cup brandy, warmed*
3 *tablespoons potato flour, cornstarch, or flour*
1 *teaspoon tomato paste*
1½ *cups chicken stock*
¼ *cup each of brandy, vermouth, and sherry*
1½ *cups burgundy*
1 *teaspoon red currant jelly*

1. Drop the onions in boiling water for 10 to 15 seconds. Drain and run under cold water. Remove skins. Wash and remove stems from the mushrooms.
2. Heat the olive oil in a heavy skillet and sauté Canadian bacon until crisp. Remove bacon and set aside.
3. Add the chicken and brown slowly for about 25 to 30 minutes. Turn frequently. Remove to a separate dish.
4. Add the onions and sugar and brown, stirring frequently. Add mushrooms and garlic. Return chicken to the pan and add the warmed brandy. Ignite and tilt the pan to burn off all the alcohol.
5. Remove the chicken and vegetables and stir the potato flour and tomato paste into the pan juices. When smooth add the chicken stock, brandy, wines, and bring to a boil. Reduce the heat and stir in the red currant jelly until dissolved. Return the chicken and onions to the pan. Place in a 375° oven for 35 minutes. Add bacon and mushrooms and cook for 10 more minutes.
6. Remove chicken and vegetables to a serving platter. Skim all fat and pour sauce over chicken and serve. This is excellent made the day before.

Sesame Chicken
Serves 4

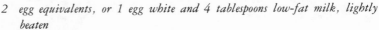

So simple and so good.

> 1 *frying chicken, cut up*
> ½ *cup sesame seeds*
> ¼ *cup flour*
> 2 *egg equivalents, or 1 egg white and 4 tablespoons low-fat milk, lightly beaten*
> 4 *tablespoons margarine*

1. Place sesame seeds on a baking sheet and toast in a 425° oven for 10 minutes.
2. Put the flour in a paper bag. Shake the chicken in the bag, a few pieces at a time, to coat thoroughly.
3. Dip the floured chicken pieces in the egg mixture and then the seasame seeds. Make sure they are thoroughly coated with sesame seeds.
4. Melt the margarine in a baking dish and add the chicken pieces. Roll the chicken pieces in the margarine and bake in a 325° oven for 1 hour or until tender.

Chicken Cynthia
Serves 6

This is from Paul Mayer's outstanding cooking school in San Francisco. Simply elegant.

> 3 *tablespoons vegetable oil*
> 1 *frying chicken, cut up*
> 2 *teaspoons potato flour*
> 6 *ounces dry champagne or dry white wine*
> 1 *chicken bouillon cube*
> *juice of ½ lemon*
> 2 *tablespoons curaçao liqueur*
> *salt and pepper*
> 24 *seedless grapes*
> 24 *mandarin orange sections*
> 4 *tablespoons margarine*

1. Heat the oil in a heavy, ovenproof pan. Add chicken and brown slowly for

10 minutes. Place in a 350° oven for 50 minutes, turning chicken occasionally. When the chicken is done remove to a separate dish and skim any excess fat from the pan.

2. Add flour to pan juices and blend well.
3. Add champagne, bouillon cube, lemon juice, curaçao, salt, and pepper. Stir over medium heat until the sauce boils and thickens. Add grapes and orange sections and stir in the margarine until melted.
4. Place chicken on a serving platter and cover with the sauce. Serve hot.

Chicken Cacciatore
Serves 6

This improves with age so if possible, prepare the day before.

1 large frying chicken, cut up
flour
salt and pepper
3 tablespoons vegetable oil
1 large green pepper, chopped
2 medium yellow onions, chopped
2 cloves garlic, sliced
1-pound can plum tomatoes
1 teaspoon salt
freshly ground pepper
1 teaspoon Italian seasoning
pinch cayenne pepper
1 pound mushrooms, quartered

1. Place the chicken in a paper bag and add flour, salt, and pepper. Use just enough flour to lightly coat the chicken pieces when you shake the bag.
2. Heat the oil in a large skillet and add the chicken pieces. Sauté until golden, turning frequently. Sauté slowly, browning the chicken for 20 to 25 minutes.
3. Remove the chicken to a separate dish and add the green pepper, onions, and garlic. Sauté until the onions are soft but not brown. Return the chicken to the pan and add the tomatoes, salt, pepper, Italian seasoning, and cayenne. Simmer the chicken for 35 minutes.
4. Add the mushrooms and continue cooking for 15 minutes or until the chicken is tender. Serve with cracked wheat or rice.

Sherried Chicken and Rice
Serves 4

Elegant but easy.

1   *frying chicken, cut up*
¼   *cup margarine*
1   *teaspoon paprika*
½   *teaspoon marjoram*
½   *teaspoon thyme*
½   *teaspoon salt*
1   *medium onion, diced*
1½ *cups uncooked rice*
2½ *cups chicken stock*
½   *cup sherry*

1. Wash and dry the chicken pieces. Melt the margarine in a heavy skillet and add the chicken. Turn several times to coat thoroughly. Brown slowly for about 15 minutes.
2. Sprinkle the paprika over the chicken turning to coat completely. Add the marjoram, thyme, salt, and onion.
3. When the onions have softened but not browned, remove the chicken to a separate dish and add the rice to the skillet. Cook the rice and onions for 3 minutes while stirring.
4. Add the chicken stock and sherry and stir. Add the chicken and cover tightly. Cook over low heat for 30 minutes or until chicken and rice are done. Serve immediately.

Chicken Paprikash
Serves 4

1 *frying chicken, cut up*
3 *tablespoons vegetable oil*
2 *onions, diced*
1 *green pepper, diced*
1 *tomato, peeled, seeded, and chopped*
2 *tablespoons paprika*
1 *tablespoon tomato paste*
1 *cup water*
1 *cup Cottage Cream (see Saucery)*

1. Wash and dry the chicken. Heat the vegetable oil in a skillet and sauté the chicken pieces slowly until golden brown, about 15 minutes.
2. Add the onions, green pepper, and tomato. Continue to sauté the chicken and vegetables for 30 minutes, turning the chicken frequently and stirring the vegetables.
3. Stir in the paprika, tomato paste, and water. Stir until smooth and simmer the chicken for another 15 minutes or until tender. Add more water if necessary.
4. When the chicken is done, remove it to a separate dish and remove the vegetables. Skim the fat. Stir the Cottage Cream into the sauce. If the sauce separates, whirl in a blender until smooth. Return the chicken and vegetables to the sauce and reheat gently.

Tangy Chicken
Serves 4

This is great when prepared a day ahead.

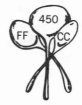

 1 *frying chicken, cut up*
 1 *tablespoon vegetable oil*
 ½ *cup mayonnaise*
 1 *cup plain low-fat yogurt*
 3 *teaspoons fresh parsley, finely minced*
 ⅓ *teaspoon rosemary*
 1 *teaspoon sweet basil*
 1 *teaspoon salt*
 freshly ground pepper
 ¼ *cup orange juice*
 3 *large sprigs parsley*
 orange slices

1. Remove the skin from the chicken pieces. Heat the oil in a skillet and add the chicken. Cook 10 minutes on each side. Arrange in a baking dish.
2. Blend together the mayonnaise, yogurt, parsley, rosemary, sweet basil, salt, pepper, and orange juice.
3. Cover the chicken with sauce and bake at 325°, covered, for about 1 hour. Uncover and bake for a few more minutes. Skim any fat and garnish with parsley and orange slices.

Cornish Game Hens with Wild Rice Stuffing
Serves 6

For a holiday celebration try these golden birds instead of the traditional turkey.

1 *cup wild rice*
4 *cups chicken stock*
2 *tablespoons onions, chopped*
2 *tablespoons celery, chopped*
3 *tablespoons water chestnuts, diced*
2 *tablespoons margarine*
6 *Rock Cornish game hens*
Orange Sauce for Fowl (see Saucery)
red crab apples
parsley sprigs

1. Put the wild rice in a saucepan with enough cold water to cover it. Bring to a boil and strain. Return rice to the saucepan and add the chicken stock. Bring to a boil again. Reduce heat and simmer for about 35 minutes until all the liquid is absorbed.
2. Sauté onions in margarine over low to medium heat until soft and transparent. Do *not* brown. Toss with celery, chestnuts, and wild rice.
3. Salt the cavity of the hens, and fill with dressing. Place in a 350° oven for 1 hour, basting with orange sauce. Turn the oven to 400° for 10 minutes more. Remove to a serving platter. Garnish with apples and parsley.

Marinated Turkey Legs
Serves 6

rind from 1 lemon (about 1 tablespoon)
1 *cup vegetable oil*
½ *cup lemon juice*
3 *tablespoons oregano, crushed*
3 *cloves garlic, mashed*
¾ *cup white wine*
½ *cup chicken stock*
6 *turkey legs*

1. Combine the lemon rind, vegetable oil, lemon juice, oregano, garlic, wine, and chicken stock.
2. Place the turkey legs in a shallow dish and pour the marinade over them. Refrigerate for 4 hours or overnight, turning the turkey legs occasionally.
3. The turkey legs may be barbecued or baked in a 325° oven for 2 hours.

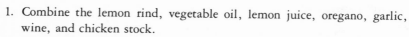

Duck with Olives

Serves 6

2   Long Island ducklings, quartered
3   tablespoons flour
1½ cups chicken stock
¾   cup white wine
salt and pepper
1   herb bouquet (1 large sprig of parsley, ½ teaspoon thyme, 1 bay leaf)
24 green olives, pitted

1. Place the duck quarters on a rack in a roasting pan. Bake in a 450° oven for 30 minutes.
2. Remove skin from the duck and skim all fat but 3 tablespoons from the pan. Add the flour and stir over heat for 2 minutes.
3. Add chicken stock and wine and bring to a boil. Reduce heat and stir until thickened. Season with salt and pepper and add herb bouquet. Return duck to the pan, cover and cook at 350° for 1 hour.
4. Parboil olives for 10 minutes and set aside.
5. Remove the duck from the oven and strain the sauce and let it settle for 10 minutes and skim off all fat from the surface.
6. Add the olives to the sauce and rewarm. Pour over the duck and serve.

Roast Turkey

Serves 8

For moistness and flavor, this method of roasting is unmatched. The dressing is cooked separately and lightly stuffed into the bird for the last hour of cooking or the bird can be left unstuffed.

1 turkey, 10 to 12 pounds
salt and pepper
1 large onion, peeled and quartered
1 large orange, quartered
2 carrots, washed and quartered

1. Clean and rinse the turkey. Lightly salt and pepper the cavity. Place the onion, unpeeled orange, and carrots in the cavity.
2. Place the bird on a rack in a roasting pan and cover with aluminum foil or brown paper. Cook 15 minutes per pound at 300 to 325° and then add an extra 20 minutes. The turkey is done when the juice runs clear, but don't poke too many holes in it or it will dry out. Remove the cover during the last 40 minutes and baste with the pan juices frequently for a lovely, golden color. Turkey may be stuffed for the last hour of cooking with cooked dressing after removing the onion, orange, and carrots.

12
Fish for Compliments

THE FISHING BOAT coming back into the harbor loaded with the day's catch provides a treat for any chef.

The challenge of the fisherman is in filling his nets. The test of the cook is in preparing the catch properly. To do justice to a freshly caught fish, regard it lovingly and cook it briefly. It is fragile and must be treated with care. Fish is extremely perishable and will let you know if you've put off cooking it too long. It should go into the pan the day it's caught, if possible, and should not wait more than 2 days at most. When buying fish look for clear, bulging eyes, a fresh, unobjectionable odor, and smooth, rather than slimy, skin.

Now that you've been cautioned to the care of the fish, what to do with it? If it is whole, stuff it or poach it; if it's summer, barbecue it; and if you are rushed for time, broil it. Fish lends itself to so many dishes that the choice may be difficult. Do you like fruit? Then cook it with grapes or pineapple. If you prefer vegetables, Sole with Asparagus is the dish for you.

There are many regional species so your geography may determine what will be available in your market. Many varieties are now commercially frozen for those living inland. Generally speaking, most recipes can be adapted to accommodate local specialties. Here are some suggestions for cooking any fish. Follow these rules and be rewarded with the delicacies from the sea.

1. Do not overcook it, regardless of what fish you use. As soon as it is firm and has changed color it is done.
2. When poaching fish do not let the liquid bubble. A very slow simmer is all that is required or the fish will break apart.
3. Refrigerate fish until cooking. Do not let it stand at room temperature for any length of time and do not keep it for more than 2 days at most.

Cioppino
Serves 8

San Francisco is justly famous for this incomparable crab stew.

2   *tablespoons vegetable oil*
2   *tablespoons olive oil*
1   *large onion, coarsely chopped*
1   *large green pepper, coarsely chopped*
½   *cup green onions, coarsely chopped*
3   *cloves garlic, sliced*
⅓   *cup fresh parsley, minced*
2   *cups tomato purée*
1   *cup tomato sauce*
1   *large tomato, peeled, seeded, and chopped*
1   *cup red wine*
2   *cups water*
½   *bay leaf*
3   *teaspoons salt*
¼   *teaspoon pepper*
pinch of cayenne
pinch of rosemary
pinch of thyme
¼   *teaspoon Italian seasoning*
1   *medium crab*
1   *dozen prawns, uncooked*
1   *dozen clams, minced*
1½ *pounds snapper or other firm-fleshed fish*

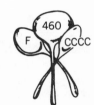

1. Heat the oils in a large pot. Add the onion, green pepper, scallions, and garlic. Sauté until the onion is soft but not brown.
2. Add the parsley, tomato purée, tomato sauce, tomato, red wine, water, bay leaf, salt, pepper, and herbs. Bring to a boil and immediately reduce the heat. Simmer for 30 to 45 minutes. Taste for seasoning.
3. Crack the crab into 2-inch pieces or have this done by the market. Scrub the clams free of all sand and grit. Peel and devein the prawns. Cut the fish into large chunks. Add all the seafood to the simmering sauce and cook gently until the clams are open and the prawns are pink. Do not let the simmering sauce bubble while the fish is cooking and do not over-cook. Serve very hot with lots of French bread.

Fisherman's Stew

Serves 6 to 8

2 tablespoons vegetable oil
1 large onion, finely chopped or grated
1 clove garlic, minced
1 tablespoon oregano, dried
1 tablespoon crushed basil, dried
1 tiny red chili pepper, crushed or, ½ teaspoon Tabasco sauce
1 cup dry white or red wine
1 46-ounce can tomato juice
1 8-ounce can tomato sauce
1 6-ounce can clams
1 6-ounce bottle or can clam juice
1 teaspoon salt
pinch of saffron (optional)
2 pounds fish fillets: fresh or frozen, cod, haddock, sole (cut in bite-size pieces)

1. Heat the oil in a large pot. Add the onion and garlic and cook slowly until soft but not brown.
2. Add oregano, basil, red pepper, and wine. Simmer until reduced by one-half. Add tomato juice, tomato sauce, clams, clam juice, salt, and saffron. Simmer for 30 to 45 minutes. Add fish pieces. Cook until just done — about 15 minutes longer. Serve with French bread.

Oyster Stew

Serves 4

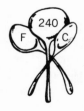

1 cup nonfat milk
1 cup buttermilk
2 tablespoons margarine
1 tablespoon celery, finely chopped
2 potatoes, peeled and thinly sliced
2 dozen oysters, shucked
salt and pepper to taste
paprika

1. Place the milk and buttermilk in a saucepan. Bring to a boil, stirring constantly. Reduce the heat immediately after reaching the boil.

2. Add the celery and potatoes. Cook for 5 minutes or until the potatoes are tender.
3. Add the oysters and simmer 3 to 4 minutes. Season to taste. Serve with a garnish of paprika.

Bouillabaisse
Serves 10

This seafood classic is made with any available freshly caught fish. Use at least one lobster tail, a few clams, and whatever ocean fish is available in the market that day. The base can be made ahead and reheated just before adding the saffron and fish. It can be an easy family or company meal. Serve with hot French bread and a large, crisp, green salad.

2	*tablespoons vegetable oil*
1	*cup onion, diced*
1	*cup leeks, washed and sliced*
3	*cloves garlic, mashed*
2	*cups canned tomatoes, or fresh, chopped*
1½	*quarts water*
3	*sprigs parsley*
½	*teaspoon basil*
1	*slice orange peel, or ½ teaspoon grated peel*
1	*tablespoon salt*
2	*pounds fish trimmings, bones, head, etc.*
1	*8-ounce bottle clam juice*
⅛	*teaspoon saffron (optional)*
4	*pounds assorted firm-fleshed fish*
2	*lobster tails*
2	*dozen clams, well scrubbed*

1. Heat the oil in a skillet and add the onion and leeks. Sauté until soft but not brown. Add the garlic and tomatoes and simmer for 5 minutes. Add the water, herbs, orange peel, salt, fish trimmings, and clam juice and simmer for 35 to 40 minutes.
2. Remove the fish trimmings from the stock and add the saffron and fish. Simmer until the clams are open and fish is tender. Serve very hot.

Beer Soufflé
Serves 6

A few shrimp, a well-flavored sauce base, and a slight tang of beer make a perfect marriage in this unusual soufflé.

vegetable oil
⅓ pound medium shrimp
1   cup water
¼ cup vermouth or white wine
6   peppercorns
1   bay leaf
5   tablespoons margarine
3   tablespoons flour
¼ cup light beer
salt and pepper
2   egg equivalents
⅓ cup Parmesan cheese, grated
4   egg whites
¼ teaspoon cream of tartar

1. Preheat oven to 375° and oil a 6-cup soufflé dish or baking dish.
2. Shell, drain, and chop the shrimp. Place the shells in a saucepan with the water, wine, peppercorns, and bay leaf. Boil gently until the shells have turned pink and the liquid reduced to ½ cup. Drain, reserving liquid, and discard shells and seasonings.
3. Melt 2 tablespoons of the margarine in a saucepan. Add the chopped shrimp and toss quickly over a medium heat until pink. Remove the shrimp and reserve.
4. Melt the rest of the margarine in the same saucepan over low heat. Add the flour, blend well, and cook over low heat for 2 minutes, stirring constantly. Remove from the heat and quickly stir in the drained shrimp stock and beer. Bring to a boil over high heat, and stirring constantly reduce the heat and cook until thickened. Stir in the egg equivalent and cheese. Salt and pepper to taste, and set aside.
5. Beat the egg whites until foamy and add the cream of tartar. Gradually increase the speed and beat until stiff and glossy. Do not overbeat.
6. Stir ¼ of the egg whites into the sauce and blend. Fold into the remaining egg whites and gently fold in the shrimp. Pour into the prepared soufflé dish and bake for 40 minutes. Serve immediately.

Broiled Halibut in Vermouth
Serves 4

4 tablespoons margarine
½ cup dry vermouth
4 halibut steaks
1 teaspoon salt
freshly ground pepper
½ cup green onions, finely chopped
¼ cup Parmesan cheese, grated
¼ cup bread crumbs

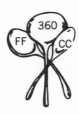

1. Melt the margarine in a saucepan. Add the vermouth.
2. Place the halibut steaks close together in a shallow pan and pour the vermouth and margarine over them.
3. Season with salt, freshly ground pepper, and sprinkle with half the chopped onions.
4. Broil for 7 to 8 minutes, basting once or twice.
5. Turn over in the pan, season, sprinkle with the remaining chopped onions, and broil for another 5 to 7 minutes. Baste several times while cooking.
6. Mix Parmesan cheese with the bread crumbs. Sprinkle lightly over cooked fish. Broil for 1 minute more and serve.

Halibut Maltaise
Serves 4

1½ pounds halibut steaks
¼ cup white wine
2 tablespoons margarine, melted
½ teaspoon dill weed
Sauce Maltaise (see Saucery)

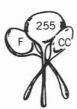

1. Place the halibut steaks on a baking sheet. Combine the wine, margarine, and dill weed, and brush on the fish.
2. Place in a 350° oven for 25 minutes or until fish flakes easily with a fork. Brush frequently with the wine mixture.
3. Remove to a serving dish, cover with Sauce Maltaise and serve.

Fish in Beer Sauce
Serves 4

Any firm-fleshed fish such as cod, snapper, or halibut is suitable for this lovely, tangy sauce.

4 *fish fillets*
4 *tablespoons margarine*
¼ *cup onion, diced*
¼ *cup mushrooms, sliced*
2 *tablespoons flour*
12-ounce can of light beer
2 *cloves, 6 peppercorns, 1 bay leaf, 1 sprig of parsley, wrapped in cheesecloth*
   or Handi-wipe for easy removal
1 *tablespoon sugar*
1 *teaspoon salt*
lemon slices
fresh parsley

1. Wash the fish and pat dry with a paper towel.
2. In a shallow skillet or heatproof dish, melt the margarine over low heat. Add the onions and mushrooms and sauté for 5 minutes over low heat. Add the flour and stir for at least 2 minutes. Stir in the beer and bring to a boil. Reduce the heat and stir until slightly thickened. Add the spices and herbs wrapped in cloth, the sugar, and salt and simmer for 15 minutes.
3. Add the fish to the sauce and simmer until firm and white. Do not overcook or the fish will fall apart. Do not let the sauce boil at any time. Turn the fish once. When cooked through, remove the seasonings. Arrange the fillets on a serving platter and cover with the sauce. Garnish with parsley and lemon slices.

Curried Halibut
Serves 4

1½ *pounds halibut steaks*
½ *cup white wine*
1 *cup water*
1 *bay leaf*
1 *small onion, quartered*
6 *peppercorns*
sprig of parsley

½   cup celery, coarsely chopped (leaves may be included)
½   teaspoon salt
4   tablespoons margarine
1   small onion, diced
½   green pepper, diced
1   stalk celery, diced
3   tablespoons flour
¾   teaspoon curry powder
¾   cup dry white wine
2   tablespoons fresh parsley, chopped

1. Place the halibut steaks in a shallow pan and add the wine and water. Add more liquid if necessary to cover the steaks. Add the bay leaf, onion, peppercorns, parsley, celery, and salt and simmer slowly until done, about 8 minutes. Do not let the liquid bubble or the fish will break apart. Remove the fish to a warm platter and strain the stock.
2. Melt the margarine in a skillet and sauté the onion, pepper, and celery over medium heat about 5 minutes or until soft. Add the flour and curry powder and stir until smooth, at least 2 minutes. Stir in the strained stock and white wine and bring to a boil stirring constantly. Reduce the heat and simmer for 10 minutes or until the alcohol flavor of the wine has evaporated. Add the parsley and pour over the halibut. Serve hot.

Dilled Halibut
Serves 4

1½ pounds halibut steaks
margarine
½   teaspoon salt
1   teaspoon dried dill weed
¾   cup buttermilk
¾   cup white wine
1   tablespoon green onions, minced

1. Rinse halibut under cool water and pat dry. Place halibut in shallow baking pan, which has been lightly greased with margarine. Sprinkle with salt and dill weed.
2. Mix the buttermilk, wine, and green onions. Pour this mixture over the halibut.
3. Bake at 400° for approximately 20 minutes. Spoon sauce over fish when served.

Salmon with Cucumber Sauce
Serves 6

1½ *pounds salmon steaks*
salt and pepper
½ *cup plain low-fat yogurt*
¼ *cup mayonnaise*
1 *large cucumber, peeled, seeded, and grated*
salt and pepper
1 *teaspoon dill weed (optional)*
fresh parsley

1. Lightly sprinkle the salmon steaks with salt and pepper. Broil or barbecue until moist and tender but not dry, about 10 minutes each.
2. Blend the yogurt, mayonnaise, and cucumber. Season to taste with the salt, pepper, and dill.
3. Arrange the cooked salmon on a serving platter and garnish with parsley. Pass the sauce separately.

Salmon Moutarde
Serves 4

1 *cup imitation sour cream*
½ *cup green onions, minced*
1½ *tablespoons Dijon-type mustard*
1 *tablespoon fresh parsley, chopped*
½ *teaspoon salt*
½ *teaspoon thyme*
½ *teaspoon marjoram*
dash of pepper
salt and pepper
4 *salmon steaks*
paprika

1. Combine the imitation sour cream, green onions, mustard, parsley, salt, herbs and pepper. Set aside.
2. Lightly salt and pepper the salmon steaks and place under the broiler for approximately 7 minutes.
3. Turn the steaks, cover with the sauce, sprinkle lightly with paprika and broil until flaky, about 5 minutes. Serve hot.

Red Snapper Aloha
Serves 6

 1½ pounds red snapper
 Teriyaki Sauce (see Saucery)
 6   pineapple rings

1. Arrange the snapper in a shallow dish and cover with the Teriyaki Sauce. Cover and let stand in the refrigerator for 2 hours.
2. Barbecue the fish, brushing frequently with the Teriyaki Sauce, about 20 minutes or until done. The snapper may also be cooked under the broiler.
3. Brush both sides of the pineapple slices with the sauce. Place on the barbecue or under the broiler until heated through.
4. Arrange the cooked fish on a serving platter. Place a pineapple slice on each piece of fish and serve immediately.

Baked Red Snapper
Serves 4

You may use red snapper slices or a small, whole fish may be prepared in the same way.

 4   thick slices of red snapper
 aluminum foil, 4 pieces, each 2½ times the size of the fish
 1   tablespoon margarine
 1   teaspoon salt
 ¼ teaspoon pepper
 1   teaspoon marjoram, crushed
 1   cup Court Bouillon (see Saucery)
 1   recipe Herbed Fish Sauce (see Saucery)

1. Place a slice of fish in the center of each piece of foil. Brush lightly with melted margarine.
2. Combine salt, pepper, and marjoram and sprinkle each piece of fish with this mixture.
3. Pour ¼ cup of Court Bouillon over each and fold the edges of the foil tightly to seal completely.
4. Place on a baking sheet and bake in a 350° oven for 25 minutes.
5. Serve in the foil with Herbed Fish Sauce.

Spinach Stuffed Red Snapper
Serves 8

Any firm-fleshed fish may be substituted. This is a marvelous way to prepare the one that didn't get away.

2   tablespoons vegetable oil
2   tablespoons margarine
3   tablespoons green onions or shallots, chopped
½   cup mushrooms, chopped
1   large bunch spinach
1½ to 2 cups freshly made bread crumbs
4   tablespoons nondairy creamer
1   teaspoon lemon juice (optional)
salt and pepper
4 to 5 pounds, red snapper, cod, sea bass, or similar fish
4   tablespoons margarine, melted
1   cup dry white wine
parsley and lemon slices

1. Heat the oil and margarine in a skillet. Add the scallions and mushrooms and sauté until soft.
2. Soak the spinach briefly in vinegar water. Rinse well to remove any sand. Trim the stems and chop the leaves very finely. Add to the scallions and mushrooms and stir over high heat until all moisture has evaporated.
3. Remove from the heat and add enough bread crumbs and nondairy creamer to make a loose but moist consistency. Season to taste with lemon juice, salt, and pepper.
4. Clean the fish and remove the backbone if possible. Fill the cavity with the stuffing and close with skewers and string. Lightly brush the top of the fish with melted margarine, brush the bottom of a large baking dish, which can also double as a serving dish. If the fish is to be transferred to a serving platter, line the baking dish with cheese cloth for easy removal.
5. Place the fish in the baking dish, and cover with the remaining margarine and the wine. Bring to a simmer on top of the stove and then place in a 375° oven for 35 to 40 minutes or until firm. Baste frequently with the cooking juices. Remove to a serving platter.
6. Boil the cooking juices until thickened. Garnish the fish with parsley and lemon slices and pass the sauce in a separate bowl.

Plaki
Serves 8

This wonderful Greek dish is a meal in itself.

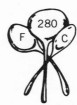

1/4 *cup vegetable oil*
2 *onions, diced*
2 *medium leeks, chopped*
10 *green onions, chopped*
large sprig of fresh parsley
2 *bunches spinach, washed, drained, and chopped*
1 *tablespoon mint, chopped*
2 *cups plum tomatoes, whole*
3 *slices sea bass*
salt and freshly ground pepper
6 *lemon slices*

1. Heat the oil in a skillet and add the onions, leeks, and green onions. Sauté until soft. Add the parsley, spinach, mint, and tomatoes. Simmer for 30 minutes.
2. Place half the vegetable mixture on the bottom of a roasting pan. Arrange the sea bass on top, sprinkle with salt and pepper, and cover with the remaining vegetables. Arrange the lemon slices on top and bake in a 350° oven for 15 to 20 minutes or until fish is done. May be served hot or cold.

Scampi
Serves 4

The beauty of simplicity is demonstrated in this heavenly dish. Reserve this for the week when your intake of cholesterol and saturated fat has otherwise been low.

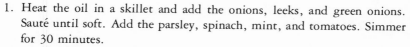

1 *pound medium to large prawns, shelled and deveined, uncooked*
1/2 *cup margarine*
2 *cloves garlic, minced*
salt and pepper to taste

1. Wash the prawns and make a slice around the outside, lengthwise. This incision will allow the prawns to curl or "butterfly" during cooking.
2. Melt the margarine in a skillet and add the garlic. Toss the prawns and stir for 5 minutes or until pink. Do not overcook or they will toughen. Season and serve immediately spooning the sauce over the scampi. Serve lots of French bread to dip in the garlicky sauce.

Sea Bass à l'Espagnole
Serves 8

3 pounds sea bass steaks or whole piece
salt and pepper
vegetable oil
1 teaspoon thyme, crushed
2 bay leaves
pinch of saffron (optional)
8 cloves garlic, minced
3 tablespoons vegetable oil
1 large onion, diced
2 green peppers, diced
6 large tomatoes, peeled, seeded, and diced
3 medium potatoes, peeled, and diced
2 cups Fish Stock (see Saucery) or clam juice
2 cups dry white wine
3 tablespoons fresh parsley, chopped

1. Season the fish with salt and pepper. Arrange on a lightly oiled roasting pan. Sprinkle with the crushed thyme, bay leaves, and saffron, and 1 teaspoon of the garlic.
2. Heat the oil and sauté the onions and peppers until soft but not brown. Add the remaining garlic and cook 2 more minutes. Add the tomatoes and simmer for 15 minutes, stirring frequently.
3. Cook the potatoes in boiling water for 1 minute, drain thoroughly, and add to the sauce.
4. Cover the fish with the vegetable mixture. Add the Fish Stock and wine, and bring to a boil. Cover with foil and bake at 375° for 25 minutes. Baste frequently with the juices.
5. When done, remove fish to a serving platter. Bring the vegetables and sauce to a boil and cook until juices have reduced to half. Spoon over the fish, sprinkle with parsley, and serve.

Flaming Shrimp
Serves 6

This is a French version of scampi.

¼ cup margarine
shelled and deveined shrimp, about 6 medium per person
salt and pepper to taste

2   *tablespoons shallots, minced*
1   *teaspoon lemon juice*
3   *tablespoons warmed brandy or cognac*

1. Melt the margarine in a chafing dish or skillet and when hot add the shrimp. Toss until pink on each side.
2. Add salt and pepper, shallots, and lemon juice, cooking and stirring for 2 minutes.
3. Spoon cognac over shrimp and ignite. Burn off all the alcohol and serve with French bread.

Sole Apollo
Serves 8

½   *cup water*
1   *cup dry vermouth*
bouquet garni (1 bay leaf, 1 sprig parsley, 6 peppercorns, ½ teaspoon of thyme
    wrapped in cheesecloth)
2   *pounds fillet of sole*
½   *cup low-fat milk*
3   *tablespoons margarine*
¼   *pound mushrooms, finely diced*
2   *tablespoons flour*
salt and pepper to taste
sprigs of parsley

1. Bring the water, vermouth, and bouquet garni to a boil in a shallow baking dish. Reduce heat and simmer for 5 minutes.
2. Add the sole, immersing it completely in the liquid. Poach the fish gently until it begins to turn white and looks flaky, approximately 5 minutes. **Do not overcook.** Do not let liquid bubble.
3. Remove fish to a separate platter, cover and keep *warm*, not hot.
4. Reduce the poaching liquid by boiling it rapidly until you have ¾ cup. Add ½ cup milk and heat.
5. Melt the margarine and sauté the mushrooms until soft. Add the flour and stir over low heat for at least 2 minutes. Remove from heat and add the hot liquid in a slow steady stream, stirring constantly until smooth. Bring the sauce to a boil and cook for 1 minute stirring frequently. Taste for seasoning.
6. Place the sole in a serving dish and spoon the hot sauce over the fish. Decorate with parsley and serve.

Shrimp Tuscany
Serves 6

May be served with rice, spaghetti, or French bread.

4	tablespoons vegetable oil
¼	cup shallots, chopped
2	bunches green onions, chopped
1	bunch leeks, chopped
3	cloves garlic, minced
2	tablespoons lemon juice
1	cup tomato sauce
4	tomatoes, peeled, seeded, and chopped
1	green pepper, seeded and chopped
1	tablespoon fresh oregano, or ½ tablespoon dried
1	tablespoon fresh basil, or ½ tablespoon dried
¼	cup dry red wine
1½	pounds shrimp, shelled and deveined
2	tablespoons chopped parsley

1. Heat the oil and add the shallots, green onions, leeks and garlic. Sauté until all are soft but not brown, about 15 minutes.
2. Stir in the lemon juice, tomato sauce, tomatoes, green pepper, herbs and wine. Simmer over low heat for 30 minutes.
3. Just before serving, add the shrimp and simmer, stirring continuously, until they become bright pink, about 5 to 8 minutes. Sprinkle with chopped parsley and serve.

Rock Cod with Tartar Meringue
Serves 6

2	pounds rock cod
	salt and pepper
⅓	cup mayonnaise
2	tablespoons plain low-fat yogurt
¼	cup pickle relish
2	tablespoons fresh parsley, chopped
1	tablespoon lemon juice
¼	teaspoon salt
	dash of cayenne pepper
2	egg whites

1. Lightly sprinkle the fish with salt and pepper. Broil 7 minutes or until almost done.
2. Gently mix the mayonnaise, yogurt, pickle relish, parsley, lemon juice, salt, and cayenne together.
3. Beat the egg whites until stiff but not dry. Fold in the mayonnaise mixture and spread over the fish. Broil until puffy and golden. Serve immediately.

Sole Asparagus
Serves 6

The green tips of the asparagus spear peeking out of the sole, covered with the delicately flavored sauce, is an elegant presentation for a dinner party.

1½ *pounds fillet of sole*
1   *teaspoon lemon rind, grated*
1   *pound asparagus spears, peeled and trimmed*
1   *teaspoon vegetable oil*
salt and pepper
12   *large mushrooms*
2   *tablespoons margarine*
2   *tablespoons flour*
1½ *cups low-fat milk, heated*
salt and pepper to taste
½   *cup sherry*

1. Sprinkle the sole with the lemon rind. Partially cook the asparagus spears. Place 2 or 3 on each sole fillet, cutting the spear in half if necessary. Roll the fish around the spears. Coat a shallow baking dish with 1 teaspoon of oil and arrange the sole in the dish. Sprinkle lightly with salt and pepper and place the mushrooms on top. Cover with foil. Place in a 375° oven for 10 to 15 minutes. The sole should be moist and tender but not dried out or flaking apart.
2. Melt the margarine in a saucepan over low heat. Add the flour and stir continuously for 2 minutes over low heat. Remove from the heat and stir in the milk. Return to the heat and bring to a boil. Reduce the heat and stir until thickened and smooth. Season to taste and add the sherry and continue to cook over low heat for 3 to 4 minutes.
3. Arrange the sole and asparagus rolls on a serving platter. Spoon the sauce over them and serve immediately.

Sole à la Florentine
Serves 4

1	cup water
1	cup white wine
1	bay leaf
½	teaspoon salt
6	cloves
6	peppercorns
1	pound fillet of sole
1½	pounds fresh spinach, thoroughly rinsed
4	tablespoons margarine
4	tablespoons flour
1	cup nonfat milk, heated
¼	cup buttermilk
salt and pepper	
⅓	cup Parmesan cheese, grated

1. Bring the water, wine, bay leaf, salt, cloves, and peppercorns to a boil in a skillet. Reduce heat and simmer for 10 minutes, then add the sole. Simmer for 5 minutes without letting the liquid bubble. Remove the sole to a shallow baking dish. Reserve the fish stock for future use.
2. Soak the spinach briefly in vinegar water and rinse well. Steam until limp, about 4 minutes, and drain thoroughly. Chop coarsely and place on top of the sole.
3. Melt the margarine over low heat. Stir in the flour and cook for 2 minutes, stirring constantly. Remove from the heat and stir in the heated milk. Bring to a boil and reduce the heat. Stir until thickened. Add the buttermilk, stir until smooth, and remove from the heat. Season with salt and pepper.
4. Pour the sauce over the fish and spinach and sprinkle with Parmesan cheese.
5. Place in the oven and bake for 5 minutes at 375°, then place under the boiler until the top is browned. Serve immediately.

Trout Stuffed with Mushrooms
Serves 4

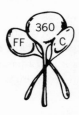

4	trout, approximately ½ pound each
3	tablespoons margarine
½	cup onion, minced
1	cup mushrooms, minced
3	tablespoons Madeira wine (optional)

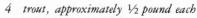

4   tablespoons fine bread crumbs
¼ cup Parmesan cheese, freshly grated
3   tablespoons fresh parsley, minced
3   tablespoons evaporated skim milk
salt and pepper
flour
3   tablespoons vegetable oil
parsley sprigs

1. Bone the trout if not done by your butcher.
2. Melt the margarine in a skillet and add the onions. Sauté until soft but not brown. Add the mushrooms and sauté until soft. Stir over high heat until the moisture has evaporated. Stir in the Madeira wine and cook rapidly until almost evaporated.
3. Remove from the heat and stir in the bread crumbs, cheese, and parsley. Add milk but the mixture should remain firm. Season with salt and pepper.
4. Fill the trout with this mixture. Roll the fish in flour and pat off excess.
5. Heat the oil in a skillet and sauté the trout about 5 minutes on each side. Do not overcook. Remove to a platter, garnish with parsley and serve.

Squid Cutlets
Serves 4

1   pound fresh squid
1   cup bread crumbs
½ cup Parmesan cheese, grated
1   tablespoon fresh parsley, minced
2   cloves garlic, minced
2   egg whites, lightly beaten with 1 teaspoon water
4   tablespoons margarine
lemon wedges for garnish

1. To prepare the squid, cut off the head and tentacles. Insert the blade of a knife into the body, slicing it open. Scrape the opened, flattened squid clean with blade of the knife, removing the gray-pink skin and the "cuttle bone." Wash under cold water and drain. Pat dry. Cut in half.
2. Mix the bread crumbs, cheese, parsley, and garlic.
3. Dip each squid cutlet into the crumb mixture, then into the egg whites, then back into bread crumb mixture. Coat thoroughly.
4. Melt margarine and sauté the squid 2 to 3 minutes on each side. Serve immediately with lemon wedges.

Sole Meunière
Serves 6

1½ pounds fillet of sole
low-fat milk to cover
flour
salt and pepper
6   tablespoons margarine
1   tablespoon lemon juice
chopped parsley
lemon slices

1. Cover the sole with low-fat milk and soak for approximately 15 minutes.
2. Pat dry. Blend the flour, salt, and pepper together. Roll the fillets in this mixture, shaking off any excess.
3. Melt 3 *tablespoons* of the margarine in a skillet. Add the fillets and cook until golden, 3 to 4 minutes on each side. Do not overcook or they will break apart. Remove to a warm serving dish.
4. With a paper towel, wipe out the skillet and add the remaining margarine and when it just starts to brown remove from the heat and stir in the lemon juice. Pour over the cooked fish and sprinkle with chopped parsley. Garnish with lemon slices and serve.

Trout with Almond Sauce
Serves 4

4   trout, boned, approximately ½ pound each
salt and pepper
flour
3   tablespoons vegetable oil
4   tablespoons margarine
½ cup almonds, ground
lemon slices

1. Lightly salt and pepper the inside of each trout. Roll each one in flour, patting off the excess.
2. Heat the vegetable oil in a large skillet and add the trout. Cook for 6 minutes on each side or until flesh is firm and white. Do not overcook or the fish will fall apart. The fish is done when the eyes have turned white.
3. Remove fish to a serving platter and cover with foil to keep warm.
4. Melt the margarine in the same skillet and add the almonds. Stir until bubbly. Add more margarine if the almond sauce appears too thick. Spoon over the trout and garnish the head and tail with a lemon slice. Serve immediately.

13
Meaty Subject

WHEN YOUR APPETITE has been whetted by a discriminating selection of canapés or a creamy soup, the meat course must do justice to the rest of your menu.

In traveling across the globe, there is disagreement about the proper way to fix a "bit of beef." Americans barbecue steaks, Chinese stir-fry thin strips with crisp vegetables, the French sauce it with burgundy and mushrooms and the English roast it with Yorkshire pudding. Which is best? You decide, but doubtless you will have a difficult time choosing a favorite.

Beef adapts well to many dishes. Budget cuts are disguised with spirits and herbs and transformed into delectable ragouts. Beef Bourguignon and Beef Carbonnade are simply beef stews with a special touch. Hamburger can be given royal treatment with Mushroom Sauce or crowned with a spicy meringue. For special celebrations choose the tenderest fillet and serve it as a tart and slightly dilled Stroganoff.

Still can't make up your mind? Then perhaps your taste runs to roast lamb with a tangy Cumberland Sauce or richly flavored Lamb Shanks. Veal is one of the most versatile of the meats and has much less fat than the others. Get out your repertoire of sauces because veal is made for them. From a light sprinkling of lemon in Veal Piccata to the rich flavoring of wine and herbs in Scallopine, veal loves to be dressed up.

Meats can be cooked in fruits, wines, or stocks to produce different but equally delicious tastes.

Remember some basic rules when preparing meats.

1. Do not overcook roasts, broiled, or barbecued meats. They will dry out and become tough and flavorless.
2. Do not overcook stews and ragouts, or the meat will be stringy.

3. Do not pierce meat with a fork before or during cooking. Use tongs for turning and moving meat or it will lose its juices and dry out.

4. Do cook the meat according to the cut. For example, do not expect lamb stew meat to be tender after a quick sauté, for it requires long, slow cooking. Sirloin tips, on the other hand, become stringy in braised dishes, such as Beef Bourguignon.

Suitable cooking methods for most cuts are listed.

Baking: This method is used for ground meat cooked with a mixture of ingredients such as meat loaf, stuffed zucchini or lasagna.

Braising: This is best for less tender cuts such as chuck, brisket, and shoulder. When preparing, add liquids and seasonings for a long, slow, moist cooking. Skim all fat off before serving.

Broiling: Use this method for quick cooking of the more tender cuts such as chops, steaks, and ground meat. Fat is greatly reduced by this method.

Pot roasting: This is for cooking the less tender roasts such as chuck, rump, or brisket in liquid which will result in surprisingly tender meat.

Oven roasting: For cooking tender roasts such as leg of lamb, sirloin or loin of pork in dry heat in the oven.

Sautéing: This method is for cooking tender cuts quickly over medium heat in a skillet.

Searing: This is a quick browning of meats to be followed by another method, such as seared cubes of beef or veal for stew. This step seals in the juices.

Remember to choose the cut of meat best suited to your recipe, trim off all fat and serve 3-ounce cooked portions. Then the meat will make your meal.

Brittany Beef
Serves 4

2   tablespoons margarine
2   tablespoons vegetable oil
1   pound fillet of beef, sirloin or other tender cut, sliced in thin strips
¼   pound mushrooms, sliced
½   cup onions, diced
salt and pepper
1   tablespoon flour
½   cup burgundy
1   medium tomato, peeled, seeded, and chopped

1   *cup Brown Sauce (see Saucery)*
1   *cup string beans, cooked*
½   *cup Swiss cheese, grated*

1. Heat margarine and oil in a skillet. Add the beef and sauté until browned. Do not overcook. Remove to a side dish. Add the mushrooms and onions and sauté until soft. Season to taste with salt and pepper.
2. Add the flour to the skillet and stir over low heat for at least 2 minutes.
3. Add the wine, tomato, Brown Sauce, and beans and bring to a boil. Simmer for 15 minutes. Transfer beef and sauce to an ovenproof dish and cover with the cheese. Place under the broiler until cheese has melted and serve hot.

Beef Bourguignon
Serves 6

This is excellent made the day before and should be served with lots of French bread and a green salad.

2   *tablespoons vegetable oil*
2   *cups onion, sliced*
2   *pounds beef chuck, cut into 1-inch cubes*
2   *tablespoons flour*
salt and pepper to taste
½   *teaspoon marjoram*
½   *teaspoon thyme*
½   *cup beef bouillon*
1   *cup dry red wine*
1   *pound fresh mushrooms, sliced*

1. Heat the vegetable oil in a skillet. Add the onion and sauté until soft but not brown. Remove to a separate dish.
2. Add the beef and sear over high heat on all sides until brown. Sprinkle with the flour, salt, pepper, and herbs and stir to coat the pieces.
3. Add the bouillon and red wine and reduce the heat to barely a simmer and cook uncovered for 3 hours. Add more bouillon and wine if necessary to keep the meat barely covered.
4. Return the onion to the skillet and add the mushrooms. Cook for another 45 minutes or until the meat is tender but not stringy and the sauce thick and brown. Serve hot.

Beef Carbonnade
Serves 6

>   2 pounds beef chuck
>   1 tablespoon vegetable oil
>   1 pound onion, sliced
>   3 cloves of garlic, minced
>   1 cup beef stock, hot
>   2 cups light beer
>   1 tablespoon brown sugar
>   herb bouquet (1 large sprig of parsley, ½ teaspoon thyme, bay leaf tied in
>   cheesecloth)
>   1 tablespoon cornstarch
>   2 tablespoons wine vinegar
>   coarse ground pepper

1. Trim all visible fat from the beef and cut into 1-inch pieces. Heat the oil in a heavy bottomed skillet or ovenproof casserole with a tight fitting lid. Brown the meat, turning to sear all sides.
2. Set the beef aside and add the onions and garlic to the skillet. Sauté until soft but not browned.
3. Arrange the browned beef and onions in the ovenproof dish and add the hot stock. You may use canned broth or bouillon, or concentrated stock base (do not use consommé). Add the beer and brown sugar, and bury the herb bouquet in the middle.
4. Bring to a simmer, cover and place in a 325° oven for 1½ hours or until beef is tender. Cook longer if necessary but do not at any time let the heat come above a simmer. Remove from the oven and discard the herb bouquet. Remove the beef and onions with a slotted spoon and skim all the fat from the liquid and pour sauce over beef. The dish may be prepared ahead up to this point and refrigerated. The congealed fat is easier to remove when cold. Combine the cornstarch and vinegar and beat into the hot liquid. Simmer for 5 minutes or until sauce has nicely thickened. Taste for seasoning and pour over the beef and onions. Serve.

Beef Esterhazy
Serves 6

The Esterhazy family were patrons of the arts in Austria for many centuries. They justly deserve this culinary tribute.

2 *pounds top round steak*
salt and freshly ground pepper
flour
3 *tablespoons vegetable oil*
1½ *cups onion, diced*
1 *clove garlic, minced*
½ *cup carrots, finely diced*
3 *tablespoons flour*
3 *cups beef bouillon*
⅛ *teaspoon ground allspice*
3 *bay leaves*
6 *peppercorns*
½ *teaspoon thyme*
¼ *teaspoon lemon peel, grated*
¼ *cup Canadian bacon, chopped*
2 *tablespoons fresh parsley, chopped*
¼ *cup wine vinegar*
2 *parsnips*
1 *carrot*
¾ *cup nondairy creamer*
1 *teaspoon lemon juice*

1. Cut the beef into 2-inch strips. Lightly dust with the salt, pepper, and flour. Heat the oil in a skillet and brown the strips on each side. Remove to a side dish.
2. In the same skillet, add the onion, garlic, and diced carrots and sauté until the onions are soft but not brown. Stir in the flour and cook over low heat for at least 2 minutes. Remove from the heat and stir in the beef bouillon. Return to the heat and bring to a boil, stirring constantly. Reduce heat and stir until thickened and smooth.
3. Add the allspice, bay leaves, peppercorns, thyme, grated lemon peel, Canadian bacon, parsley, and wine vinegar. Add the cooked beef and bring to a boil once more. Reduce the heat to a simmer and cook uncovered for 1 hour or until the beef is very tender.
4. Peel the parsnips and carrot and cut into thin strips. Cook in boiling water until slightly tender, about 5 minutes. Drain. Arrange the beef, carrot, and parsnips on a serving platter.
5. Strain the sauce and skim all fat from the surface. Stir in the nondairy creamer and lemon juice and simmer over low heat for 2 minutes. Do not let the sauce bubble. Pour over the beef and vegetables and serve immediately.

Beef Stroganoff
Serves 4

The best of two worlds, Russian seasoning and French cooking technique, results in an international classic.

1   *pound tender beef, sirloin or fillet*
2   *tablespoons vegetable oil*
½   *pound mushrooms, sliced*
1   *large onion, sliced*
salt and pepper to taste
3   *tablespoons margarine*
3   *tablespoons flour*
1½ *cups beef bouillon, hot*
½   *cup buttermilk, warm*
½   *teaspoon dill weed*
¼   *teaspoon mustard*

1. Slice the beef into ½-inch strips.
2. Heat 1 tablespoon of the vegetable oil and sauté the mushrooms and onion until soft. Season with salt and pepper to taste.
3. Melt the margarine in a saucepan over low heat and add the flour. Stir over low heat for at least 2 minutes.
4. Remove from heat and stir in the hot beef bouillon. Bring to a boil and stir over heat for 1 minute or until thickened. Reduce heat and cook for 5 minutes. Stir in the warmed buttermilk, dill weed, and mustard.
5. Heat the remaining oil in a skillet and quickly sauté the beef strips on both sides. Do not overcook. The meat should be pink inside. Add meat, mushrooms, and onion to the sauce. Serve hot with noodles or rice.

Stir-Fried Beef and Broccoli
Serves 4

This is a delicious "one pan" meal. Have *all* ingredients ready before starting the cooking. Everyone should be available and ready to eat as it does not keep.

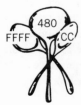

1 *pound beef flank steak or brisket*
1 *bunch broccoli*
1 *onion*
1 *cup beef bouillon*
2 *tablespoons cornstarch*
2 *tablespoons soy sauce*
4 *tablespoons corn oil*
1 *tablespoon sesame oil (optional)*

1. Cut the beef across the grain into ¼-inch slices. Cut the slices into narrow strips 2 to 3 inches long.
2. Trim 1 inch off each end of the broccoli stalks. Cut stalks, leaves, and flowerettes into 1-inch pieces at diagonal angle. Cut the onion into narrow wedges and separate. Combine the beef broth, cornstarch, and soy sauce in a cup.
3. Heat the oil in a skillet or wok until very hot. Add beef and stir-fry until just brown (2 to 3 minutes). Remove from pan.
4. Add onion and broccoli to pan and stir-fry for 2 to 3 minutes.
5. Add the soy sauce mixture to the vegetables, add the beef, and cook covered for 2 minutes. Stir until the sauce thickens. Serve at once.

Flank Steak Mary Linda
Serves 6

   ¼ cup prepared mustard
   ¼ cup soy sauce
   2 pounds flank steak

1. Combine the mustard and soy sauce. Coat one side of the steak with the sauce and place *that* side down on the grill, or up under the·broiler.
2. Broil 5 minutes, coat the other side with the sauce, and turn. Repeat basting and turning until cooked to the desired degree of doneness.
3. Remove and slice on the diagonal across the grain in ¼-inch strips. Serve at once.

Flank Steak Teriyaki
Serves 6

This marinade can be used for beef, chicken, or fish. It can be reused and stores well in a covered jar in the refrigerator. If, however, it has been used for fish do not use it again for meat or fowl.

   2 pounds flank steak, trimmed of any visible fat
   1 recipe Teriyaki Sauce (see Saucery)

1. Place the flank steak in a shallow dish and cover with the Teriyaki Sauce. Marinate for at least 3 hours. Turn at least once.
2. Place under the broiler for 10 to 12 minutes on each side or to the desired degree of doneness. Turn the meat with tongs rather than a fork, so as not to pierce the surface and lose the juices. Baste every 5 minutes with the sauce. When done, remove to a carving platter. Slice thinly across the grain and serve.

Meat Loaf Meringue
Serves 4

A tangy crown of seasoned meringue surrounds each individual loaf. Once tried you may never have meat loaf without it.

1¼ *pounds ground meat, beef; or beef, lamb, and veal in equal proportions*
1   *sliver fresh ginger or ½ teaspoon ground*
1   *clove garlic, finely minced*
1   *tablespoon sherry*
1   *medium onion, diced*
1   *tablespoon cornstarch*
1   *teaspoon salt*
freshly ground pepper
1   *teaspoon soy sauce*
½   *cup oatmeal*
¼   *cup tomato juice*
2   *egg whites*

MERINGUE:
2   *egg whites*
¼   *teaspoon cream of tartar*
¼   *teaspoon salt*
¼   *cup barbecue or chili sauce*

1. Combine all ingredients, except those for meringue, in a bowl and blend thoroughly. Divide into 4 equal portions and shape into oblong loaves 1½ inches thick and 3 inches long.
2. Place on a rack on a cookie sheet and bake in a 350° oven for 25 minutes. Cool for 5 minutes.
3. Make meringue. Beat egg whites until frothy, add cream of tartar and salt. Beat until stiff peaks form but still appear moist.
4. Gently fold in barbecue sauce and cover each meat pattie with the meringue. Bake 15 minutes. Serve immediately.

Hamburger with Mushroom Sauce
Serves 4

1   *pound ground beef, very lean*
salt and pepper
2   *tablespoons margarine*
½   *cup mushrooms, sliced*
½   *cup red wine*

1. Season the ground beef with the salt and pepper. Form into 4 patties.
2. Panfry in a skillet to the desired degree of doneness. Remove to a separate platter and keep warm.
3. Melt the margarine in the skillet and scrape up the coagulated juices from the beef. Add the mushrooms and sauté until tender.
4. Add the red wine and cook over high heat until reduced by one-half. Spoon the mushroom sauce over the beef patties and serve.

Veal Marengo
Serves 6

Marengo indicates tomatoes in the sauce. Chicken can be substituted for the veal.

1½ *pounds veal shoulder, boned and cut into 2-inch pieces*
2   *tablespoons vegetable oil*
2   *onions, sliced*
3   *tablespoons flour*
6   *large tomatoes, peeled, seeded, and coarsely chopped*
2   *cloves garlic, sliced*
1   *teaspoon orange rind, grated (optional)*
½   *cup chicken or veal stock*
⅔   *cup vermouth or other white wine*
1   *tablespoon tomato paste*
salt and pepper
2   *tablespoons margarine*
1   *cup mushrooms, sliced*

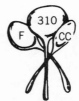

1. Remove any fat from the veal. Heat the vegetable oil in a large skillet or Dutch oven. Add the veal and brown lightly on all sides. Remove veal to a side dish.
2. Add the onions to the pan and sauté until soft but not brown. Add the flour and cook for 2 minutes, stirring constantly. Add all the remaining ingredients except the margarine and mushrooms. Cover and simmer until the veal is tender, about 1½ hours.
3. Melt the margarine in a skillet and toss the mushrooms briefly. Add them to the veal and cook another 20 minutes.
4. Remove veal and vegetables from the pan. If the sauce is thin, increase the heat and boil rapidly until reduced by one-half. Drain veal and vegetables once more to prevent sauce from thinning and arrange on a serving platter. Spoon sauce over the top and serve hot.

Veal Goulash
Serves 8

The dollop of Sour Topping at the end is not necessary but is a nice finishing touch.

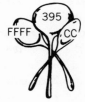

4   *tablespoons vegetable oil*
2   *onions, diced*
2   *cloves garlic, diced*
2½ *pounds veal shoulder, boned and cubed in 2-inch pieces*
2   *tablespoons paprika*
¼   *teaspoon caraway seeds*
herb bouquet (½ teaspoon each, marjoram, thyme, parsley and 1 bay leaf wrapped in cheesecloth)
salt and pepper
1   *pound mushrooms, quartered*
2   *red peppers, chopped*
2   *green peppers, chopped*
6   *medium to large tomatoes, peeled, seeded, and coarsely chopped*
½   *cup Sour Topping (see Saucery)*

1. Heat the vegetable oil in a skillet and add the onions and garlic. Sauté until soft but not brown. Add the veal and brown on each side.
2. Add the paprika and blend thoroughly. Add all the remaining ingredients but the sour topping, bring to a simmer, cover, and cook very gently for 2 hours or until the veal is very tender. Skim any fat and serve with a small dollop of Sour Topping.

Swiss Steak
Serves 4

2   *tablespoons flour*
½   *teaspoon salt*
dash of freshly ground pepper
1½ *pounds Swiss steak, cut into 3-inch strips*
2   *tablespoons vegetable oil*
½   *cup green pepper, diced*
½   *cup onion, diced*
1   *clove garlic, minced*
1   *cup beef bouillon*
½   *cup tomato sauce*

1. Blend the flour, salt, and pepper together.
2. Pound the Swiss steak into thin strips with a mallet or the edge of a saucer and lightly dust with the flour.
3. Heat the vegetable oil in an ovenproof dish with a tightly fitting cover. Add the steak and brown on both sides. Add the green pepper, onion, and garlic and stir briefly.
4. Pour the bouillon and tomato sauce over the meat and vegetables, cover and bake for 1 hour or until the beef is tender. Serve hot.

Veal Scallopine Ryan
Serves 6

1½ *pounds veal round, cubed*
flour
salt and pepper
¼ *cup vegetable oil*
2   *cloves garlic, diced*
1   *large onion, sliced*
¾   *cup white wine*
½   *cup water*
2   *tablespoons lemon juice*
1   *bay leaf*
4   *cloves*
salt and pepper
¾   *cup mushrooms, sliced*
2   *tablespoons stuffed green olives, sliced (optional)*

1. Dredge the veal in the flour, salt, and pepper.
2. Heat the vegetable oil in a heavy skillet and add the veal. Brown slowly on each side. Add the garlic, onion, ¼ cup of the wine, water, lemon juice, bay leaf, cloves, and salt and pepper to taste. Cover and simmer for 1 hour, stirring occasionally. Add more water and wine if necessary.
3. When the veal is tender add the mushrooms and remaining wine. Cook for another 30 minutes. Remove the garlic, cloves, and bay leaf. Season to taste and serve with rice. For very special occasions serve with wild rice.

Veal Piccata
Serves 4

The veal must be sliced *very* thin, it must be cooked *very* quickly, and it will be enjoyed *very* much.

> *1 ¼ pounds veal cutlet, cut into ¼-inch slices*
> *flour*
> *salt and papper*
> *4   tablespoons margarine*
> *2   tablespoons lemon juice*
> *chopped parsley*
> *lemon slices*

1. Pound each slice of veal lightly to ¼- to ⅜-inch thickness.
2. Lightly dust each slice with flour. Pat off excess. Do not use too much flour. Lightly salt and pepper each slice.
3. Melt the margarine in a large skillet. Add the veal slices but do not overlap or crowd them. If the skillet is not large enough to cook them all at once, then do 2 batches. Cook quickly, no more than 2 minutes on each side, and remove to a warm serving platter.
4. Remove any browned bits from the skillet and swirl the lemon juice into the margarine, adding a little more margarine if necessary until you have a light sauce. Pour over the warm veal, sprinkle lightly with the chopped parsley, and garnish with lemon slices.

Veal Quincy
Serves 4

Veal and cheese are often teamed but never as well as in this combination.

> *1 pound veal scallops, sliced in 8 pieces*
> *4 ounces mozzarella cheese, sliced paper thin*
> *4 ounces prosciutto, sliced paper thin*
> *3 tablespoons vegetable oil*
> *1 cup bread crumbs*
> *2 tablespoons Parmesan cheese, freshly grated*
> *1 teaspoon oregano*
> *salt and pepper*

1. Pound the veal scallops very thin. Place a slice of mozzarella cheese and

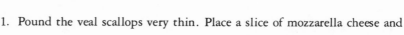

prosciutto on top of each. Roll up together tucking in the ends. Secure with a string or small skewers.

2. Brush each veal roll with vegetable oil. Combine the bread crumbs, Parmesan cheese, oregano, salt, and pepper and roll each one in this mixture. Chill for at least 15 minutes. May be prepared several hours in advance up to this point.

3. Place the veal rolls under the broiler, turning frequently for 7 minutes or until golden brown. Remove string or skewers. Serve with Allison's Favorite Tomatoes (see From the Garden).

Veal Smetana
Serves 6

Smetana indicates sour cream but a substitute works very well in this dish.

12 *veal scallops, no more than ½ inch thick*
1   *teaspoon salt*
3   *teaspoons flour*
6   *tablespoons margarine*
1   *cup onion, finely minced*
1   *pound mushrooms, sliced*
3   *tablespoons brandy*
1   *cup sour cream substitute, or Cottage Cream (see Saucery)*
parsley sprigs
lemon slices

1. Cut the veal into serving pieces. Blend the salt and flour together. Dip the veal into the flour and shake off excess.

2. Melt the margarine in a skillet and brown the veal about 3 minutes on each side. Do not overcook them. Remove them to a warm platter.

3. Add the onion to the skillet, adding a little more margarine if necessary. Sauté onion until soft but not brown. Add the mushrooms and sauté until tender.

4. Add the brandy and ignite it with a match. Shake the pan over the heat until the flame is extinguished. That indicates that all the alcohol has burned off. Stir in the sour cream substitute. Taste for seasoning. Return the scallops to the pan and just reheat them. Do not let the sauce boil. Serve with a garnish of parsley and lemon slices.

Veal Tarragon
Serves 6

6   veal chops
1   tablespoon margarine
1   tablespoon vegetable oil
3   tablespoons green onions, minced
1   clove garlic, diced
½   cup dry white wine
1   teaspoon fresh tarragon, chopped, or ½ teaspoon dried
¼   cup chicken stock
2   tablespoons margarine
1   cup mushrooms, sliced

1. Dry the veal thoroughly. Heat the margarine and oil in a skillet and brown the veal. Place in an ovenproof casserole.
2. Sauté the green onions in the same skillet until soft. Add the garlic, white wine, and tarragon. Simmer for 2 minutes, stirring with a wooden spoon and scraping up the juices. Pour this over the veal and cover. Place in a 325° oven until the veal is tender, about 20 minutes.
3. Remove the cooked veal to a serving platter. Add the chicken stock to a skillet and boil rapidly until reduced to half. Melt the margarine in a skillet and sauté the mushrooms until tender. Add the reduced stock, stir until blended, and pour over the veal. Serve hot.

Roast Lamb with Mint Sauce
Serves 6

½   cup mint jelly
½   cup Cointreau
mint, fresh if available
1   leg of lamb
1   clove garlic, quartered

1. Combine mint jelly and Cointreau in a saucepan and simmer until jelly has melted.
2. Mince 2 or 3 mint leaves and add to sauce. Set aside.
3. Make a cut in the lamb on each side and insert a piece of garlic. Place on a rack in a roasting pan and roast 12 to 14 minutes per pound until medium rare.
4. Baste lamb with sauce during cooking and serve remainder in a sauce boat with the lamb.

Rack of Lamb Cumberland
Serves 4

The tangy Cumberland Sauce perfectly complements the roast lamb. Leg of lamb can also be served this way.

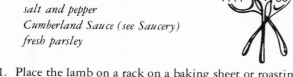

1 rack of lamb
salt and pepper
Cumberland Sauce (see Saucery)
fresh parsley

1. Place the lamb on a rack on a baking sheet or roasting pan. Sprinkle very lightly with salt and pepper. Place in a 350° oven for 1 hour or until it has reached the desired degree of doneness. Do not overcook.
2. Place the lamb on a serving platter and garnish with parsley. Pass the Cumberland Sauce separately in a sauce boat.

Shish Kabob
Serves 6

Serving cracked wheat with this succulent dish will make an authentic Middle Eastern meal.

1	*medium onion, sliced*
3	*cloves garlic, diced*
¼	*teaspoon ground cumin*
3	*tablespoons olive oil*
1	*tablespoon vegetable oil*
3	*tablespoons fresh lemon juice*
1	*teaspoon salt*

freshly ground pepper
1½ teaspoons paprika
1½ pounds boned leg of lamb, cut in 1-inch cubes
mushrooms, cherry tomatoes, green pepper, boiling onions

1. Combine all ingredients except the lamb and vegetables. Toss the lamb with the marinade. Cover and refrigerate for 24 hours. Baste occasionally.
2. Wash the mushrooms, tomatoes, and peppers. Cut the peppers into strips. Peel the small white onions and parboil. Just before barbecuing remove the lamb from the marinade and place on skewers alternating with a mushroom, tomato, onion, and strip of pepper. Broil or barbecue until the lamb is cooked to desired degree of doneness. Remove from the skewers and serve.

Spring Lamb with Vegetables
Serves 6

This elegant stew takes advantage of the spring harvest to produce a delectable one-dish meal. It may be prepared in advance and reheated before serving.

2½ *pounds lamb stewing meat, neck, shoulder, breast, or ribs*
2   *tablespoons vegetable oil*
1   *tablespoon sugar*
salt and pepper to taste
3   *tablespoons flour*
2½ *cups beef bouillon*
3   *tablespoons tomato paste*
2   *cloves garlic, minced*
sprig of thyme or rosemary
1   *bay leaf*
6   *red potatoes*
6   *carrots*
6   *turnips*
12   *small white boiling onions*
1   *cup fresh green peas*

1. Trim all visible fat from lamb and cut into 1-inch cubes and dry thoroughly.
2. Heat the vegetable oil in a covered ovenproof skillet and add the lamb. Brown on all sides. Pour off any fat. Sprinkle the sugar over the meat and continue to brown the lamb until the sugar is melted and caramelized. Add the salt, pepper, and flour, stirring constantly. Continue to cook over medium heat for 5 minutes.
3. Remove any accumulated fat. Add the beef bouillon. Bring to a boil, stirring continuously. Add the tomato paste, garlic, and herbs. Make sure the lamb is covered with liquid, adding more bouillon if necessary. Cover and place in a 325° oven for 1 hour. Lower heat if necessary so that liquid does not boil.
4. Remove any bones from the meat and skim all fat from the sauce. Peel and quarter potatoes, carrots, and turnips. Peel the boiling onions and pierce the bottom with a long-tined fork or make an "X" on the bottom with a knife to prevent them from falling apart during cooking. Add onions to the cooked meat, turning them in the sauce. Heat to a simmer, cover, and return to the oven and continue to simmer for 1 hour or until the lamb and vegetables are tender. Add the peas about 15 minutes before serving, but do not overcook them. Serve hot.

Lamb Boulangère
Serves 6

Steamed asparagus and a crisp salad would complement this spring dish.

> 6   *loin lamb chops*
> 2   *tablespoons vegetable oil*
> 1   *pound potatoes, peeled and thinly sliced*
> 1   *pound onions, peeled and sliced*
> 1   *teaspoon rosemary*
> 1   *small clove garlic, quartered*
> 1   *teaspoon salt*
> *freshly ground pepper*
> 1½ *cups beef bouillon or chicken stock*
> 2   *tablespoons parsley, minced*
> 4   *tablespoons bread crumbs*
> 2   *tablespoons margarine*

1. Trim all fat from the lamb chops. Heat the oil in a large covered skillet and add the lamb. Brown chops lightly on both sides for 10 minutes.
2. Place the sliced potatoes, onions, rosemary, garlic, salt, and pepper over the chops. Pour the bouillon or stock over the top and bring to a simmer. Cover and cook 30 minutes or until lamb is tender.
3. Mix the parsley and bread crumbs together. Melt the margarine in a small skillet and add the bread crumb mixture. Cook over high heat briefly until very lightly browned.
4. Remove cover from the lamb. Sprinkle with the bread crumbs and place under the broiler until the top is nicely browned. Serve hot.

Noisettes of Lamb
Serves 6

This simple treatment of lamb is a perfect foil for an eggplant casserole or stuffed tomatoes.

> 3 *pounds boned leg of lamb or eye of rack of lamb, cut in strips*
> *salt and pepper*
> *marjoram*
> 2 *tablespoons olive oil*
> *fresh parsley*

1. Sprinkle lamb with salt, pepper, and marjoram.
2. Roll slices of lamb into small rounds. Secure with a toothpick.
3. Heat oil in a pan. Add noisettes and cook 4 to 5 minutes on each side. Serve with a garnish of parsley.

Butterflied Barbecued Lamb
Serves 8

This is an incomparable marinade for lamb. Have your butcher bone and butterfly the lamb for you, the day before. Butterfly means to slice down the middle and spread the meat out in butterfly fashion.

> *1   leg of lamb, approximately 6 pounds, boned and butterflied*
> *½ cup dry red wine*
> *¼ cup vegetable oil*
> *sprig of parsley*
> *sprig of fresh thyme, or ½ teaspoon dried*
> *2   bay leaves*
> *1   clove of garlic, sliced in quarters*
> *1   small onion, sliced*
> *1   tablespoon sugar*
> *1   teaspoon salt*

1. Trim any excess fat from the lamb. Place lamb in a shallow dish.
2. Combine the remaining ingredients and pour over the lamb. Cover and refrigerate for 24 hours, turning once.
3. Cook the marinated lamb over barbecue coals until pink. This dish is also excellent served cold.

Lamb Curry
Serves 6

> *1   tablespoon vegetable oil*
> *1   tablespoon margarine*
> *2½ pounds boned lamb, cut in 1-inch cubes*
> *1   large onion, diced*
> *1   green pepper, diced*
> *¾ cup celery, diced*
> *2   cloves garlic, minced*
> *2   cups chicken stock*
> *2   ounces raisins*
> *⅓ cup plain low-fat yogurt*
> CURRY BLEND:
> *4   tablespoons curry powder*
> *½ teaspoon ginger*
> *½ teaspoon tumeric*
> *¼ teaspoon paprika*

¼   *teaspoon ground clove*
2   *tablespoons flour*
½   *teaspoon salt*
¼   *teaspoon pepper*

CONDIMENTS:
¼ *cup each: diced cucumber, currants, green pepper, chopped peanuts, chutneys, mango, fruit, or Major Gray*

1. Combine the oil and margarine in a large skillet and heat. Add the lamb and sauté until well browned. Remove the lamb to a separate dish and add onion, pepper, celery, and garlic to the skillet. Cook over low to moderate heat until the onions are soft and transparent, about 8 minutes.
2. Add the stock and ¼ of the curry blend. Simmer for 5 minutes and taste. Add more curry as desired. Any remaining curry blend may be kept covered for future use. Cover the curry and simmer for 15 minutes.
3. Return the lamb to the skillet and add the raisins. Cook over low heat until the lamb is tender, about 1 hour.
4. When the lamb is tender, add the yogurt and stir until smooth. Serve over rice. Pass the condiments and chutneys at the table.

Dilled Lamb Boats
Serves 4

4   *small baking potatoes*
3   *tablespoons vegetable oil*
¾   *pound lean lamb, ground*
1   *small clove garlic, sliced*
¼   *cup onion, diced*
1   *teaspoon dill weed*
salt and pepper to taste

1. Scrub the potatoes and bake until tender. Slice in half lengthwise and scoop out the pulp. Reserve skin.
2. Heat the vegetable oil in a skillet and add the ground lamb, garlic, onion, and dill weed. Sauté, stirring until the lamb is cooked and the onion is soft. Drain off any fat.
3. Coarsely chop the potato pulp and add it to the skillet. Do not use more than 1 cup of potato. Cook until the potato is very lightly browned. Taste for seasoning. Fill the potato skins with the lamb mixture and heat in a 400° oven for 10 minutes. Serve immediately.

Lamb Shanks
Serves 4

>   2   *tablespoons vegetable oil*
>   4   *lamb shanks, lightly dusted with flour*
>   1   *medium can of tomatoes (1 pound)*
>   1   *cup celery, chopped*
>   3   *tablespoons parsley, chopped, fresh if possible*
>   2   *medium onions, sliced*
>   1   *large clove garlic, minced*
>   1   *teaspoon Worcestershire sauce*
>   1   *tablespoon horseradish*
>   1   *cup dry red wine*
>   ½   *pound whole, fresh mushrooms*
>   1   *tablespoon potato flour, mixed with 2 tablespoons water, if needed to thicken*

1. Heat the oil in a heavy-bottomed pan. Brown the lamb shanks, turning on all sides.
2. When nicely browned, add tomatoes, celery, parsley, onions, garlic, Worcestershire sauce, horseradish, and red wine. Cover and let simmer for 2 hours.
3. Add mushrooms, which have been thoroughly washed. Simmer for an additional 30 minutes.
4. Remove the lamb from the pan. Skim carefully to remove any fat. If the sauce is too thin, add 1 tablespoon of potato flour mixed with 2 tablespoons water, and heat to thicken. Pour over the lamb shanks and serve.

Pork Roast with Prunes
Serves 6

Pork always tastes better when served with fruit. This combination is unbeatable.

>   1   *12-ounce package of pitted prunes*
>   1   *cup port wine, or to cover*
>   3 to 4 *pound pork roast, boned*
>   1   *tablespoon potato flour or cornstarch*
>   *juice of 1 orange*
>   1   *tablespoon red currant jelly*

1. Cover the prunes with the port and soak for 1 hour in a saucepan. Then simmer for 30 minutes.

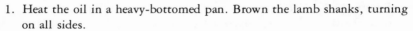

2. Place ⅓ of the prune mixture in the center of the pork, roll up, and tie securely with twine. Place in a 325° oven for approximately 2 hours or 35 minutes per pound. When done remove to a serving dish and keep warm.

3. Skim all but 2 tablespoons of fat from the roasting pan. Add the potato flour or cornstarch and stir. Add a little water if necessary to make a smooth consistency.

4. Strain the remaining prunes and add liquid to the sauce. Stir over medium heat until the sauce has thickened. Add the orange juice and red currant jelly and stir until jelly has dissolved. Arrange the prunes around the pork and serve with the sauce.

Pork Steaks Jaime
Serves 4

Succulent and tangy, this sauce can be used for barbecuing as well as for broiling.

4   *pork steaks*
2   *heaping tablespoons apricot preserves*
1   *teaspoon soy sauce*
¼   *teaspoon ginger*
¼   *teaspoon garlic salt*

1. Trim all visible fat from the meat. Place on broiler pan under broiler or over hot coals on a barbecue grill.

2. Combine preserves, soy sauce, ginger, and garlic sauce in a small bowl. Brush sauce on meat as it cooks.

3. Broil each side 12 to 15 minutes, brushing with sauce frequently.

14
From the Garden

THERE IS SUCH infinite variety in the selection and preparation of vegetables to qualify this area of cooking as an art in itself. Each type of vegetable has its own requirements to bring out the individual color, texture, and flavor that makes it unique. Generally speaking, the most common errors in the preparation of vegetables are overcooking, and using too much liquid, which is then discarded along with the color, taste, and nutrients. Vegetables can be poached, braised, broiled, sautéed, sauced, deep-oil fried, seasoned, herbed, steamed, served in a casserole, or stuffed. They can be served as a main course, first course, hors d'oeuvre, garnish, soup course, or accompany the entrée. They can provide subtle contrast to a highly flavored meat dish or be boldly prepared to stand on their own as the highlight of a meal. Creativity and care in preparation is necessary to raise them from the daily required yellow and green vegetable to the level of a separate course eagerly anticipated.

Vegetables provide a natural emphasis in a restricted cholesterol and fat diet. In their natural state they do not contain any cholesterol and very few contain saturated fat. Most of our essential vitamins and minerals are to be found in the garden. Menus planned around vegetables can eliminate the need for meat at some meals, cutting costs and also reducing high-fat foods in our diet. Dishes such as Vegetable Carousel and Ratatouille are hearty enough to be main courses when French bread and fruit complete the meal. Dieters will find an endless variety of interesting dishes for their low-calorie regimen by seeking out the treasures of the garden. Most vegetables can be eaten in sufficient quantity to be filling and satisfying to any weight watcher without sabotaging a weight reduction plan.

Vegetables that go directly from the garden to the stove are in a special category and those fortunate to have access to their own gardens will undoubtedly enjoy produce that is far superior to that of many markets. Modern refrigeration and transportation systems as well as greenhouse gardening make most types of vegetables available all year round in our markets. Frozen vegetables may be quite helpful both as timesavers as well as providing variety when fresh vegetables are out of season. Canned products rarely capture the taste, color, or texture of the fresh version and require some help in the way of seasoning if they are to be used.

Careful attention must be paid to the preparation of vegetables for they are fragile when exposed to heat and they lose texture, flavor, and nutritive value when they are overcooked. The taste of fresh broccoli that has been steamed for a bare minimum of time is a delightful surprise to the palate. Its crisp and crunchy, alive, fresh taste will discourage preparing overcooked, watery vegetable dishes. Some vegetables are better suited to certain types of cooking than others although there are no hard and fast rules. Spinach, for example, is obviously more easily braised than broiled. A handy trick for cleaning produce, berries as well as greens, is to soak them briefly in a bowl of cold water with approximately ¼ cup of vinegar added. A soft vegetable brush helps remove grit lodged in the crevices. A quick rinse with cold water then removes any vinegar taste, and gently shaking and draining on a paper towel removes excess water. The following are the suitable methods for preparing vegetables.

Baking: This method is suitable for starchy vegetables such as carrots, winter squash, potatoes, and turnips. The vegetables are placed whole on a baking sheet or pared and sliced and placed in a baking dish with a small amount of oil or water. The cooking time is longer than other methods.

Blanching: Plunge vegetables into a large amount of rapidly boiling water and cook for the specified time. Food is then drained or chilled with cold water depending on use. This sets color and preserves nutrients. Used as a preparation for freezing.

Boiling: Although this is probably the easiest cooking method since it requires only a saucepan and water, it can be the reason why vegetables are not always popular. Too much water makes the vegetable mushy, watery, and almost devoid of color, texture, and flavor. The pot can be covered to speed cooking time if necessary, but only for root vegetables. Green vegetables tend to darken when covered. If the vegetables are not to be served immediately, the cooking process can be stopped by placing them under running cold water and draining. This will prevent continued cooking and keep them from becoming gummy and mushy. The vegetables can be reheated in a small amount of liquid or sauce just prior to serving.

Green vegetables require a shorter boiling time and should not be covered after cooking or they will turn from a beautiful emerald color to army green, which is fine on blankets but most unattractive on the dinner table. The cooking time should be as short as possible to prevent unnecessary loss of flavor, texture, and nutrients. Many vitamins are water soluble and are lost when cooking liquid is discarded. Green vegetables such as beans, broccoli, and asparagus should be served slightly crisp. Cook root vegetables such as potatoes and carrots until tender. Do not add baking soda to green vegetables for it makes them soft and destroys vitamin C. White vegetables will retain their brightness with the addition of a pinch of cream of tartar and red vegetables retain their color with a bit of acid, i.e., vinegar, lemon, or a slice of apple.

Braising: This is an excellent technique for some, not all, vegetables. Those with high cellulose and fiber content are well suited for this method: spinach, lettuce, leeks, cabbage, celery, and endive for example. The vegetables are usually blanched and then placed in a covered baking dish with liquid, water or stock, and seasonings and then given a long, slow cooking. During this process the liquid reduces in volume and concentrates in flavor and produces its own sauce, beautifully glazed. Some color is sacrificed but the resulting taste is worth it.

Broiling: This is usually a finishing step to brown or crisp vegetables that have been prepared in one of the foregoing methods.

Deep-oil frying: This method of preparation will have a higher calorie content and more saturated fat than vegetables prepared other ways. But if done properly it need not be ignored on a controlled saturated fat and cholesterol program. Unsaturated vegetable oils are more suited to this technique than butter, margarine, or olive oil. The saturated fats cannot tolerate the high temperature necessary for deep-oil frying without burning and smoking whereas the vegetable oils can. Temperature is extremely important in frying. The hot oil should sear the outside of the food and the cooking is done by the heat of the moisture inside which actually steams the vegetables. If the temperature is too low, the searing effect will not occur and the vegetables will absorb the oil with a greasy, soggy result. If the oil is too hot, it will smoke and burn, cooking unevenly. The food will be crusty on the outside and underdone on the inside. A frying thermometer is most helpful in checking the temperature of the oil before and during cooking. About 2 to 3 inches of oil in the pan is sufficient to produce a good product. An electric skillet is suitable for deep-oil frying and the temperature more easily controlled.

If you do not have a thermometer, put a small cube of bread in the heated oil. If it sizzles in the oil, the temperature is about 375°.

After the oil has come slowly to the proper temperature, add the food which has been warmed to room temperature. Cold foods lower the temperature of the oil and slow cooking. Foods should be added in small amounts, since large quantities cool the oil and will not cook evenly. There should be enough oil so that the foods can move freely and not touch the bottom of the pan or they may stick.

When the food is golden brown and crisp, remove it with a slotted spoon to a crumpled paper towel to drain thoroughly. Do not salt deep-fried food until ready or the food will become soggy. Place the fried food in a 200° oven in an uncovered dish until ready to serve. Some vegetables may need to be tenderized by parboiling before final cooking. Most deep-oil fried foods are coated with flour or a batter. This will be discussed in the sections on individual vegetables.

Steaming: For retaining color and texture in asparagus, celery, broccoli, endive, and other high cellulose vegetables, steaming is by far the best method. A small amount of water is brought to a boil in a covered steamer or pot fitted with a rack or mesh basket. The vegetables are placed on the rack above the water and cooked covered for just a few minutes until tender.

Stir-fry: This oriental method of preparing vegetables produces very crisp vegetables while losing none of the flavor and nutrients. The food is chopped or sliced into small pieces and placed in a wok or skillet containing a small amount of very hot oil. The vegetables are stirred quickly over high heat for several minutes until partially done. A sauce of cornstarch, soy sauce, stock, and sherry is added and the skillet is covered to finish the cooking.

Artichokes

When in bloom the artichoke is a beautiful lavender blue thistle. When harvested before the blooming stage it yields a delicate morsel at the end of each leaf.

Selection: The artichoke should be chosen when it has firm leaves and good color. Artichokes that have been touched by frost will have dark and sometimes grayish spots on the leaves but this does not affect the taste. Size will vary from very small to up to 4 inches in diameter and all are good. Artichoke hearts are available marinated and frozen, and artichoke bottoms are commercially canned.

Storage: Artichokes will keep for a week to 10 days in the crisper of the refrigerator.

Nutrition: Artichokes contain such minerals as iron and calcium as well as vitamins A and B complex.

Preparation: Remove the stalk and bottom row of small leaves. Snip the thorny tip from each leaf and rinse thoroughly under running water.

Serving: Boiling, steaming, and baking are suitable cooking methods for whole artichokes. They can be served hot or cold with a dipping sauce. The bottoms can be removed and served with a purée of peas or spinach and covered with hollandaise sauce. The hearts can be marinated or used in casseroles. Whole artichokes can be stuffed and served as an entrée or simply dressed with mayonnaise and served as a vegetable.

Boiled Artichokes

Allow one artichoke per person and trim them as directed. All recipes calling for cooked artichokes will be prepared in this manner whether served hot or cold.

1 large kettle of boiling water
2 cloves garlic, sliced in about 4 pieces each
1 teaspoon vegetable oil
1 bouillon cube (optional)

1. Bring the water in a large pot or kettle to a boil.
2. Add the garlic, oil, and bouillon cube. Boil until the bouillon cube dissolves, then reduce the heat and add artichokes.
3. Do not cover but boil gently for 25 to 30 minutes or until the center of the artichoke is quite tender when poked with a fork. They will become mushy with overcooking. Drain thoroughly.
4. Separate the leaves and scrape the fuzzy choke in the center away with a spoon. Serve with a dipping sauce of mayonnaise or use in subsequent recipes.

Artichoke Parmesan
Serves 4

The artichoke is the sauce boat for the tangy tomato and cheese sauce. The amount of cheese used is small but necessary for the taste. Both sauce and artichoke can be prepared ahead and assembled just before serving.

4 *cooked artichokes*
¼ *cup mayonnaise*
1 *tablespoon tomato paste*
4 *teaspoons Parmesan cheese, grated*

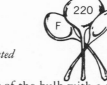

1. Scrape the choke from the center of the bulb with a spoon, but keep the leaves intact to form a cup.
2. Combine the mayonnaise (homemade is the tastiest) with the tomato paste.
3. Place ¼ of the tomato sauce in the center of each artichoke.
4. Sprinkle 1 teaspoon of the grated Parmesan cheese on top.
5. Place in a 350° oven for 15 minutes or until the cheese has melted. Serve immediately.

Shrimp Stuffed Artichokes
Serves 4

When you are splurging on shrimp, combine it with the artichoke and you have a sauce for the leaves.

4 *artichokes, boiled and trimmed of chokes*
3 *tablespoons margarine*
2 *tablespoons olive oil*
2 *cloves garlic, minced*
3 *tablespoons green onions, minced*
1 *pound shrimp, shelled and deveined, or frozen*
salt and pepper to taste

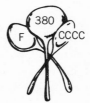

1. Cook the artichokes, remove the fuzzy choke, and spread the leaves apart.
2. Melt the margarine in a skillet and heat with the olive oil. Add the garlic and onions and stir for 1 minute.
3. Add the shrimp and stir until they turn pink. This should only take a few minutes.
4. Add the salt and pepper and taste.
5. Fill the artichokes with the shrimp mixture; be sure to use all the garlic-flavored oil. Serve.

Artichoke Bottoms Stuffed with Spinach
Serves 4

This combination of artichoke bottoms sauced with puréed spinach makes an elegant accompaniment to a simple entrée such as roast chicken or leg of lamb. While it appears a special dish it requires little extra in the way of preparation. Both the artichokes and spinach can be prepared ahead and assembled at the last minute.

4 artichoke bottoms
1 cup Puréed Spinach (see pages 198–99)
1 teaspoon lemon juice

1. Remove the outer leaves from 4 cooked artichokes and scrape away the choke. If the artichokes have cooled, place in a covered dish in a 350° oven for 10 minutes until they are hot.
2. Prepare the Puréed Spinach as directed and add the lemon juice. Taste for seasoning and add more lemon juice if desired.
3. Place the artichoke bottoms in a shallow baking dish and cover with the spinach.
4. Place under the broiler just until the top has browned slightly. Serve immediately.

Asparagus

Asparagus is the harbinger of spring. The long, slender stalks bring the promise of sunny days and all the colors and fragrances of the new harvest.

Selection: Choose firm, green stalks with tightly closed tips. There is also a white variety, extremely good. Size varies from ¼ to ¾ inch in diameter and it is a matter of taste as to which you choose. Asparagus spears are available frozen and canned although the canned variety has an altogether different taste.

Storage: Store in a plastic bag in the crisper of the refrigerator.

Nutrition: Asparagus is a source of minerals and vitamins and being a fibrous watery vegetable, is quite low in calories.

Preparation: Cut off the white tough ends of the stalks. Peel the stalks with a potato peeler. They may be cooked whole or cut into 2-inch pieces.

Serving: Steaming, boiling, and stir-frying are good methods for preparing asparagus. Whichever you choose, just be sure you don't overcook it.

Asparagus Benedict
Serves 4

Asparagus benedict is a combination of several delicious dishes that omit the onerous poached egg but leaves the heavenly flavors of hollandaise, asparagus, Canadian bacon, and English muffin. This would be an ideal brunch dish but watch the other items on the menu as it is higher in cholesterol than some other recipes. An arrangement of fresh fruit or a bowl of fresh berries with a carafe of steaming coffee made from freshly ground beans complete an elegant luncheon menu.

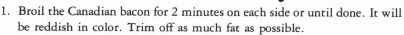

1 pound cooked asparagus, hot
4 slices Canadian bacon
Hollandaise Sauce (see Saucery)
4 English muffins, split

1. Broil the Canadian bacon for 2 minutes on each side or until done. It will be reddish in color. Trim off as much fat as possible.
2. Toast the English muffin halves and place on serving plate.
3. Place the Canadian bacon on the muffins between the 2 halves.
4. Place the asparagus spears on top of the bacon and cover with the Hollandaise Sauce.

Asparagus in the Chinese Manner
Serves 4

water to cover
1 pound of asparagus, trimmed
½ teaspoon sugar
3 tablespoons soy sauce
1 tablespoon cornstarch
1 tablespoon water

1. Bring enough water to barely cover the asparagus to boil in a large, flat skillet.
2. Add the asparagus, sugar, and soy sauce to the water and when the water is boiling again reduce the heat to moderate.
3. Cook over medium heat until the asparagus is just barely tender, about 5 minutes.
4. Mix cornstarch and water into a smooth paste and stir into the cooked vegetable. Cook until slightly thickened and serve. There will be a light coating of soy sauce clinging to the spears.

Asparagus Newburg
Serves 4

An elegant luncheon dish or a Sunday supper. A tossed green salad and a fruit compote would complete the menu.

1	tablespoon vegetable oil
3	tablespoons margarine
½	pound mushrooms, sliced
¼	cup almonds, slivered
3	tablespoons flour
1	cup low-fat milk, hot
1½	tablespoons sherry
4	toast squares
1	pound asparagus, cooked and drained

1. Heat the vegetable oil in a skillet and add 1 tablespoon of the margarine. When melted add the mushrooms and stir over high heat until all liquid has evaporated. Set aside.
2. Melt the remaining margarine in a saucepan and add the almonds. Cook for 1 minute and add the flour. Stir thoroughly over low-medium heat for **at least** 2 minutes.
3. Remove from the heat and in a slow steady stream, add the hot milk while stirring.
4. Return to the heat and bring to a boil, stirring. Reduce the heat and stir until the sauce has thickened and is smooth. If the sauce lumps, force it through a sieve and pick out the almonds.
5. Add the mushrooms and stir, then add the sherry and cook gently for 3 minutes.
6. Trim the crust from 4 slices of toast and cut them diagonally. Arrange them on a serving plate.
7. Arrange the asparagus on the toast and cover with the sauce. Serve immediately.

Asparagus Papillote
Serves 4

This is a variation of steaming. Papillote means cooking in a case or bag.

4	teaspoons margarine
¼	cup shallots or green onions, minced
1	teaspoon sugar
1	pound asparagus, trimmed

1   *cup peas, fresh or frozen*
4   *12-inch squares of aluminum foil*

1. Melt margarine in a skillet and add shallots or green onions. Sauté until soft but not brown. Stir in sugar and cook for 30 seconds.
2. Place ¼ pound of asparagus and ¼ cup of peas on each square of foil. Top each square with ¼ of the cooked onions.
3. Seal each square by folding the edges over and pinching together to make a tightly closed envelope.
4. Place in a steamer or large pot with a rack on the bottom. Add about 1 inch of water for steaming. Cover and steam for 30 minutes.
5. Remove papillotes from steamer and place on a serving plate. Cut a hole in the top of each exposing the steaming vegetables. Serve.

Asparagus Parmesan
Serves 4

1   *pound asparagus, cooked*
¼   *cup mayonnaise*
1   *tablespoon tomato paste*
¼   *cup Parmesan cheese, grated*

1. Place the cooked asparagus in a shallow baking dish.
2. Combine the mayonnaise and tomato paste and spread over the asparagus.
3. Sprinkle the grated Parmesan cheese over the tomato sauce and place in a 350° oven until the cheese has melted, about 10 minutes. Serve hot.

Asparagus Piccata
Serves 4

This is an adaptation of a famous veal dish served at New York's Colony restaurant. The very thin spears are best for this dish and they should be peeled to cook quickly.

1   *pound asparagus, trimmed*
4   *tablespoons margarine*
1   *tablespoon lemon juice*

1. Slice the asparagus in 2-inch strips.
2. Melt the margarine in a skillet and when hot add the asparagus. Toss in the skillet until slightly tender, about 3 minutes.
3. Add the lemon juice and gently coat the asparagus with the lemon juice and margarine. Serve.

Asparagus and Mushrooms Stir-Fry
Serves 4

> 3 *tablespoons vegetable oil*
> 1 *pound asparagus, trimmed, peeled, and sliced in 2-inch pieces*
> ½ *pound mushrooms, sliced*
> 1 *tablespoon soy sauce*
> 1 *thin slice fresh ginger*
> ½ *cup chicken stock*
> 2 *teaspoons cornstarch*
> 3 *tablespoons cold water*

1. Heat the oil in a wok or skillet. The oil should be very hot but not smoking.
2. Add the asparagus and stir-fry for 1 minute.
3. Add the mushrooms and stir-fry for 1 more minute.
4. Add the soy sauce, ginger, and chicken stock and bring to a boil. Cover and reduce the heat, simmer until the asparagus is tender but still bright green. It should remain crisp.
5. Mix the cornstarch and water and add to the skillet, stirring until the mixture thickens. Serve immediately.

Asparagus Polonaise
Serves 4

Vegetables Polonaise indicate they are finished with a topping of bread crumbs and sieved hard-boiled egg. In our version we simply omit the egg yolk.

> 1 *pound asparagus, cooked*
> 3 *tablespoons margarine*
> 4 *tablespoons bread crumbs, freshly made if possible*
> 1 *hard-boiled egg white, grated or finely chopped*

1. Arrange the hot, cooked asparagus on a serving platter.
2. Melt the margarine in a skillet. Add the bread crumbs and toss until lightly browned.
3. Stir in the egg white and sprinkle the mixture over the asparagus. Serve.

Asparagus Vinaigrette
Serves 4

This dish can be served as a salad or as a summer vegetable. The asparagus can also be sliced into 1-inch pieces and served on toothpicks as an hors d'oeuvre.

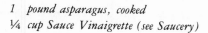

1 *pound asparagus, cooked*
¼ *cup Sauce Vinaigrette (see Saucery)*

1. Place the asparagus in a shallow dish and pour the sauce over it, turning the asparagus to completely coat all the spears.
2. Refrigerate for at least 1 hour, or overnight.
3. Remove the asparagus to a serving dish and cover with the remaining sauce. Serve.

Dried Beans or Legumes

This diverse class of food is a staple all over the world. The Orient, Central and South America, Mediterranean Europe, and Africa are just a few areas that incorporate the broad family of dried beans into their diet.

Selection: In this country we usually find packaged dried beans readily available. Some types are also available frozen, notably lima beans and black-eyed peas. Some prepared dishes, such as canned refried beans, can also be found.

Storage: Store dried beans in a covered canister, box, or paper bag in a cool, dry place.

Nutrition: Beans offer an alternative to meat and fish as a source of protein in our diet. Soybeans, in particular, are widely used as an inexpensive protein substitute. They also furnish fiber, iron, and other minerals, as well as vitamin B complex.

Preparation: Dried beans are usually soaked for several hours in cold water to soften them and reduce the cooking time. Dried beans require long cooking times in a covered pot.

Serving: Beans may be served boiled, baked, puréed, or in soups and salads.

Boston Baked Beans
Serves 6

The judicious use of seasonings converts canned baked beans to an epicurean delight.

1 30-ounce can baked beans
1 teaspoon prepared mustard
¼ teaspoon garlic salt
2 tablespoons brown sugar
½ cup catsup
1 teaspoon Worcestershire sauce
2 tablespoons molasses

1. Place beans in a large pot.
2. Add the seasonings and mix thoroughly.
3. Bring to a boil and reduce heat. Cook for 20 minutes. Serve.

Chili with Beans
Serves 4

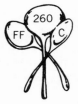

1 pound ground beef
2 medium onions, chopped
3 large cloves garlic, minced
1 tablespoon chili powder
½ cup chili sauce
1 large can tomatoes
1 teaspoon oregano
salt and pepper to taste
2 15-ounce cans red kidney beans, drained

1. Brown the ground beef, add the onions, garlic, and chili powder. Stir frequently until the onions are soft but not brown.
2. Add the chili sauce, tomatoes, oregano, salt, and pepper, and kidney beans and simmer for 1 hour.
3. Taste for seasoning during this time and add more chili powder, or garlic if necessary.
4. Serve with saltine crackers.

Fava Beans Extraordinaire
Serves 4

Lima beans may be substituted if you cannot locate favas. Favas are delicious but need to be well cooked to rid them of their possible toxic effects.

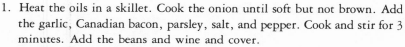

1   tablespoon olive oil
2   tablespoons vegetable oil
1   cup onion, chopped
2   cloves garlic, minced
½ cup Canadian bacon, chopped and cooked
¼ cup parsley, minced
1   teaspoon salt
½ teaspoon pepper
½ cup fava beans, shelled and washed, or frozen lima beans
1   cup vermouth or white wine

1. Heat the oils in a skillet. Cook the onion until soft but not brown. Add the garlic, Canadian bacon, parsley, salt, and pepper. Cook and stir for 3 minutes. Add the beans and wine and cover.
2. Cook for 1 hour. Serve hot.

Garbanzos Elena
Serves 4

Elena Zelayeta was a Mexican cook extraordinaire. She overcame blindness to run a restaurant, teach Mexican cooking, and run a frozen food business. This is a variation on one of her themes.

2   tablespoons vegetable oil
2   small cans garbanzo beans or chick peas
2   cloves garlic, minced
1   cup onion, diced
1   15-ounce can plum tomatoes, drained
1   teaspoon salt
½ teaspoon pepper
½ cup pimiento-stuffed olives, chopped

1. Heat the oil in a large skillet. Add garbanzos, garlic, and onion. Sautée, stirring gently, until the onion is soft but not brown.
2. Add the tomatoes, salt, and pepper and simmer for 45 minutes.
3. Add olives and when heated through, serve.

Green Beans

Whether you refer to them as green, string, French, or snap, fresh beans are a delightful addition to any menu. They make an appearance in numerous dishes, from the very simple to the most elaborate.

Selection: Fresh beans are available year round. Choose firm, crisp beans with no discolorations. Beans are also available canned and frozen.

Storage: Beans should be left unwashed in a plastic bag in the refrigerator until ready for use.

Nutrition: Beans are fairly low in calories, contain a moderate amount of fiber, and are good sources of all the minerals and vitamins.

Preparation: Most varieties require only trimming the ends, however some need to have the heavy string along the side removed. Beans can be cooked whole, sliced lengthwise (julienned), or sliced.

Serving: Beans can be served simply prepared with a garnish of herb "butter" or combined with other vegetables in casseroles and soups. They are complemented by herbs, flavored stocks, and sauces.

Green Beans Amandine
Serves 4

   2 *tablespoons margarine*
¼ *cup slivered almonds*
   1 *pound crisp beans, cooked*

1. Melt the margarine in a skillet. Add the almonds and stir over high heat until the almonds and margarine are quite brown but do not let them burn.
2. Toss with the cooked beans and serve.

Green Bean Casserole
Serves 4

   1 *pound fresh green beans*
   2 *tablespoons vegetable oil*
   1 *red onion, sliced*
½ *pound fresh mushrooms, sliced*
   1 *cup chicken stock*
   1 *teaspoon cornstarch*
   1 *teaspoon water*

1. Trim the ends of the beans and slice in half lengthwise. Place in a baking dish.
2. Heat the oil in a skillet and add the onion. Sauté until soft but not brown. Add the mushrooms and stir-fry until soft. Add the chicken stock. Mix cornstarch and water to form a paste. Add to the skillet and bring to a boil.
3. Pour over the beans and bake in a 350° oven until the beans are tender, about 25 minutes. Serve hot.

Herbed Green Beans
Serves 6

> 1½ *pounds fresh green beans*
> ⅓   *cup bread crumbs*
> ¼   *cup margarine*
> 1   *clove fresh garlic, sliced or,* ½ *teaspoon garlic powder*
> 3   *tablespoons Parmesan cheese, grated*
> ⅛   *teaspoon basil*
> ¾   *teaspoon salt*

1. Wash and trim beans. Steam until barely tender.
2. Place bread crumbs in a 400° oven for 5 minutes.
3. Melt the margarine and add garlic. Sauté until soft and remove the garlic slices.
4. Add the cheese, bread crumbs, basil, and salt to the margarine. Toss this mixture with the beans. Serve hot.

Green Beans Ravigote
Serves 4

> 1 *pound green beans, cooked, hot, and cut in 2-inch pieces*
> 4 *tablespoons Sauce Ravigote (see Saucery)*

1. Toss the hot beans with the cold Sauce Ravigote. Serve immediately.

Green Beans with Mushrooms and Onions
Serves 4

This cooking method is a modified Chinese style stir-fry.

1 pound fresh green beans
1 pinch ground ginger (about ⅛ teaspoon) or 1 thin slice fresh ginger
½ cup water or chicken stock
2 teaspoons soy sauce
¼ teaspoon sugar
1 teaspoon salt
½ teaspoon pepper
2 cups water
½ cup green onions, sliced
½ pound mushrooms, sliced

1. Slice the beans into 1-inch diagonal pieces.
2. Combine the ginger, water or chicken stock, soy sauce, sugar, salt, and pepper in a saucepan and simmer for 1 minute.
3. Bring the 2 cups of water to a boil and cook the beans and onions for 5 minutes. Drain.
4. Add beans, onions, and mushrooms to soy sauce mixture and heat for 1 minute. Serve.

Beets

This delicious, sweet root thrives in chilly climes and is edible from its leafy top to the bottom of its bulb.

Selection: Choose fresh beets with small firm roots and crisp, reddish green foliage. Beets are available fresh and canned. Frozen beets have not been found to be satisfactory.

Storage: Store in the crisper of the refrigerator.

Nutrition: Beets are low in calories and a good source of all the minerals and vitamins, particularly vitamin A in beet greens.

Preparation: Trim the greens just above the top. Do not cut into the skin or the color will leak into the water during cooking. Peel and slice *after* boiling.

Serving: Beets, like most tubers, are best boiled or baked. They can then be added to soups, salads, and sauced as a vegetable. The green tops can be served as a vegetable or used as a seasoning.

Minted Beets
Serves 4

1	pound fresh beets, peeled and shredded
2	tablespoons margarine
3	tablespoons lemon juice
1	teaspoon salt
½	cup water
1	tablespoon onion, grated
1	tablespoon sugar
1	tablespoon mint, chopped

1. Shred the beets on the coarse section of a cheese grater.
2. Melt the margarine in a saucepan. Add the lemon juice, salt, and beets. Cover the pan and cook over low heat for 30 minutes. They should be very tender. Check them twice during cooking, stirring them to keep from sticking.
3. Add the water, onion, sugar, and mint and cook for another 10 minutes. Serve.

Beets Moldau
Serves 4

1	pound beets, unpeeled
1	large onion, peeled and sliced very thin
2	tablespoons lemon juice
2	teaspoons sugar
1	teaspoon salt
½	teaspoon pepper
¼	cup mayonnaise
¼	cup plain low-fat yogurt
	chopped fresh parsley

1. Boil the beets until tender, about 30 minutes. Drain, cool, and peel.
2. Slice the beets and place in a shallow dish. Cover with the onion.
3. Combine the lemon juice, sugar, salt, pepper, mayonnaise, and yogurt. Spread this mixture over the beets and onions and refrigerate until well chilled.
4. Serve with a garnish of chopped parsley.

Harvard Beets
Serves 4

> 2   teaspoons cornstarch
> 2   teaspoons water
> ⅓   cup sugar
> ⅓   cup vinegar, wine vinegar is preferred
> 1   tablespoon margarine
> ½   teaspoon salt
> 2   cloves, whole
> 2   cups beets, cooked, peeled, and sliced

1. Combine the cornstarch and water to make a smooth paste.
2. In a saucepan, add the sugar, vinegar, margarine, salt, and cloves.
3. Add the cornstarch mixture and heat until the sauce is transparent.
4. Add the beets and cook until heated through. Serve hot.

Baked Beets
Serves 4

A simple way to prepare beets that brings out their sweet flavor uses small beets. The baking time is almost twice that of potatoes.

> 8   small beets, golf ball size
> salt

1. Preheat oven to 400°.
2. Trim the root ends and greens from the beets. Scrub skins.
3. Place on a baking sheet in preheated oven for 25 to 30 minutes or until tender when pierced with a knife.
4. When done remove from oven and slide skins off. They should slip easily.
5. Lightly salt the beets and serve hot.

Beets à l'Orange
Serves 4

This dish has a subtle taste of orange which does not mask the sweetness of the beets.

> 2   cups beets, whole and unpeeled
> 1   cup boiling water
> 1   tablespoon white sugar

1   tablespoon brown sugar
1   tablespoon wine vinegar
¼   teaspoon cream of tartar
½   cup orange juice

1. Place the beets in the boiling water until tender, about 8 minutes. Drain thoroughly, peel, and slice.
2. Combine the sugars, wine vinegar, and cream of tartar in a saucepan and place over a high flame until the sugars melt and caramelize. Do not let the syrup get too dark in color. Remove from the heat and stir in the orange juice.
3. Bring to a boil and add the beets. Heat thoroughly. Serve hot.

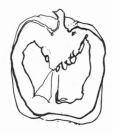

Broccoli

Broccoli is a member of the cauliflower family. It was first cultivated in this country in California in 1920. There are several ornamental varieties as well as two edible kinds, the familiar green and the purple Venetian type.

Selection: Choose compact heads with tightly closed buds and dark green stalks. Avoid broccoli that is turning yellow.
Storage: It keeps well unwashed in a plastic bag in the refrigerator.
Nutrition: Broccoli is low in calories, high in vitamins A and C and in minerals.
Preparation: Just prior to cooking, wash the broccoli thoroughly, trim off the end of the stems and peel the stalk. Stalks may be sliced lengthwise for steaming or cut into 2-inch pieces for stir-frying.
Serving: Steaming is by far the best method of preparing broccoli. It is also very good stir-fried and adapts well to casseroles and sauces.

Steamed Broccoli
Serves 4

This is a method of preparation for any recipes calling for cooked broccoli.

> *boiling water*
> *1½ pounds broccoli, trimmed and cut in 1-inch pieces, or thin spears*

1. Bring water to boil in large cooking pot. Use a steamer or large, flat skillet with a rack on top.
2. Place broccoli in the steamer or skillet and cover.
3. Steam for 5 minutes. **Do not overcook.** Broccoli should be firm, bright green, and crisp.
4. Serve hot with lemon juice and salt. Or, cold with homemade mayonnaise as an hors d'oeuvre or salad.

Broccoli Amandine
Serves 4

The surprise in this recipe is the almost scorched almonds. They should be a deep brown but snatch them from the heat before they burn.

> *8 stalks of broccoli, trimmed and cut in 1-inch pieces, or thin spears*
> *3 tablespoons margarine*
> *¼ cup slivered almonds*
> *2 teaspoons lemon juice*

1. Place broccoli on a rack in a steamer or large flat skillet. Pour boiling water 1-inch deep in the pan.
2. Cover and let steam until just tender but not soft, about 7 minutes. Remove from steamer and keep warm.
3. Melt the margarine in a small skillet. Add the almonds and stir until they are the color of a paper bag. The margarine also takes on a brown color.
4. Stir in the lemon juice and toss over broccoli. Serve immediately.

Cold Broccoli with Warm Hollandaise
Serves 4

This has to be the eighth wonder of the world; the colors and tastes are superb. **Do not** overcook the broccoli.

> *1 pound broccoli spears, cooked and cold*
> *½ cup Hollandaise Sauce (see Saucery)*

1. Slice broccoli spears in half. For very special occasions serve only the flowerettes and save the bottom half of the stalks for another meal.
2. Arrange broccoli on serving platter, cover with sauce, and serve. For an appetizer, place the sauce in a separate bowl and serve as a dip for chilled, cooked broccoli.

Broccoli Sauté
Serves 4

> 1½ *pounds broccoli, trimmed*
> 2 *tablespoons olive oil*
> 1 *tablespoon vegetable oil*
> 2 *cloves garlic, minced*
> 1 *teaspoon oregano, fresh, or ½ teaspoon oregano, dried*

1. Cut the broccoli into ½-inch pieces.
2. Heat the oil in a skillet but do not let it smoke.
3. Add the garlic and cook for 1 minute.
4. Add the broccoli and oregano and stir until the broccoli is tender but not soft.
5. Remove any garlic pieces and serve hot or cold.

Broccoli Smetana
Serves 6

Smetana usually indicates a dish is made with sour cream. Substitute half yogurt and half mayonnaise.

> ¼ *cup plain low-fat yogurt*
> ¼ *cup mayonnaise*
> 1 *teaspoon horseradish*
> 1 *teaspoon sugar*
> 1½ *pounds broccoli, cooked*

1. Combine the yogurt, mayonnaise, horseradish, and sugar.
2. Place mixture in the top of a double boiler over very hot but not boiling water. Stir until warm and smooth.
3. Arrange the broccoli in a serving dish and pour the warm sauce over the hot broccoli. Serve immediately.

Creamed Broccoli
Serves 4

2   tablespoons margarine
¼   cup onion, diced
2   tablespoons flour
¾   cup low-fat milk, hot
salt and pepper to taste
1½   pounds broccoli, cooked
2   ounces Parmesan cheese, grated

1. Melt the margarine in a skillet. Add the onion and sauté over low heat until soft and transparent but not brown.
2. Add the flour and stir thoroughly for **at least** 2 minutes over low heat. Remove from the heat.
3. Stir the hot milk in a slow steady stream into the mixture and return the sauce to the stove. Stir constantly until it boils and then reduce the heat. Stir until it thickens and is smooth.
4. Salt and pepper to taste.
5. Arrange the broccoli in a shallow baking dish and pour the sauce over it, then sprinkle with the Parmesan cheese.
6. Place in a 350° oven for 12 minutes or until the cheese has melted. Serve hot.

Broccoli Moutarde
Serves 6

4   large stalks broccoli
1   cup boiling water
¼   cup mayonnaise
1   teaspoon mustard
1   tablespoon lemon juice
½   teaspoon Worcestershire sauce
½   teaspoon garlic salt
1   teaspoon salt
½   teaspoon pepper

1. Peel the tough outer layer from the broccoli stalks and slice into 1-inch pieces.
2. Place the pieces in a shallow, covered skillet in an even layer and add 1

cup of boiling water. Cover and boil vigorously for 5 minutes or until barely tender. Do not overcook. Drain immediately and place in serving dish.

3. Combine the mayonnaise, mustard, lemon juice, Worcestershire sauce, garlic salt, salt, and pepper. Mix well. Spoon over the hot broccoli. Serve immediately.

Brussels Sprouts

Sprouts are often maligned because they are improperly cooked. The baby cabbages, named after the Belgian capital, require care to bring out their full flavor.

Selection: Choose compact, bright green sprouts, firm and unwrinkled. They are also available frozen.

Storage: Store unwashed in a plastic bag in the refrigerator. Fresh sprouts should be used soon after purchase and not kept more than 1 or 2 days.

Nutrition: Brussels sprouts are a source of minerals and vitamins A and B complex.

Preparation: Wash and trim stems off each sprout. Remove limp outer leaves. Large sprouts may be cut in half.

Serving: Sprouts should be cooked in boiling salted water until tender, about 10 minutes. Long cooking will render them bitter.

Brussels Sprouts with Caraway Seeds
Serves 4

½ cup chicken stock
1 package frozen Brussels sprouts, or ¾ pound fresh sprouts, trimmed
2 tablespoons margarine
1 teaspoon caraway seeds

1. Bring the stock to a boil and add the sprouts.
2. Reduce the heat to medium and cook until tender, about 8 minutes. Drain thoroughly and set aside.
3. Melt the margarine in the same pot. Add sprouts and caraway seeds. Toss well and serve.

Brussels Sprouts Supreme
Serves 4

> *1½ pounds Brussels sprouts, trimmed*
> *1   tablespoon margarine*
> *½   cup small white boiling onions, sliced*
> *⅓   cup chicken stock*
> *1   teaspoon salt*
> *½   teaspoon pepper*
> *1   tablespoon parsley, minced*
> *1   tablespoon Parmesan cheese, grated*

1. Place the Brussels sprouts in a saucepan with 1 cup of boiling, salted water. Boil uncovered for 5 minutes. Drain.
2. Melt the margarine in a skillet and add the onion. Sauté until soft but not brown. Add the stock, salt, and pepper, and simmer for 2 minutes. Add the Brussels sprouts and parsley. Simmer until the sprouts are tender. Do not let them get soft and mushy.
3. Place in a shallow baking dish and spoon stock over the sprouts. Sprinkle with cheese.
4. Place under the broiler just until the cheese melts. Serve immediately.

Cabbage

Cabbages are colorful and versatile. Varieties range from smooth red and green heads to the crinkled pale green Chinese kind.

Selection: Choose cabbage heads that are firm and fresh and of medium size.
Storage: Store unwashed in a plastic bag in the refrigerator.
Nutrition: Cabbage is high in minerals, vitamin B complex, some vitamin A, and in the raw state, vitamin C.
Preparation: Discard wilted outer leaves and rinse well. Cut into wedges; slice, or shred as needed.
Serving: Cabbage may be served stuffed, boiled or sautéed. Do not cover cabbage during cooking as it develops an unpleasant odor and taste. Raw cabbage is crisp and tasty in salads or in cole slaw. Certain varieties are used for brining in sauerkraut.

Cabbage Royale
Serves 6

> 3   tablespoons vegetable oil
> 1   small head cabbage, shredded
> 1   large onion, chopped
> ½ cup chicken stock
> 1   teaspoon wine vinegar
> 3   tablespoons Canadian bacon, chopped
> 1   teaspoon caraway seeds
> salt and freshly ground pepper

1. Heat the vegetable oil in a skillet. Add the cabbage and onion and sauté over medium heat, stirring frequently for 5 minutes.
2. Add the chicken stock and vinegar and continue cooking until the vegetables are tender.
3. Sauté the Canadian bacon until crisp and add to the cabbage mixture with the caraway seeds, salt, and freshly ground pepper.

Colcannon
Serves 6

This heavenly Irish dish can be prepared as follows, but if you are boiling a ham or spareribs, add the potatoes and cabbage to the cooking liquid during the last 15 minutes of cooking, then continue with step 2.

> 4   medium boiling potatoes, peeled and quartered
> 1   head cabbage, trimmed and chopped
> 4   tablespoons margarine
> 1   teaspoon salt
> freshly ground pepper

1. Place potatoes and cabbage in two separate pots. Cover with water and boil gently until tender, 25 to 30 minutes. Drain thoroughly.
2. Mash the potatoes and beat until smooth.
3. Melt half the margarine in a skillet and add the cabbage. Stir and sauté for 5 minutes.
4. Add the potatoes, salt, pepper, and rest of the margarine. Mix thoroughly and test for seasoning. Add more salt if necessary. Serve hot.

Cabbage Tarragon
Serves 6

> 1 medium head cabbage
> 4 tablespoons margarine
> 1 teaspoon tarragon
> 1 cup vermouth
> 1 teaspoon salt
> freshly ground pepper

1. Trim the outside leaves if they are wilted and chop the cabbage coarsely.
2. Melt the margarine in a skillet and add the cabbage. Sauté, stirring frequently, for about 8 minutes or until soft.
3. Add the tarragon, vermouth, salt, and pepper and simmer over medium heat until the cabbage is tender, about 8 to 10 minutes. Serve hot.

Red Cabbage and Apples
Serves 4

This classic combination has a different twist. The port and red currant jelly add an interesting flavor.

> 1   head red cabbage, grated
> 3   tart apples, peeled and grated
> 1   onion, chopped
> 1½ tablespoons red currant jelly
> ¼   cup port wine
> 2   tablespoons wine vinegar
> ¼   cup Canadian bacon, cooked and chopped
> 1   teaspoon salt
> ½   teaspoon pepper to taste

1. Place the cabbage, apples, and onion in a covered casserole.
2. Place the currant jelly, port, vinegar, and Canadian bacon in a saucepan. Heat until the jelly has melted. Pour over the cabbage mixture and mix thoroughly. Add salt and pepper.
3. Cover and cook over low heat for 1 hour.
4. Stir once or twice and serve when cabbage and onion are tender.

Carrots

A fresh, tender young carrot is exquisitely sweet. Who would guess it is related to the deadly hemlock. The garden variety, however, is as healthful as it is delicious.

Selection: Choose firm, medium-sized carrots. Greens should be fresh and full. Carrots are also available canned and frozen.

Storage: Store carrots in the crisper of the refrigerator. Limp carrots may be "crisped" by placing them in ice water in the refrigerator for an hour.

Nutrition: They are an excellent source of vitamin A, minerals, and fiber.

Preparation: Remove tops and discard. Peel large carrots. Small young ones can be scrubbed vigorously and left unpeeled. They may be sliced, diced, shredded, and grated.

Serving: Carrots can be boiled, baked, steamed, mashed, creamed, and puréed. They are excellent in soups and as a flavoring in many stews.

Deviled Carrots
Serves 4

1	pound carrots, peeled
1	cup boiling water
3	tablespoons margarine
1	tablespoon vegetable oil
2	tablespoons brown or raw sugar
2	teaspoons mustard
½	teaspoon salt
	dash of pepper

1. Slice the carrots into ¼-inch slices. Place in a covered saucepan and add boiling water. Cover and cook until barely tender, about 5 minutes. Drain thoroughly.
2. Melt the margarine in a covered skillet. Add the carrots, oil, sugar, mustard, salt, and pepper and toss well.
3. Cover the skillet and cook over moderate heat until the carrots are tender, about 5 more minutes. Serve hot.

Glazed Carrots
Serves 4

1	pound carrots, peeled and sliced
1	cup boiling, salted water
1	tablespoon margarine
¼	cup brown sugar, firmly packed

1. Cook the carrots in the boiling, salted water until just tender. Drain.
2. Melt the margarine in a saucepan and add the brown sugar. Cook until it forms a syrup.
3. Place the carrots in a shallow baking dish and cover with the syrup. Bake at 350° for 10 minutes. Serve hot.

Baked Carrots and Apples
Serves 6

> 1 *pound carrots, peeled and cut into ½-inch slices*
> 1 *pound green apples, cored, peeled, and sliced*
> 6 *tablespoons water*
> 1 *tablespoon lemon juice*
> 1 *tablespoon margarine*
> 2 *teaspoons brown sugar*

1. Place the carrots in boiling water for 5 minutes and cook until barely tender. Drain in a colander.
2. Place alternating slices of apples and cooked carrots in a shallow baking dish.
3. Combine water, lemon juice, margarine, and brown sugar in a small saucepan and heat until margarine melts.
4. Pour this mixture over the apples and carrots and place in a 350° oven for 15 minutes. Serve.

Baked Garlicky Carrots
Serves 4

This is a favorite carrot dish. It goes well with roast meats, hamburger, and poultry.

> 1 *pound carrots, peeled*
> 1 *cup boiling water*
> 3 *cloves garlic*
> 2 *tablespoons margarine*
> 3 *tablespoons hot water*

1. Slice the carrots in quarters and then each quarter into 6 strips. This is called julienne and the carrots will look like match sticks.
2. Place the carrots in a covered saucepan with the boiling water and cook over medium heat until tender, 3 to 5 minutes. Drain thoroughly. Arrange in a shallow baking dish.
3. Slice each clove of garlic into 4 pieces. Bury in the carrot sticks. Be sure you distribute them evenly.
4. Dot with the margarine and pour the hot water over the carrots.
5. Bake in a 350° oven for 20 minutes or until tender. Remove the garlic before serving.

Scalloped Carrots and Potatoes
Serves 4

1   *pound carrots, peeled and sliced*
3   *small potatoes, peeled and sliced*
½   *cup onions, chopped*
2   *tablespoons flour*
2   *cups low-fat milk*
1   *teaspoon salt*
½   *teaspoon pepper to taste*
2   *tablespoons margarine*

1. Place the carrots, potatoes, and onion in a shallow baking dish.
2. Blend the flour with ¼ cup of the milk to make a smooth paste. Gradually stir in the rest of the milk and salt and pepper and pour over the carrot mixture. Dot with margarine.
3. Place in a 350° oven for 45 minutes or until carrots and potatoes are tender. If they seem to scorch on the top reduce the heat to 325°.

Cauliflower

Cauliflower is a member of the cabbage family and a close relative of broccoli. There are many colorful ornamental varieties but the most common is white with green foliage.

Selection: Choose compact heads with tight, creamy white flowerettes free of bruises or discoloration. Leaves should be bright green, not yellowed. Cauliflower is available frozen.
Storage: Store in the refrigerator in a plastic bag.
Nutrition: Cauliflower is high in vitamin C, minerals, and relatively low in calories.
Preparation: Wash thoroughly and remove stem and outside leaves. The head may be cooked whole or divided into flowerettes. Any remaining cauliflower should be stored in the refrigerator.
Serving: Cauliflower can be baked, steamed, boiled, or cooked, cooled and served as a salad. It is also refreshing served raw as an appetizer, or sliced into a mixed vegetable salad. If it is to be baked it is best to parboil it first.

Cauliflower Amandine
Serves 6

> 1   *head of cauliflower*
> *boiling, salted water*
> 2   *tablespoons margarine*
> ½   *cup slivered almonds*
> 1   *tablespoon lemon juice*

1. Trim the cauliflower and break into flowerettes. Drop into the boiling water and reduce the heat to a low boil. Cook for 12 minutes or until just tender. Do not overcook. When done drain thoroughly.
2. Melt the margarine in a small skillet and add the almonds. Stir until they have browned but do not let them scorch. Add the lemon juice and mix thoroughly.
3. Spoon over the drained cauliflower and serve hot.

Cauliflower with Salsa Verde
Serves 6

Try this in the summer time. It can be served as a cold salad or as a hot vegetable.

> 1   *head cauliflower*
> *boiling water*
> ½   *pound spinach*
> ⅓   *cup vegetable oil*
> ⅔   *cup olive oil*
> ¼   *cup lemon juice*
> 2   *tablespoons capers, finely minced*
> 2   *tablespoons parsley, finely minced*
> 2   *tablespoons watercress, finely minced*
> 2   *tablespoons black olives, finely minced*
> 2   *tablespoons green stuffed olives, finely minced*
> *salt and pepper to taste*

1. Trim cauliflower and break into flowerettes. Cook in boiling water until just tender. Do not overcook. Drain thoroughly and chill.
2. Wash and thoroughly drain the spinach. Arrange the leaves on a serving platter. Place paper towel over the spinach and chill.
3. Combine remaining ingredients, mix thoroughly, and chill.
4. Just before serving, drain the cauliflower again and arrange on the spinach leaves. Mix the salsa verde again and spoon over the cauliflower.
5. Serve with the remaining sauce in a separate bowl.

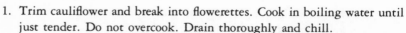

Cauliflower Pudding
Serves 4

1 head cauliflower
2 cups boiling water
1 egg, slightly beaten or egg equivalent
½ cup sour cream or ¼ cup plain yogurt, mixed with ¼ cup mayonnaise
1 teaspoon salt
⅛ teaspoon pepper
½ cup cheddar cheese, grated

1. Trim the cauliflower and cut into flowerettes.
2. Place in a saucepan with 2 cups boiling water and boil gently until tender, about 8 to 10 minutes. Drain.
3. Place cooked cauliflower in a shallow baking dish.
4. Combine the beaten egg and sour cream (or yogurt and mayonnaise mixture) and season with salt and pepper and spread this mixture over the cauliflower.
5. Sprinkle with the grated cheese and bake at 350° for 20 minutes. Serve hot.

Celery

Celery first appeared in this country in the 1800s. It is now a mainstay in almost every kitchen. It makes a subtle appearance in soups, stews, and casseroles. It is a marvelous snack food because it is so low in calories and can stand on its own as a vegetable course.

Selection: Choose bright, crisp, firm stalks with full leafy tops.
Storage: Celery will keep in the refrigerator for 7 to 10 days in a plastic bag. Celery can be crisped by placing it in a tray of ice water for an hour or so.
Nutrition: Celery is high in vitamins A and C, very low in calories, and an excellent source of fiber.
Preparation: Trim the leaves and stem of the stalk. Remove any thick strings from the outside stalk with a potato peeler. Slice, dice, or use whole. The leaves may be chopped and added to soups and stews.
Serving: Celery may be served braised, boiled, or raw. Raw celery may be stuffed and served as an appetizer or served with a dip.

Braised Celery
Serves 4

> 1   bunch celery
> *boiling, salted water*
> 2   *tablespoons lemon juice*
> ½   *cup chicken stock*
> 2   *tablespoons margarine*

1. Trim celery of leaves and root end. Slice in 3-inch pieces. Place in boiling water for 3 minutes. Drain. Place in shallow baking dish.
2. Add lemon juice, chicken stock, and margarine. Bring to a boil. Place a piece of wax paper, cut to fit the dish, directly on the celery and then cover. This permits faster cooking. A small hole cut in the center of the paper helps to retain the color.
3. Place over low heat and simmer for approximately 30 minutes, or until tender.
4. A sauce can be made by removing the celery to a serving dish, boiling the stock rapidly until it has reduced to approximately ⅓ cup, and spooning this over the celery before serving hot.

Celery Vinaigrette
Serves 4

This elegant dish can be served as an appetizer or a luncheon dish. The beauty of it is that it must be prepared ahead of time, so you can assemble this at your leisure.

> 2   *bunches celery*
> 1½ *cups chicken stock*
> *herb bouquet of 1 large sprig of parsley, 1 bay leaf,*
>   *and ½ teaspoon thyme, tied together*
> ¼   *cup olive oil*
> 1½ *tablespoons wine vinegar*
> *salt and freshly ground pepper*
> *sliced pimiento*

1. Trim the celery and slice large stalks in half. Place in a covered skillet and add the stock and herb bouquet. Bring to a boil and then reduce to a simmer. Cover and simmer for 30 minutes or until the celery is very tender. Drain and chill for 3 to 4 hours.
2. Combine the oil, vinegar, salt, and pepper. Cover the celery with this mixture just before serving.

3. Arrange the celery on serving dishes. Crisscross 2 strips of pimiento on the top of each serving.

Corn

Corn is a new world vegetable. A staple in Mexican and Indian diets, it appears in many forms. Corn meal, masa, and tortillas form the basis for many of their dishes. For northerners, no summer barbecue would be complete without fresh corn on the cob.

Selection: Sweet ears of corn are one of the most rapidly deteriorating vegetables on the market. The sugar in the kernel begins to convert into starch almost immediately after picking. Purists will tell you that the only way to serve corn is to first boil the water, *then* pick the corn. If possible, choose corn picked the same day. Peel back a few inches of husk and check for smooth, plump kernels with no evidence of worm damage. Corn is also available frozen and canned.

Storage: Corn may be stored for very short periods in the husks in the refrigerator but it will lose some of its sweetness.

Nutrition: Corn contains small amounts of vitamins A and B.

Preparation: To serve corn on the cob, remove the husks and silk just prior to cooking. The kernels may be removed from the cob by scraping with a sharp knife.

Corn ears are cooked in boiling **unsalted** water until tender. Salt will cause the kernels to wrinkle. Corn ears may also be wrapped in foil and baked in the oven or on the barbecue. Corn kernels can be boiled, scalloped, or served in soups.

Serving: Corn is most popular served on the cob but the kernels can be removed and combined with other vegetables, creamed, or used in stuffings.

Corn on the Barbecue
Serves 6

6 *ears corn in husk*

1. Soak corn ears in cold water for 1 hour before cooking.
2. Remove, shake dry, and grill over barbecue coals or bake in oven for 20 to 30 minutes. The water in the corn will steam the ears for a delicious flavor. Aluminum foil may be substituted for the corn husk or wrapped around the corn husk if the barbecue fire is very hot.

Corn Creole
Serves 6

2   *tablespoons margarine*
¼   *cup green pepper, chopped*
1   *tablespoon flour*
1   *large can (16 ounces or No. 303) tomatoes, drained*
½   *cup Cheddar cheese, grated*
1   *can (12 ounces) corn niblets, drained*
1   *can whole boiling onions, drained*
salt
pepper to taste

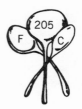

1. Melt the margarine in a saucepan. Add the green pepper and cook for 5 minutes. Add the flour, cook, and stir over low heat for 2 minutes.
2. Add the tomatoes and stir until smooth. Add the cheese and stir until it has melted and the sauce is smooth.
3. Add the corn and onions and season with salt and pepper.
4. Pour into a 2-quart baking dish and place in 350° oven for 20 minutes. Serve hot.

Corn Fritters
Makes 16 2-inch fritters

These are delicious lightly salted or if you are not watching your waistline serve with syrup.

1   *cup corn kernels, fresh or canned*
6   *tablespoons flour*
1   *teaspoon salt*
⅓   *teaspoon pepper*
½   *teaspoon baking powder*
1   *teaspoon sugar*
2   *egg whites*
oil or margarine for frying

1. Place all ingredients, except oil, in a blender and whirl at high speed until smooth.
2. Heat oil or margarine to 375°. Do not add too much oil, just a liberal coating. Add corn batter by large spoonfuls. Cook until browned on the underside. Turn and cook on the other side, but do not overcook. Serve hot.

Corn Puffs
Makes about 16

> 1 cup corn kernels, fresh or canned
> ¼ cup onion, grated
> 4 tablespoons flour
> ½ teaspoon baking powder
> ½ teaspoon salt
> 2 tablespoons low-fat milk
> 1 egg white
> oil for frying

1. Combine corn, onion, flour, baking powder, salt, and milk in a blender and whirl until smooth.
2. Beat egg white to form stiff peaks and fold into the corn mixture.
3. Heat oil to 375°, follow instructions for deep-oil frying (pages 158–59).
4. Drop large spoonfuls of batter into the hot oil and when golden brown and puffy, turn and brown the other side. They can also be panfried as for fritters but they will not be puffy.
5. Salt and serve immediately.

Cucumbers

The long slender green cucumber is one of man's oldest vegetables, going back to biblical times. It has long been highly regarded by epicures.

Selection: There are many sizes and shapes of cucumbers, ranging from the small, yellow lemon cucumbers prized in salads, to the coiling English and Armenian types. There are special varieties used for pickling but the most familiar is the long, green type found in the markets. Choose a cucumber with a firm skin and no soft spots.

Storage: Store in a plastic bag in the refrigerator.

Nutrition: Cucumbers are extremely low in calories and contain vitamins C and B complex and minerals.

Preparation: Commercial cucumbers have a waxy coating which is edible but may be scrubbed away. Peel the skin for cooking or serving raw sticks. For salads it is not necessary to peel but cut in thin slices. Seeds may be removed by slicing the cucumber lengthwise and scraping with a spoon.

Serving: Braised cucumbers are a gourmet treat. They may be boiled or sautéed. Cucumbers are best known for their distinctive taste in cool, crispy salads.

Sautéed Cucumbers
Serves 4

> 2   *tablespoons margarine*
> 3   *cucumbers, peeled and thinly sliced*
> 1   *teaspoon salt*
> ½ *teaspoon pepper*
> 2   *tablespoons parsley, minced*

1. Melt margarine in a skillet and add the cucumbers. Stir over medium heat for 3 to 4 minutes or until they turn translucent. Do not overcook.
2. Season with salt and pepper and sprinkle with parsley.

Marinated Cucumbers
Serves 8

> 40 *small pickling cucumbers, 3 inches long*
> 5 to 10 *sprays dill weed, fresh*
> 4   *quarts water*
> 1   *cup kosher salt*
> 4   *garlic cloves*
> 4   *tablespoons vinegar*
> 2   *bay leaves*
> 1   *teaspoon mustard seed*
> 4   *hot green peppers*

1. Wash and dry the cucumbers and place whole in a crock with dill weed. Set aside.
2. Boil 4 quarts water with salt and cool.
3. Add garlic, vinegar, bay leaves, mustard seed, and green peppers and pour over cucumbers. Be sure the liquid covers them. Cover the crock and marinate for at least 2 weeks. The cucumbers should be turned from time to time.

Eggplant

Eggplant is surely the most beautiful of all the vegetables. Its smooth, lustrous purple skin inspired Edward Weston, the photographer, to make classic studies of eggplants and peppers. When he was through with his arrangement he served them for his supper.

Selection: Choose firm, small eggplants with shiny, purple, unwrinkled skins.

Storage: It keeps best in a cool, dry, storage area or it can be refrigerated.

Nutrition: Eggplant is a source of minerals and some vitamin B complex.

Preparation: The eggplant should be washed just prior to serving and the ends trimmed. If it is not going to be baked whole, peel with a potato peeler and slice. Sliced eggplant should be salted and placed in a bowl for 20 minutes. Discard any liquid that may collect. This removes any bitterness from the eggplant.

Serving: Eggplant lends itself to a variety of preparations. It can be baked whole, stuffed, fried, broiled, and served in combination with other vegetables. It performs equally well as an appetizer, vegetable, or main course.

Eggplant Parmesan
Serves 6

You can make your own tomato purée for this or, as in this recipe, perk up the canned sauce.

> 3   *tablespoons vegetable oil*
> 1   *clove garlic, minced*
> ½ *onion, diced*
> 1   *large eggplant, peeled and sliced*
> 2   *cans tomato sauce*
> ½ *teaspoon oregano*
> ½ *teaspoon basil*
> *salt and pepper to taste*
> 2   *ounces mozzarella cheese, sliced*
> ¼ *cup Parmesan cheese, grated*

1. Heat the oil in a skillet and sauté the minced garlic. Do not let it brown. Add the onion and sauté until soft but not brown. Add the eggplant slices and sauté briefly on each side. Transfer to a shallow baking dish.
2. Heat the tomato sauce and add the oregano, basil, salt, and pepper. Pour over the eggplant and onion.
3. Place the mozzarella slices over the sauce and sprinkle the Parmesan cheese over all.
4. Bake in a 350° oven for 30 minutes. Serve hot.

Imam Bayildi
Serves 6

A story is told about a Middle Eastern holy man who fainted dead away on being presented with this dish. Hence, its name, Imam Bayildi, or "The Priest Fainted." Whether or not the story is true, it is a heavenly creation.

> 3   small eggplants, unpeeled
> boiling water
> 2   tablespoons olive oil
> 4   tablespoons vegetable oil
> 2   onions, sliced
> 1   green pepper, seeded and chopped
> 2   cloves garlic, minced
> 1   teaspoon salt
> ¼   teaspoon pepper
> ½   teaspoon sugar
> ½   teaspoon oregano
> ½   teaspoon basil
> 4   tomatoes, peeled, seeded, and coarsely chopped
> 2   tablespoons lemon juice
> chopped fresh parsley
> 2   ounces pine nuts

1. Place eggplants in boiling water to cover for 5 minutes. Cool. Slice in half and scoop out the pulp, leaving ½ inch in the shell. Chop the pulp. Refrigerate the shells.
2. Heat half the oil in a large skillet. Add onions, green pepper, and garlic and sauté until soft but not brown. Add the eggplant and cover. Cook for 5 minutes or until the eggplant is soft. Add the salt, pepper, sugar, oregano, and basil and cook for another 2 minutes.
3. Add the tomatoes, remaining oil, and lemon juice. Toss well and chill.
4. Fill each eggplant shell with the mixture and sprinkle with the parsley and pine nuts before serving.

Ratatouille
Serves 10

The aroma is tantalizing as the taste. Add garlic freely if you have a Mediterranean soul. This is even better when made the day before.

> 2   tablespoons olive oil
> 2   tablespoons vegetable oil
> ½   pound eggplant, peeled and sliced

½ pound zucchini, peeled and sliced
2 large yellow onions, peeled and thinly sliced
2 green peppers, sliced in thin strips
3 cloves garlic, mashed
3 to 4 medium firm, ripe, red tomatoes, peeled,
   seeded, and sliced salt and pepper
1 tablespoon parsley, minced

1. Heat the oils in a large skillet. Eggplant soaks up cool oil so it must be hot but not smoking. Sauté the eggplant and zucchini in the hot oil until lightly browned. Add more oil sparingly if necessary. Remove to a heated side dish.
2. In the same skillet, cook the onions and peppers slowly for 10 minutes or until tender but not browned. Stir in the garlic.
3. Place the tomato slices over the onions and peppers. Season with salt and pepper. Cover the skillet and cook over low heat for 5 minutes. The mixture should be quite liquid. Uncover, baste the tomatoes with the juices. Over high heat, boil for several minutes until the juice has almost entirely evaporated.
4. Place a third of the tomato mixture in the bottom of an ovenproof casserole and sprinkle with the parsley. Layer the eggplant, zucchini, and remaining tomato mixture, then cover and simmer over low heat for 10 minutes. Uncover and baste with the juices. Raise heat slightly and cook uncovered for another 15 minutes or until most of the juice has evaporated. May be baked in a 350° oven for 30 minutes. Serve hot or cold.

Vegetable Carousel
Serves 6

Simplicity is the main ingredient in this fragrant marriage of fresh vegetables.

1 medium eggplant, peeled and sliced
3 large tomatoes, peeled and quartered
1 pound zucchini, cut in strips
2 large onions, peeled and sliced
1 large green pepper, cut in strips
1 sprig fresh oregano or marjoram or ½ tablespoon dried

1. Arrange all the vegetables in a large covered casserole. Place the herbs in the center. Do not add any liquid.
2. Cover and cook over medium heat for 40 minutes or until the vegetables are tender and have produced a fragrant sauce. Serve hot.

Endive

There is a great deal of confusion surrounding endive. Its name is used interchangeably with chicory and escarole. The endive referred to in these recipes is, oddly enough, related to the daisy family and commands high prices in the markets. It is grown in the dark which prevents photosynthesis, accounting for its whiteness. The slightly pungent taste is highly prized by lovers of haute cuisine.

Selection: Choose endive with tightly closed heads. Older heads start to spread open at the top and become bitter.

Storage: Wrap tightly in foil or plastic wrap and refrigerate. Use as soon as possible.

Nutrition: A good source of vitamin A, and minerals such as calcium and potassium.

Preparation: Remove any bruised leaves and trim ¼ inch from the stem. For salads, pull the leaves apart and rinse well.

Serving: Endive is best simply prepared. It makes a superb salad with a good Vinaigrette Dressing or is a good accompaniment to roast meats and poultry when braised in a good chicken stock.

Braised Endive Hearts
Serves 4

    8 *firm, fresh endive hearts*
    3 *tablespoons margarine*
    ½ *cup chicken stock*

1. Trim and rinse the endive. Place in a shallow, covered baking dish.
2. Dot with the margarine and cover with the chicken stock.
3. Cover and bring to a boil. Reduce the heat to a simmer and cook for approximately 30 minutes.
4. When the hearts are tender and most of the liquid has been absorbed, remove from the heat and serve.

Endive par Excellence
Serves 4

    8 *endive hearts or 2 to 3 heads*
    boiling, salted water
    3 *tablespoons margarine*
    salt and pepper to taste
    2 *tablespoons Parmesan cheese, grated*

1. Trim and wash the endive, then coarsely chop the leaves.
2. Plunge into the boiling, salted water and cook for 2 minutes or until barely wilted. Do not overcook.
3. Drain thoroughly. Stir in the margarine, salt and pepper to taste.
4. Place in a serving dish and sprinkle with the Parmesan cheese. Serve hot.

Greens

Swiss chard, spinach, and the many varieties of lettuce are familiar greens to most of us. But the choice is much wider. Mustard greens, dandelion greens, beet tops, and wild greens can add snap to your menu. Wild greens generally have a sharp flavor and you may want to experiment to find the ones to your liking.

Selection: Look for leaves with a good color that are fresh, tender, and free from blemishes. Some varieties can be found growing wild but be sure you know what you are picking for some wild greens may be poisonous. Consult local gardening books for harmless varieties.

Storage: Wash greens in vinegar water, rinse thoroughly, and dry. Store in a plastic bag until ready to use.

Nutrition: All greens are excellent sources of vitamins A, B complex, and C, and most minerals. They are also very low in calories.

Preparation: Cut off the roots and any tough stems. Rinse thoroughly in vinegar water. Greens for a salad should be thoroughly dried. Oil dressings will not cling to wet leaves. An old pillowcase or linen tea towel is perfect for shaking greens dry. Wild greens should be slightly parboiled to remove any bitterness, and then chilled.

Serving: The many varieties of lettuce are usually used in salads, either singly or in combinations. However, raw spinach makes an excellent salad, and braised lettuce a delicate vegetable.

Steamed Spinach
Serves 4

> 2 pounds spinach, fresh
> 3 tablespoons margarine
> salt and pepper to taste

1. Trim the root ends of the spinach. Wash in vinegar water and rinse.
2. Place spinach in a saucepan. Do not add any extra water. The water clinging to the leaves is sufficient to cook the spinach.
3. Toss over high heat until the spinach has wilted. Remove from heat immediately.
4. Drain thoroughly and toss with margarine and salt and pepper. Serve hot.

Braised Spinach
Serves 4

> 2 pounds spinach, fresh, or 2 packages spinach, frozen, whole leaf
> 2 tablespoons margarine
> 1 yellow onion, diced
> ½ cup chicken stock

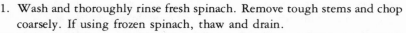

1. Wash and thoroughly rinse fresh spinach. Remove tough stems and chop coarsely. If using frozen spinach, thaw and drain.
2. Melt the margarine in a covered skillet or casserole. Add diced onion and sauté until soft and transparent but do not let them brown.
3. Add the spinach and chicken stock.
4. Place in a 350° oven for 20 to 25 minutes.
5. Remove the spinach to a serving dish and boil remaining stock until it has reduced to 2 tablespoons. Mix thoroughly with spinach. Serve.

Puréed Spinach
Serves 4

An elegant dish easily prepared but be sure the spinach has been thoroughly drained.

> 1 large bunch spinach, washed and trimmed, or 1 package frozen spinach, chopped
> 3 tablespoons margarine
> 3 tablespoons flour
> 1 cup low-fat milk

½ teaspoon salt
dash of pepper

1. Place fresh spinach in a saucepan. Do **not** add any additional water as the water clinging to the leaves is sufficient. Toss over high heat until the spinach has thoroughly wilted. Drain and cool slightly. Squeeze the spinach between your hands and remove all the moisture. Chop very fine or run through a grinder. Toss over high heat again to evaporate any remaining liquid. If you do not do this the sauce will be watery. (If frozen spinach is used, thaw and squeeze between your hands to remove all the moisture. Do not do any further cooking.)
2. In the same saucepan add the margarine to the spinach and stir until it has melted. Add the flour and stir over medium heat for **at least** 2 minutes.
3. Add the milk in a slow steady stream and stir until it comes to a boil. Reduce the heat and continue stirring for 4 to 5 minutes or until thickened and smooth. Add salt and pepper. Taste for additional seasoning.
4. For an extra smooth purée, whirl through a blender before serving.

Mixed Greens
Serves 4

Any greens can be prepared in this way. Use them singly or in combinations, for example kale and spinach are very good together.

1 pound of greens (spinach, chard, kale, beet tops)
boiling, salted water
3 tablespoons Canadian bacon, finely diced
1 tablespoon margarine
2 tablespoons Parmesan cheese, grated
salt and pepper to taste
1 tablespoon lemon juice

1. Wash the greens thoroughly in vinegar water and rinse well.
2. Plunge the greens in a large amount of boiling, salted water and cook until tender. The time will vary with the greens; beet tops cook quickly, 5 to 8 minutes, and kale will take 20 to 25 minutes.
3. Drain thoroughly and place in a serving dish.
4. Cook the Canadian bacon in margarine briefly and toss with greens.
5. Sprinkle with the Parmesan cheese, add salt, pepper, and lemon juice. Mix thoroughly and serve hot.

Spinach Timbale
Serves 4

The spinach must be drained of all liquid or this dish will be runny.

1   *pound spinach, fresh*
½   *cup mushrooms, chopped*
2   *tablespoons margarine*
½   *cup onion, chopped*
2   *tablespoons flour*
¾   *cup evaporated skim milk, heated*
1   *whole egg, lightly beaten*
1   *teaspoon salt*
    dash of freshly ground pepper
    dash of nutmeg

1. Soak the spinach and mushrooms briefly in vinegar water to remove the sand. Rinse the spinach several times. Place the spinach in a saucepan over high heat. Do not add any water, the water clinging to the leaves is sufficient. Toss with a wooden spoon until the spinach is limp. Turn into a colander and press out all the water. Finely chop the spinach and toss over high heat once more to evaporate any additional liquid.
2. Melt the margarine in a skillet and add the onion. Sauté until soft but not brown and add the mushrooms. Cook until soft and then toss over high heat to evaporate any liquid.
3. Stir in the flour and cook over low heat for at least 2 minutes. Add the evaporated skim milk and bring to a boil, stirring. Reduce heat and stir until thickened. Beat in the egg. Season with salt, pepper, and nutmeg. Pour into a lightly oiled or sprayed shallow baking dish. Bake in a 350° oven for 35 minutes or until firm. Cut into squares and serve.

Kohlrabi

Kohlrabi is a member of the cabbage family although its round shape resembles a turnip. Both the bulb and pungent greens are edible.

Selection: Choose small- or medium-sized, firm bulbs with fresh-looking leaves.
Storage: They may be stored in the crisper of the refrigerator for a week.
Nutrition: Kohlrabi is a good source of vitamin C and some minerals, and is low in calories.

Preparation: Remove the leaves and stems and peel the bulb with a potato peeler. Leaves and stems can be chopped and cooked. Kohlrabi is also good peeled and served raw in slices or quarters.

Serving: Kohlrabi is delicious boiled until tender and then mashed and served with an herb "butter" (margarine of course). The greens can be boiled until tender and served as a green vegetable or chopped raw in salads.

Sunkissed Kohlrabi
Serves 4

> 1 *pound kohlrabi*
> *water to cover*
> *salt and pepper*
> 1 *tablespoon lemon juice*
> 1 *tablespoon orange juice*
> 2 *tablespoons margarine*
> *dash of nutmeg*

1. Remove the leaves and stems from the kohlrabi and peel. Dice into ½-inch squares.
2. Cook in boiling water for 15 to 20 minutes or until tender. Leaves may be added to this.
3. When done, drain and season with salt and pepper and stir in the lemon juice, orange juice, margarine, and nutmeg. Heat thoroughly and serve.

Herbed Kohlrabi
Serves 4

> 1 *pound kohlrabi, peeled and cubed*
> *boiling, salted water*
> 3 *tablespoons margarine*
> ½ *teaspoon tarragon*
> *salt and pepper to taste*

1. Cook the kohlrabi in boiling, salted water until tender, about 10 minutes. Drain thoroughly.
2. Mash with a potato masher or ricer.
3. Stir in the margarine; add tarragon, salt, and pepper. Test for seasoning and serve hot.

Kohlrabi au Gratin
Serves 6

1   *pound of kohlrabi, peeled and sliced*
boiling, salted water
2   *tablespoons margarine*
1   *tablespoon flour*
¾ *cup low-fat milk*
½ *teaspoon mustard*
1   *teaspoon salt*
½ *cup Cheddar cheese, grated*

1. Cook the kohlrabi in the boiling, salted water until tender. Drain thoroughly.
2. Melt the margarine in a saucepan over low to medium heat. Add the flour and stir for 2 minutes. Remove from the heat and add the milk, stirring constantly.
3. Return to the heat and bring to a boil. Reduce heat and stir until thickened.
4. Add the mustard, salt, cheese, and stir until the cheese has melted.
5. Add the drained kohlrabi and mix thoroughly. Serve hot.

Leeks

The leek is not fully appreciated as much as it should be. Leeks appear to be oversized scallions and belong to the onion family. They have a unique flavor, more subtle than their relatives. Leeks add a distinctive flavor to dishes such as potato soup and tomato sauce. Its use definitely should be cultivated.

Selection: Look for firm, medium-sized leeks.
Storage: Store in a plastic bag in the refrigerator.
Nutrition: Leeks are moderate sources of minerals and minimal sources of vitamins. They are low in calories.
Preparation: Use only the white portion of the leek and perhaps one inch of the green stalks. Trim the root end and the green stalks. Make a slit lengthwise half way through the leek, then separate the layers and rinse well under running water. This is necessary to remove all the sand or dirt. Shake well.
Serving: Leeks can be boiled, braised, steamed, and added to dishes such as soups and stews.

Braised Leeks Persillade
Serves 4

    2 bunches of leeks, about 8 medium-sized
    ¾ cup boiling chicken stock
    ½ teaspoon salt
    ½ teaspoon pepper
    2 tablespoons margarine
    4 tablespoons bread crumbs
    2 tablespoons parsley, minced

1. Trim and clean leeks. Place in a shallow, covered, baking dish with a tight-fitting cover. Add chicken stock, salt, and pepper.
2. Cover and simmer gently for 40 minutes or until the leeks are tender and have absorbed most of the chicken stock.
3. Melt the margarine in a skillet and add the bread crumbs and parsley. Toss until the bread crumbs are lightly browned.
4. Place cooked leeks in a serving dish and sprinkle with topping. Serve hot.

Pickled Leeks
Serves 6

This can be used as a salad or relish and is marvelous with barbecued meats. It must be prepared at least 24 hours in advance and will keep nicely for a week.

    3   tablespoons vegetable oil
    3   cloves garlic, minced
    1   tablespoon onion, chopped
    ¼   cup vinegar
    ½   teaspoon salt
    freshly ground pepper
    1½   teaspoons mustard
    1   tablespoon whole pickling spices
    1   pound leeks, about 2 to 3 bunches, cleaned and sliced
    1   onion, very thinly sliced

1. Heat the oil in a skillet and add garlic and onion. Sauté until the onion is soft. Stir in the vinegar, salt, pepper, and mustard. Wrap the pickling spices in cheesecloth or Handi-wipes and add to the mixture.
2. Add the leeks and simmer for 10 minutes or until tender when pierced with a fork. Remove the cheesecloth-wrapped spices and transfer leeks to a shallow dish. Cover with the liquid and onion slices. Marinate, refrigerated, for 24 hours. Baste occasionally. Serve chilled.

Leeks au Gratin
Serves 4

Excellent with roast meats.

2   *bunches leeks*
3   *tablespoons margarine*
2   *tablespoons flour*
1   *cup low-fat milk, heated*
¼   *cup Swiss cheese, grated*
1   *teaspoon salt*
dash of pepper

1. Trim, clean, and boil the leeks until tender. Drain.
2. Melt the margarine in a saucepan over low to medium heat. Add the flour and stir for 2 minutes. Remove from the heat.
3. Slowly add the milk, stirring constantly. Return to the heat and bring to a boil, stirring constantly.
4. Reduce the heat and add the cheese. Stir until the cheese has melted and the sauce is smooth. Season sauce with salt and pepper and spoon over the leeks. Serve hot.

Mushrooms

The mushroom is fascinating in its duplicity. There are varieties which have no equal in the preparation of fine food and others which will bring a sudden and painful death. Unless you are an **expert,** do not stalk the wild mushroom. The members available commercially will more than satisfy the gourmet palate. Cepes, morels, and chanterelles are available canned from Europe. The oriental market provides us with the black forest mushrooms, and lovely white caps are available fresh.

Selection: When choosing fresh mushrooms in the market, check to see if the gills are showing underneath. If so it is an old mushroom and should be discarded. Choose white caps, free of blemishes, tightly closed around the stem.

Storage: Mushrooms should be stored in a paper bag in the refrigerator. Plastic bags make them soggy.

Nutrition: Calories are almost nonexistent in mushrooms and they are high in vitamin D.

Preparation: Rinse mushrooms in a vinegar water and then rub 2 or 3 together briskly between the palms of your hands under running water. This will remove all the grit. Do not peel except for fancy garnishes. Trim as little of the stem as necessary. There is flavor from skin to stem. Slice lengthwise from cap to stem. To remove stems, simply loosen near the cap and snap free.

Serving: The possibilities are endless. From soup to salad, the mushroom makes a welcome appearance. They can be served raw as an appetizer, stuffed and served as a vegetable or entrée, puréed in soups, sautéed and added to sauces, and tossed in a salad.

Mushrooms Monterey
Serves 6

> 1   cup low-fat milk
> 1½ teaspoons concentrated chicken stock
> ⅓   cup margarine
> 1   teaspoon marjoram
> 1   tablespoon sherry (optional)
> 1   pound mushrooms, sliced

1. Heat the milk and blend with the concentrated chicken stock.
2. Beat the margarine until creamy. Add the marjoram and sherry.
3. Arrange the sliced mushrooms in a shallow baking dish. Spread the creamed margarine on top and cover with the chicken broth. Bake in a 350° oven until tender, about 40 minutes. Serve hot.

Sautéed Mushrooms
Serves 4

Mushrooms are always a welcome accompaniment to broiled or roast beef.

> 1 pound mushrooms, fresh
> 4 tablespoons margarine
> salt and pepper

1. Rinse the mushrooms in vinegar and water. Drain, dry, and slice.
2. Melt the margarine in a skillet and add the mushrooms. Cook over medium heat until just soft — approximately 5 minutes.
3. Season to taste and serve immediately.

Mushrooms and Green Beans
Serves 4

> 2   tablespoons margarine
> ½ pound mushrooms, sliced
> 1   teaspoon fresh thyme, or ½ teaspoon dried
> 1   pound crisp green beans, cooked and cut into 2-inch slices

1. Melt the margarine in a skillet and add the mushrooms and thyme. Stir over high heat until the moisture has evaporated.
2. Toss well with the beans and serve hot.

Mushroom and Zucchini Casserole
Serves 4

> 2   tablespoons margarine
> ½ pound mushrooms, sliced
> 1   pound zucchini, washed and sliced lengthwise into 1-inch pieces
> ¼ teaspoon dill
> 1   clove garlic
> boiling water
> 2   tablespoons flour
> ½ cup plain low-fat yogurt
> ½ cup mayonnaise
> ½ cup fresh bread crumbs
> 1   tablespoon margarine

1. Melt the margarine in a skillet and add the mushrooms. Sauté for 5 minutes.
2. Meanwhile, add the zucchini, dill, and garlic to the boiling water and cook until tender, about 5 minutes. Do not overcook. Remove garlic. Drain thoroughly.
3. Add the flour to the mushrooms; stir and cook for 2 minutes.
4. Blend together the mushrooms, zucchini, yogurt, and mayonnaise. Transfer to a baking dish.
5. Toss the bread crumbs in a skillet with 1 tablespoon margarine until lightly browned. Cover the zucchini and mushrooms with the bread crumbs and run under the broiler until golden.

Okra

Okra is grown in the southern states and wherever hot summers duplicate the climate of its homeland in Africa. When cooked it has a gluey or sticky quality which acts as a thickening agent in stews, such as gumbos.

Selection: Choose okra pods 2 to 4 inches long. They should be crisp and bright green in color.

Storage: Store in a plastic bag in the refrigerator.

Nutrition: A source of some vitamin A, small amounts of B complex and C and some minerals.

Preparation: Stem ends should be cut and trimmed. Small pods may be left whole. Large pods should be cut in ½-inch pieces.

Serving: Okra is best parboiled and can then be sautéed. It is delicious added to vegetable soups and gumbos.

Sautéed Okra
Serves 6

> 1 pound okra pods
> boiling water
> 3 tablespoons margarine

1. Wash and trim pods. If they are small, leave them whole, but slice large ones into ½-inch pieces. Drop into boiling water and cook for 3 minutes. Drain.
2. Melt the margarine in a skillet and add cooked okra. Sauté for approximately 5 minutes or until tender.

Okra Diable
Serves 4

> 3 tablespoons vegetable oil
> 1 large onion, chopped
> 1 small hot red or chili pepper, sliced, or ½ teaspoon Tabasco sauce
> 2 medium tomatoes, peeled, seeded, and chopped
> ½ pound okra, trimmed and washed
> salt and pepper to taste

1. Heat the oil in a skillet and add the onion. Sauté until soft but not brown. Add the okra, pepper or Tabasco sauce, tomatoes, salt, and pepper and cover. Cook 10 minutes or until okra is tender. Serve hot.

Onions

Where would the cook be without the onion family? Their uses are legion. They are unsurpassed as a seasoning and improve almost everything they touch. Onions can be found in appetizers, soups, sauces, stews, as a vegetable, in stuffings, and if you have a robust palate and understanding friends, they can be enjoyed raw. No newcomer to the table, onions were appreciated by the early Romans and Greeks. The many varieties add to their versatility. You can choose from red, pearl, green, yellow, and white, each with a distinctive flavor.

Selection: Choose onions that are symmetrical and have a dry, flaky skin. They should be free of spots, mold, and soft areas.

Storage: Store dry onions in a cool dry place where they will keep for several weeks. Green onions should be stored in the crisper of the refrigerator.

Nutrition: Onions are a source of vitamin B complex and some minerals, and are low in calories.

Preparation: Trim the top and bottom of the onion and peel the papery outer skin. You may have to peel several layers to get down to the shiny onion. The pungent juice is a tear jerker. There are several methods of slicing onions which will protect the eyes. Try breathing through your mouth, slicing them under water, chilling them, holding a piece of bread in your mouth, holding an extinguished match between your teeth, working quickly, or all of the above. To peel the skin easily, plunge them into boiling water for 45 seconds.

Serving: Onions can be boiled, baked, deep fried, braised, creamed, or sautéed as well as used as a distinctive seasoning in other foods.

Boiled White Onions
Serves 4

Select the smallest white onions you can find.

> 1 pound small, white boiling onions
> boiling water
> salt and pepper
> 4 tablespoons margarine

1. Plunge onions into the boiling water for 30 seconds. Drain. Remove skins and trim ends.
2. Pierce the end of each onion with the long tine of a cooking fork or a knife to prevent onion from separating.

3. Place onions in a kettle and cover with water. Bring to boil and reduce heat to medium. Cook until just tender, approximately 15 minutes. Do not overcook. Drain immediately.
4. Season with salt and pepper, add margarine and stir until well coated. Serve hot.

Steamed Green Onions
Serves 4

> *2 bunches green onions*
> *salt and pepper to taste*
> *boiling water*
> *4 tablespoons margarine*
> *1 tablespoon Parmesan cheese, grated*

1. Trim root ends and green tops leaving about 2 to 3 inches of the green.
2. Place onions in a basket and steam over ½ inch of boiling water in a tightly covered container until tender — approximately 10 minutes.
3. Sprinkle with salt, pepper, margarine, and Parmesan cheese. Serve immediately.

Baked Onions
Serves 4

> *4 medium onions*
> *4 tablespoons Parmesan cheese, grated*
> *2 tablespoons vegetable oil*
> *2 tablespoons margarine*
> *6 tablespoons bread crumbs*
> *2 tablespoons parsley*
> *paprika*

1. Peel the onions and slice off the tops. Place in a baking dish and bake in a 350° oven until tender, about 35 minutes.
2. Remove a small circle from the center of each onion. Save for soups or a casserole. Arrange the onions in a baking dish and sprinkle each with Parmesan cheese.
3. Heat the oil and margarine in a skillet and add bread crumbs and parsley. Stir until lightly browned and spoon onto the onions. Sprinkle lightly with paprika. Bake in a 375° oven for 10 minutes and serve.

Sautéed Onions
Serves 4

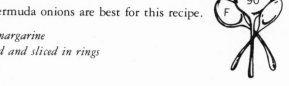

Large yellow or Bermuda onions are best for this recipe.

   3 tablespoons margarine
   4 onions, peeled and sliced in rings
   salt and pepper

1. Melt margarine in a frying pan over moderate heat. Sauté onion rings until they are soft, but not brown, and begin to look translucent, approximately 10 to 12 minutes. Stir frequently.
2. Season to taste and serve immediately.

Onions Braised with Madeira
Serves 8

   2 tablespoons olive oil
   2 tablespoons margarine
   4 large onions, peeled and sliced
   1 teaspoon salt
   ½ teaspoon pepper, freshly ground
   ¼ cup beef bouillon
   ¼ cup Madeira wine

1. Heat oil and margarine in a heavy pan. Add the onions and sauté over high heat for 2 minutes.
2. Season with salt and pepper, add broth, cover, and simmer for 10 minutes or until just tender.
3. Add the Madeira and cook over high heat until the sauce has reduced slightly. Serve immediately.

Stuffed Onions
Serves 4

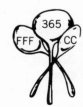

   4 large, well-shaped onions
   1 pound ground beef, lean
   1 clove garlic, quartered
   3 tablespoons tomato paste
   1 large tomato, peeled, seeded, and chopped
   1 teaspoon oregano

salt and pepper to taste
tomato sauce or Tomato-Leek Sauce (see Saucery)

1. Peel the onions and slice off the tops. Gently boil for 10 minutes. Cool slightly and scoop out the inside, leaving a ¼-inch shell. Chop the pulp.
2. Over medium heat, brown the ground beef with the garlic and chopped onion. Add the tomato paste, chopped tomato, oregano, salt, and pepper.
3. Stuff the onion shells with the beef mixture and bake in a 350° oven for 30 minutes or until onions are tender.
4. Serve with a well-flavored tomato sauce or Tomato-Leek Sauce.

Fritatta
Serves 4

This wonderful Italian omelette can be served as an entrée.

  2 *tablespoons margarine*
  2 *tablespoons vegetable oil*
  ½ *cup croutons, or fresh bread cubes*
  ½ *cup onion, diced*
  1 *clove garlic, minced*
  ½ *cup zucchini, finely diced*
  7 *egg whites*
  2 *egg equivalents (optional)*
  dash yellow food coloring (optional)
  dash red food coloring (optional)
  salt and pepper
  1 *tablespoon Parmesan cheese, grated*

1. Heat the margarine and oil and add the bread cubes. Sauté until golden and crunchy. Remove to a separate dish.
2. Add the onions and garlic. Sauté until soft but not brown.
3. Stir in the zucchini and sauté until soft.
4. Beat the egg whites and egg equivalent lightly. Omit the food coloring if you use the egg equivalent.
5. Pour the egg mixture into the onion mixture, add salt and pepper and bread cubes, and shake the pan gently until the mixture sets. Run a knife or spatula around the sides and underneath to prevent it from sticking. Invert onto a serving dish. Sprinkle with the cheese and serve.

Onion Rings
Serves 6

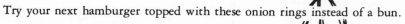

Try your next hamburger topped with these onion rings instead of a bun.

> *2 medium onions, sliced in rings*
> *beer batter for deep-oil frying (see page 82)*
> *vegetable oil*

1. Read the directions for deep frying vegetables. Prepare the beer batter.
2. Heat the oil in a saucepan. Dip the onion rings into the batter. Drop each ring separately into the hot oil and when golden turn and cook on the other side. Drain thoroughly on a paper towel, and serve.

Parsnips

The parsnip is a much neglected root vegetable. Resembling a pale carrot in appearance it has a flavor all its own. When young and tender, it is sweet and succulent. Older versions lend distinctive flavor to country stews.

Selection: Select firm parsnips with a pale orangy-beige color.
Storage: Store in the coldest part of the refrigerator. Chilling to almost freezing seems to improve their flavor.
Nutrition: Parsnips, like all root vegetables, are sources of most minerals and some vitamin B complex.
Preparation: Trim both ends and scrub well. Parsnips need not be peeled if they are young and are cleaned thoroughly. Older vegetables need to have the tough skin removed.
Serving: Do not overcook or they will become mushy. They can be boiled, baked, sautéed, or added to soups and stews.

Parsnips in Cider
Serves 4

This interesting treatment of parsnips goes well with pot roast.

> 1   *pound parsnips, peeled and quartered*
> 2   *tablespoons margarine*
> 2   *tablespoons brown sugar*

½ *teaspoon lemon juice*
½ *cup apple cider*
½ *teaspoon salt*

1. Place the parsnips in boiling water and cook until tender. Drain. Arrange them in a shallow baking dish.
2. Combine the margarine, brown sugar, lemon juice, cider, and salt and heat until the margarine has melted. Cover the parsnips with this mixture and bake in a 400° oven for 20 minutes. Baste every 10 minutes until browned and glazed. Serve hot.

Peas

Peas are one of the more popular vegetables; their sweet flavor has a universal appeal. There are several varieties, the most popular being the green or English garden pea. Chinese pea pods are a special variety with miniature seeds. Dried peas can be prepared in a number of ways.

Selection: Choose full, crisp pods. The special sugar peas or pea pods, also known as snow peas, are very slim and should not be limp. Peas adapt well to commercial processing and are quite good both frozen and canned. The canned peas have a distinctive flavor all their own.

Storage: Store in the crisper of the refrigerator.

Nutrition: Green peas are sources of vitamin B complex, some vitamin A, and minerals. They are supplementary sources of protein and provide more calories than other green vegetables.

Preparation: Shelling peas is simply done by squeezing the pod to open it and then running your finger down the middle, removing the peas. Rinse peas in cold water. Remove the strings and ends of edible pods and rinse in cool water. Dried peas should be soaked in cold water for several hours to shorten the cooking time.

Serving: Garden peas should be cooked in a small amount of water. Herbs, such as thyme or mint, complement peas very well. Steaming or stir-frying are the best methods for snow peas. Dried peas can be served as a separate vegetable or in soups.

Italian Peas
Serves 6

Canned baby peas are good for this different treatment of green peas.

3   *tablespoons vegetable oil*
1   *medium onion, chopped*
½   *cup green pepper, diced*
1   *clove garlic, minced*
1   *cup tomato sauce*
1   *cup peas*
½   *cup mushrooms, sliced*
2   *tablespoons parsley, chopped*

1. Heat the oil in a skillet. Add the onion, green pepper, and garlic. Sauté until soft but not brown.
2. Add the tomato sauce, peas, mushrooms, and parsley and simmer for 10 minutes. Serve hot.

Peas with Lettuce and Onions
Serves 6

2   *heads butter or Boston lettuce*
1   *cup pearl or small boiling onions*
2   *cups green peas .*
½   *cup chicken stock*
salt and pepper to taste
1   *tablespoon margarine*
herb bouquet (1 sprig of parsley, ½ teaspoon thyme, and 1 bay leaf wrapped in cheesecloth)
ice cubes

1. Wash and quarter the lettuce and place in the bottom of a covered saucepan.
2. If fresh onions are used, pierce the bottom with a long tined fork. Place onions, peas, stock, salt, pepper and margarine in the saucepan and bury the herb bouquet in the middle.
3. Bring to a boil and *immediately* reduce the heat to a simmer. Invert the lid and fill with ice cubes. This condenses the evaporating liquid and it falls back into the vegetables.
4. Cook for 20 minutes *only*, and serve with the liquid.

Stir-Fried Snow Peas and Water Chestnuts
Serves 4

1 tablespoon vegetable oil
1 pound snow peas, trimmed
1 cup beef or chicken broth
2 tablespoons cornstarch
2 tablespoons sweet sherry
2 tablespoons soy sauce
1 4-ounce can water chestnuts, sliced

1. Put vegetable oil in frying pan. When very hot but not smoking add snow peas and stir-fry for 2 minutes in an uncovered skillet.
2. Combine broth, cornstarch, sherry, and soy sauce and add to skillet. Add sliced water chestnuts.
3. Cover pan and cook for 2 minutes. Uncover, stir, and cook until sauce thickens slightly. Serve immediately.

Peppers

Peppers can be found on all continents, in all sizes and shapes, brilliantly colored and variously flavored. The seeds of the peppers contain the fire, so remove them if you have a tender palate.

COMMON VARIETIES:

Bell Pepper, also called green pepper or sweet pepper, changes from green to bright red when mature. This is the most common type found in produce markets.

Green Chili Peppers are fairly mild and used in Mexican dishes. Available fresh or canned, whole or diced.

Yellow Wax Peppers are moderately hot, yellow-colored and used frequently for pickling.

Long Red Cayenne, Tabasco, and Jalapeno are very hot and used primarily in sauces.

Selection: Choose well-shaped, firm peppers with smooth unblemished skins.
Storage: Store in the refrigerator, unwashed in a plastic bag. They will keep up to 2 weeks.
Nutrition: Peppers are good sources of vitamins A and C.
Preparation: They should be washed and dried just prior to use. Remove stem, cut in half lengthwise, and remove seeds; then slice, dice, or chop. For stuffing, remove stem and scoop out seeds. Parboil and stuff.

Serving: Peppers add a colorful and tasty touch to many dishes. Their shape makes them ideal for stuffing and they are a good addition to vegetable casseroles. They may also be sautéed or served raw in salads, or sautéed with other vegetables.

Corn Stuffed Peppers
Serves 4

Fresh corn is best for this dish but if the season is not cooperating, substitute frozen but do not overcook.

4	medium green peppers
1	tablespoon vegetable oil
1	medium onion, chopped
2	tablespoons margarine
1½	tablespoons flour
½	cup low-fat milk
2	cups corn
2	small tomatoes, peeled, seeded, and chopped
	salt and pepper to taste
4	tablespoons bread crumbs
1	cup boiling water

1. Remove stem end of the peppers and remove seeds. Parboil for 5 minutes. Drain. Preheat oven to 375°.
2. Heat oil in a skillet and add onions. Sauté over medium heat until soft but not brown. Add the margarine and when melted stir in the flour. Cook over low to medium heat, stirring, for at least 2 minutes. Remove from the heat and stir in the milk. Return to heat and bring to a boil; then reduce the heat. Add the corn, tomatoes, salt, and pepper. Cook for about 3 minutes until the mixture is smooth.
3. Fill the peppers with the corn mixture and sprinkle the tops with bread crumbs.
4. Place in a baking dish with 1 cup boiling water. Bake in a preheated oven for 15 minutes and serve hot.

Stir-Fried Peppers and Onions
Serves 4

4 bell peppers
2 tablespoons vegetable oil
1 large onion, peeled and sliced
2 tablespoons soy sauce
1 tablespoon water

1. Remove the top and slice pepper in half. Remove pulp and seeds and cut into ½-inch strips.
2. Heat the oil in a frying pan. When very hot but not smoking add peppers and onions, and stir-fry for 2 minutes. Add soy sauce and water and continue to cook for 3 to 4 minutes, until vegetables soften slightly. Do not overcook. Serve immediately.

Potatoes

When potatoes were introduced to European epicures during the 1600s, only the wealthiest could afford them. Spanish explorers discovered this wonderful tuber in the New World but it was not until centuries later that they attained popular status. Here's to Sir Francis Drake!

Selection: There are many varieties of potatoes and selection depends upon use. The large brown Idaho russets are excellent for baking. They have a flakier texture when cooked than other types. Small red or new potatoes are perfect for boiling and have such a delicate flavor, they are best served plain. Reserve the smooth-skinned, light-colored potatoes for scalloped dishes. Discard potatoes that have sprouted, have a green tint, or soft spots.

Storage: Store in a cool, dry place.

Nutrition: Potatoes are often shunned because of their caloric content; however they compare with apples of the same size. It is the butter and sauce that make them prohibitive on a reducing diet. They are high in essential minerals and contain goodly amounts of vitamins B and C.

Preparation: Baking potatoes should be scrubbed vigorously with a vegetable brush and rubbed lightly with vegetable oil. Potatoes can be cooked in their skins and then peeled. Do not soak peeled potatoes in water before cooking since this leaches out most of the vitamin content. New potatoes should be steamed and served in their skins which add both flavor and color.

Serving: The list is endless. The potato is one of the most versatile of vegetables, suited for appetizers, soups, and even desserts. They can be boiled, baked, fried, creamed, stuffed, mashed, and mixed with other vegetables. Leftover potatoes can be turned into potato pancakes, home fried, served au gratin, or added to some cakes and rolls for moistness.

Potatoes Florentine
Serves 4

Florentine indicates that a dish contains spinach. These spinach flecked potatoes are pretty as well as delicious.

4   *medium baking potatoes*
½   *cup spinach, cooked and chopped*
½   *teaspoon salt*
2   *tablespoons margarine*
¼   *cup skim milk*
2   *tablespoons Swiss cheese, grated*

1. Scrub potatoes and place in a 425° oven for about 40 minutes or until tender when pierced with a fork.
2. Remove from the oven and cool slightly. Slice in half lengthwise. Scoop out the cooked potato and place in a ricer or food mill or mash with a fork and potato masher.
3. Add cooked spinach, salt, margarine, and milk and beat until smooth.
4. Fill the potato skins with the spinach mixture and sprinkle with the cheese.
5. Place in a 350° oven for 15 minutes or until the cheese has melted completely. Serve hot.

Potatoes Lyonnaise
Serves 4

The term Lyonnaise indicates the presence of onions in a dish.

3   *tablespoons margarine*
1   *large onion, peeled and diced*
4   *medium potatoes, peeled and thinly sliced*
1   *tablespoon parsley, minced*
1   *teaspoon salt*
½   *teaspoon pepper or to taste*

1. Melt the margarine in a heavy skillet. Add the onion and sauté until soft. Do not let it brown.
2. Add the potatoes and cook until soft, about 10 minutes. Turn frequently.
3. Toss the onions and potatoes with the parsley and season with salt and freshly ground pepper. Serve hot.

Scalloped Potatoes
Serves 6

This dish is elegant fare with a simple entrée such as baked chicken or poached fish.

3 *cups potatoes, peeled and thinly sliced*
2 *tablespoons flour*
1 *teaspoon salt*
½ *teaspoon pepper*
4 *tablespoons margarine*
1¼ *cups low-fat milk, heated*

1. Toss the potato slices in a bowl or paper bag with the flour and salt and pepper.
2. Arrange the potatoes in layers in a shallow baking dish. Dot the layers with the margarine.
3. Pour the heated milk over the potatoes and place in a 350° oven for 1 to 1½ hours. The potatoes should be tender when pierced with a fork, and golden brown on top. The potatoes absorb the milk and are moist and tender.

Steamed New Potatoes Germaine
Serves 4

8 *small new potatoes*
1 *dozen boiling onions, peeled*
boiling water
3 *tablespoons margarine*
¾ *cup beef stock*
¼ *cup vermouth*
salt and pepper to taste
½ *teaspoon paprika*

1. Scrub the potatoes thoroughly and peel a strip from the middle, leaving the red jacket on the ends. Parboil the onions.
2. Place the onions and potatoes in a steamer or on a rack in a covered saucepan, add 1 inch of boiling water and cover. Cook over medium heat until barely tender, about 10 minutes.
3. Melt the margarine in a shallow baking dish. Add the beef stock, vermouth, salt, pepper, paprika, potatoes, and onions.
4. Cover and cook another 10 minutes or until tender.
5. Serve hot with the flavored broth.

Lemon Potatoes
Serves 4

This dish is excellent served with fish.

    4 boiling potatoes, peeled and quartered
    3 tablespoons margarine
    2 teaspoons lemon juice
    1 teaspoon lemon rind, grated
    freshly ground pepper

1. Place potatoes in a steamer or on a rack in a large saucepan over rapidly boiling water. Cover and steam approximately 12 minutes until tender.
2. Melt the margarine in a skillet and add the lemon juice and lemon rind. Add the potatoes to the skillet and toss until thoroughly coated with the sauce and sprinkle liberally with freshly ground pepper. Serve hot.

Sunshine Potatoes
Serves 4

The bright touch of orange is a delicious surprise. This is an interesting taste with roast fowl or pork.

    4 potatoes, peeled and quartered
    boiling, salted water
    1 whole egg, slightly beaten
    grated rind of 2 oranges
    4 tablespoons margarine
    salt and pepper to taste

1. Boil potatoes in salted water until tender. Drain.
2. Mash or put the potatoes through a ricer. Add the egg and beat thoroughly. Add the orange rind and margarine and beat until the potatoes are fluffy. Season to taste with salt and pepper.
3. Place large spoonfuls of the potato mixture on a well-oiled cookie sheet. Decorative mounds can be formed with a pastry bag.
4. Place in a 350° oven for 10 minutes or until lightly browned. Serve immediately.

Rice and Pasta

The evolution of rice and grains in our diet is interesting to review. Originally, these substances were the mainstay, necessary for sustaining life.

Rather than hunting for food, man could harvest his own and establish communities. In some countries rice and pastas still form the basis of the diet. In our own, weight-conscious Americans often shun them for being too caloric. Consider integrating them into your menus as appetizing meatless meals or complementing your entrée.

Selection: Grains, rice, and pasta can be bought conveniently prepackaged. Some markets carry grains and rice in bulk.

Storage: Store in tightly covered containers, particularly in the warm months when they will be invaded by weevils if left open.

Nutrition: Their contribution is mainly calories, bulk, and fiber.

Preparation: Pastas should be plunged into rapidly boiling water, cooked until "al dente," that is, soft but not mushy, then rinsed under cold water. Immediately sauce them or stir some margarine into them or they will stiffen and congeal. Rice can be steamed, boiled, or simmered in liquid.

Serving: Pastas can be served with just a dot of margarine or sauced with vegetables, meat, or herbs. Rice is incorporated into many soups, casseroles, and salads, and can be served with seasonings as pilaf, or plainly steamed. It even finds its way into desserts, proving its versatility.

Wild Rice and Pecans
Serves 6

This elegant dish was created for game hens but can be served with any roast or broiled poultry or meat.

1   cup wild rice
2   quarts cold water
4   cups chicken stock
2   tablespoons onion, chopped
2   tablespoons margarine
¼   cup pecans, halved

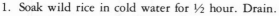

1. Soak wild rice in cold water for ½ hour. Drain.
2. Place rice in 2 quarts fresh cold water and bring to a boil, boiling for 5 minutes. Drain. Replace in saucepan and add chicken stock. Bring to a boil again. Reduce heat and simmer until broth is absorbed and rice is fluffy, about 1 hour.
3. Sauté onions in margarine until soft and transparent but not browned. Toss with pecans and add to the cooked wild rice. Serve hot or stuff cavity of 6 game hens and roast.

Steamed Rice
Makes approximately 2½ cups

>   1   *cup polished white rice, washed*
>   1½ *cups cold water*

Cooking rice is largely a matter of trial and error until you find the correct amount of water, rice, and time to suit your taste. Oriental rice is usually prepared in the same pot each time, one which cooks fairly slow. Aluminum is recommended by some Chinese chefs because the rice can stand heating for a long period of time without burning. The rice must be washed before using to get rid of the dust that covers all rice. The amount of water varies with the type of rice and the age of the rice. Japanese rice is the short grain variety which requires less water and is starchier. Chinese rice is the long grain variety and cooks drier. Older rice usually requires more water but a good rule of thumb is 1½ cups of water per cup of rice. Add the water and rice in your pot and bring to a boil, covered. Remove cover and let boil until almost all the water has evaporated. Cover again, reduce heat and steam for 10 to 15 minutes until the rice is soft and fluffy. If the rice must wait for the rest of the meal to finish cooking, let it sit on a very low flame rather than cooling and reheating it. The bottom may crust but the rice will retain its flavor and texture. After several tries you will find the right combination of rice, water, pot, and cooking time to suit your taste.

Rice Provençal
Serves 6

This is a nice dish for leftover steamed rice.

>   5   *tablespoons margarine*
>   ½   *cup onion, chopped*
>   ⅓   *cup green pepper, diced*
>   ¼   *cup parsley, minced*
>   3   *cups rice, cooked*
>   2   *tablespoons pimiento, chopped*
>   *salt and pepper*

1. Heat the margarine in an ovenproof dish with a tight-fitting cover. Add the onion and pepper and sauté until soft. Stir in the parsley.
2. Add the rice, pimiento, salt, and pepper and mix thoroughly. Cover and place in a 350° oven for 30 minutes or until heated through. Serve hot.

Pilau Istanbul
Serves 8

2	*tablespoons vegetable oil*
1	*onion, chopped*
2	*tablespoons slivered almonds*
2	*tablespoons raisins*
1½	*cups raw rice*
½	*cup vermicelli, chopped fine or run through a blender*
3	*cups chicken stock*
¼	*teaspoon anise seeds*
1	*teaspoon salt*
dash	*of pepper, freshly ground*
1	*cup water*
2	*tablespoons margarine*
2	*tablespoons pimiento, diced (optional)*

1. Heat the oil in a skillet. Add the chopped onion and sauté until soft. Add the almonds and stir until the almonds are a deep brown. Do not let them scorch.
2. Add the raisins, rice, and vermicelli, which should be chopped the size of the rice grains, and chicken stock. Stir until rice becomes milky and then add the anise seeds, salt, pepper and water. Bring to a boil and then cover and simmer until the liquid has been absorbed.
3. Fluff the rice with a fork. Stir in the margarine until it has melted. Taste for seasoning. Sprinkle with pimientos if desired and serve.

Ham Pilaf
Serves 6

    3   tablespoons margarine
    1   tablespoon onion, chopped
    1   tablespoon green pepper, chopped
    1   tablespoon chives, chopped (optional)
    1   cup cracked wheat, or rice
    ½   teaspoon salt
    ⅛   teaspoon black pepper
    1   teaspoon dry mustard
    2   cups ham, cooked and cubed
    1   cup hot chicken bouillon
    ½   cup slivered almonds, toasted
    parsley

1. Melt the margarine in heavy saucepan. Add the onion, green pepper, and chives. Cook until onion is soft but not browned. Add cracked wheat. Cook 5 to 7 minutes, stirring occasionally.
2. Stir in the salt, pepper, mustard, and ham. Place in a 1½-quart casserole and pour the chicken broth over mixture. Cover and bake in 325° oven for 45 minutes to 1 hour, or until liquid is absorbed. Sprinkle slivered almonds over top and garnish with parsley.

Grape Pilaf
Serves 6

Try this with lamb, fish, or poultry. Use beef broth with meat and chicken broth with fish or poultry.

    1   tablespoon vegetable oil
    1   medium onion, chopped
    1   cup brown rice
    2   cups beef bouillon or chicken stock
    ¼   teaspoon cinnamon
    ¼   teaspoon paprika
    salt and pepper

2   *tablespoons margarine*
2   *cups seedless grapes*

1. Heat the oil in a skillet. Add the onion and sauté until soft but not brown.
2. Add the rice and stir until lightly browned. Add the stock or bouillon, cinnamon, and paprika and bring to a boil. Cover and cook over low heat for 20 to 25 minutes until the rice is fluffy and the liquid has been absorbed. Stir occasionally. Season to taste.
3. Melt the margarine in a skillet and when bubbly add the grapes. Stir until they are just heated through and mix into the rice. Serve hot.

Risotto
Serves 6

The perfect accompaniment to fish, chicken casserole, or beef sauté.

4   *tablespoons margarine*
¼   *cup onion, finely minced*
1½   *cups clean, unwashed, raw rice*
3   *cups of boiling liquid (chicken stock, beef stock, white wine and water, or Fish Stock, depending upon what you will be serving)*
herb bouquet (2 sprigs parsley, 1 bay leaf, and ½ teaspoon thyme, tied in cheesecloth)
salt and pepper to taste

1. Preheat oven to 375°.
2. Melt the margarine in a 6-cup casserole with a tight-fitting cover. Add the onion and sauté until soft but not browned.
3. Add the rice and stir over moderate heat until the rice becomes milky in color.
4. Pour in the boiling liquid, add the herb bouquet, salt, and pepper and bring to a simmer. Stir once, cover and place in a preheated 375° oven for 5 minutes. Reduce heat to 350° and cook undisturbed for 12 minutes. Then check to see if liquid has been absorbed. If there is liquid in the bottom of the casserole return to the oven for an additional 2 to 3 minutes. For al dente rice, uncover after 17 minutes. For a softer rice cook covered for 20 minutes. Remove herb bouquet and fluff rice with a fork. Serve hot.

Spaghetti with Zucchini and Tomato Sauce
Serves 4

1	large onion, diced
3	cloves garlic, minced
¼	cup vegetable oil
3	large tomatoes, peeled, seeded, and chopped
1	pound zucchini, trimmed and chopped
2	teaspoons basil, crumbled
1½	teaspoons salt
¼	teaspoon pepper
1	pound spaghetti

1. Sauté the onion and garlic in the oil until soft but not brown.
2. Add the tomatoes, zucchini, basil, salt, and pepper.
3. Stir over low heat and let simmer for 30 minutes.
4. Cook the spaghetti according to the directions on the package. Drain, rinse under cold water, drain again, and serve with the sauce.

Linguine with Clam Sauce
Serves 4

1	medium onion, diced
3	medium cloves garlic, minced
¼	cup vegetable oil
3	tablespoons margarine
2	cans minced clams, undrained
½	cup parsley, chopped
1	pound linguine

1. Sauté the onion and garlic in the oil and margarine until the onion is soft but not brown.
2. Add the clams together with the liquid.
3. Add the parsley and stir completely.
4. Simmer over low heat for 5 minutes.
5. Cook the linguine according to the directions on the package. Drain, rinse under cold water, and drain again. Serve with the clam sauce.

Lasagna
Serves 6

1	pound ground beef, lean
2	cloves garlic, crushed
2	onions, diced
salt	
freshly ground pepper	
1	teaspoon oregano
½	teaspoon basil
2	tablespoons parsley, chopped
2	8-ounce cans stewed tomatoes
2	8-ounce cans tomato sauce
1	package lasagna noodles
1½	cups cottage cheese
½	cup mozzarella cheese, grated

1. Brown the beef in a skillet. Add the garlic, onions, salt, pepper, oregano, basil, and parsley. Sauté until the onions are soft. Drain off any fat.
2. Add the tomatoes and tomato sauce and simmer for 25 minutes.
3. Cook the noodles as directed on the package. Drain thoroughly.
4. Alternate layers of noodles, beef sauce, cottage cheese, and mozzarella cheese in a baking dish. There should be 2 layers of each. Finish with a layer of noodles and sprinkle with mozzarella cheese. Bake in a 375° oven for 20 minutes and serve.

Rutabagas

Often confused with turnips, this sweet root is delicious as well as economical.

Selection: Choose firm, unwrinkled tubers.
Storage: Store in a cool, dry place.
Nutrition: Rutabagas are relatively low in calories, and are a good source of vitamin A and minerals such as iron, calcium, and potassium.
Preparation: Trim the ends and peel the skin. They can then be sliced or cubed.
Serving: Rutabagas adapt well to boiling, baking, and frying. They are delicious mashed with other vegetables such as potatoes, carrots, or turnips. Try an unusual taste by serving raw either sliced as an hors d'oeuvre or grated in a salad.

Carrot and Rutabaga Purée
Serves 4

Sweet carrots and pungent rutabagas are beautifully paired in this dish.

1 pound rutabaga, peeled and sliced
1 pound carrots, peeled and sliced
1 teaspoon salt
2 tablespoons margarine

1. Cut the rutabaga into small pieces to speed up cooking time. Gently boil carrots and rutabaga together until tender, about 20 minutes. When quite tender, drain thoroughly.
2. Put vegetables through a food mill or mash with a potato masher. Beat with a spoon until smooth. Add salt and margarine and reheat. Serve hot.

Rutabaga au Gratin
Serves 4

¼ cup chicken stock
1 cup water
½ pound rutabagas, peeled and sliced
½ pound potatoes, peeled and sliced
3 tablespoons margarine
1 teaspoon salt
⅛ teaspoon pepper or to taste
¼ cup Cheddar cheese, grated

1. Bring the chicken stock and water to a boil. Add the vegetables, cover, and bring to a boil. Reduce heat and cook until tender, about 25 minutes. Drain thoroughly.
2. Place vegetables in a potato ricer or mash with potato masher. Stir in the margarine and season with the salt and pepper. Place in baking dish.
3. Sprinkle the cheese on top and bake, uncovered, in a 400° oven 8 to 10 minutes until cheese melts. Serve hot.

Squash

Diversity is the word for the squash family. There are numerous varieties with both soft and hard skins, harvested in winter and summer, and found all over the world. They are called crook neck, butternut, acorn,

Danish, pattypan, zucchini, banana, Hubbard, pumpkin, calabaza, and ornamental gourds, but they are all squash.

Selection: Soft skin squash generally are harvested in the summer. These include zucchini, crook neck, yellow, and scalloped or pattypan. Choose firm squash relatively small in size. They should not have soft or watery areas, tough blemished skins, or dry, black stems. Winter squash have hard shells typified by the pumpkin, Hubbard, acorn, and banana. Choose squash with hard rinds and no watery spots.

Storage: Winter squash store well in a cool, dry place. They will keep for long periods of time. Summer squash are perishable and should be stored in the crisper of the refrigerator.

Nutrition: Summer squash have a high water content and are very low in calories. They are also a source of vitamin C. Winter squash are an excellent source of vitamin A.

Preparation: Summer squash should have the ends trimmed and be well scrubbed. Do not peel. Winter squash should be cut in half or serving pieces and the seeds and string removed.

Serving: Summer squash require quick cooking by steaming or stir-frying which enhances the flavor. They can be served raw in salads or with a vegetable dip. Winter squash are best served baked or in soups.

Gracie's Baked Acorn Squash
Serves 4

Grace Ryan was an artist in the kitchen and an inspiration to me. One of her simpler dishes is offered below.

2   *acorn squash, halved and seeded*
½ *cup boiling water*
4   *tablespoons brown sugar*
4   *tablespoons margarine*

1. Place squash halves, yellow side up in a baking dish. Pour about ½ cup of boiling water in dish.
2. Place in a 375° oven for 35 minutes or until the squash is tender when pierced with a fork.
3. Remove from the oven and pour off the water.
4. Combine the brown sugar and margarine in a saucepan and when the margarine has melted, brush each portion with the mixture.
5. Place under the broiler until browned. Do not let the sugar burn. Serve hot.

Stuffed Zucchini el Rundo
Serves 8

This dish was created when a friend presented me with a 10-pound, home-grown zucchini. I had the choice of considering it a member of the family or stuffing it. If your friends don't give you a monster zucchini, then substitute several small ones.

1   *large or 4 medium zucchini*
⅛ *cup olive oil*
⅛ *cup vegetable oil*
¼ *cup onion, finely chopped*
4   *cloves garlic, minced*
½ *pound ground chuck*
2   *ounces (2 to 3 slices) Canadian bacon, finely chopped*
½ *cup bread crumbs*
6   *tablespoons Parmesan cheese, grated*
1   *teaspoon fresh oregano or, ½ teaspoon dried*
¾ *teaspoon salt*
dash of pepper
hot water
1   *recipe Tomato-Leek Sauce (see Saucery)*

1. Cut zucchini in half lengthwise and scoop out pulp leaving ¼-inch shell. Chop pulp coarsely. Remove any seeds. Lightly salt the shells.
2. Heat the oils and sauté the onions until soft but not browned and add squash pulp. Toss with the onions and add garlic. Cook for 5 minutes. Remove this mixture to a side dish.
3. Add the ground chuck and Canadian bacon to the skillet and brown lightly, stirring frequently. Drain.
4. Combine vegetables and meat in a bowl and add the bread crumbs, 2 tablespoons of the cheese, oregano, salt, and pepper. Taste for seasoning. Spoon the mixture into the zucchini shells and place in a shallow baking dish. Add ½ inch of hot water. Cover with foil and place in a 375° oven. Bake for 15 minutes and remove the foil. Sprinkle with remaining cheese and bake for another 20 minutes or until shells are soft and the top bubbly and browned.
5. Serve with Tomato-Leek Sauce.

Baked Winter Squash
Serves 4

    1 large winter squash, Hubbard, acorn, or butternut
    water
    4 tablespoons margarine
    salt and pepper to taste
    chopped parsley
    pat of margarine

1. Preheat oven to 350°.
2. Slice the squash and remove strings and seeds.
3. Place in baking dish with a small amount of water.
4. Bake for 50 to 60 minutes. When done the squash should be tender when pierced with a fork.
5. Let cool slightly, and remove the pulp. Mash lightly with the margarine, salt, and pepper.
6. Garnish with parsley and a pat of margarine and serve.

Squash à la Italienne
Serves 6

The secret of this dish is two-fold. First, use the freshest vegetable possible or home-grown squash that has been picked less than ½ hour before cooking time, and secondly, use lots of garlic.

    2 tablespoons olive oil
    2 tablespoons vegetable oil
    4 cloves garlic, minced
    1 pound zucchini, washed, trimmed, and sliced into ½-inch pieces
    1 pound yellow summer squash, washed, trimmed,
        and sliced into ½-inch pieces
    salt and pepper to taste

1. Heat the oil in a skillet and add the garlic. Add the squash and stir-fry until just tender.
2. Season with salt and pepper and serve immediately.

Baked Zucchini with Cheese Sauce
Serves 4

2   medium zucchini, grated
1   medium onion, chopped
2   tablespoons margarine, melted
3   tablespoons flour
½   cup low-fat milk
1   teaspoon salt
⅛   teaspoon pepper or to taste
½   cup Swiss cheese, grated
3   tablespoons bread crumbs

1. Sauté grated zucchini and onion in margarine for 2 minutes.
2. Add flour and continue stirring for at least 2 minutes over medium heat. Add milk and blend well. Bring to a boil and then simmer for 1 to 2 minutes.
3. Season to taste with salt and pepper. Stir in grated cheese.
4. Place in a shallow, oiled baking dish. Cover with bread crumbs, and bake at 425° for 10 minutes until browned.

Tomatoes

Thomas Jefferson, a man with tremendous foresight, harvested some of the first Yankee tomatoes. Intriguingly called a "love apple" in earlier times, it is now a universal kitchen staple.

Selection: Choose red, well-shaped, evenly colored, and firm tomatoes. Allow 1 tomato for each serving. Small cherry tomatoes are frequently used for salads. Commercially processed tomatoes in the form of purées, pastes, sauces, and solid-pack whole or sliced products are invaluable in the kitchen.

Storage: Store fresh tomatoes in the refrigerator.

Nutrition: They are excellent sources of vitamins A and C as well as B complex and minerals. They are relatively low in calories.

Preparation: Wash and trim the stem from the tomato. Tomatoes may be easily peeled by plunging into boiling water for 45 seconds or until the skin breaks and starts to peel off.

Serving: Tomatoes may be combined with a number of other vegetables and meats. They are excellent fresh, stuffed, baked, stewed, and puréed.

Allison's Favorite Tomatoes
Serves 6

These tomatoes are superb. Ask Allison.

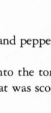

> 6   *red tomatoes, firm and ripe*
> *salt and pepper*
> 2   *cloves garlic, mashed*
> 3   *tablespoons shallots or green onions, minced*
> 4   *tablespoons fresh parsley, minced, or 2 tablespoons dried*
> ½   *teaspoon fresh basil, minced, or ¼ teaspoon dried*
> 1   *teaspoon fresh oregano, minced, or ½ teaspoon dried*
> 1   *tablespoon oil*
> ½   *cup fine, dry bread crumbs*

1. Cut tomatoes in half and scoop out the seeds. Lightly salt and pepper the shells.
2. Combine the remaining ingredients in a bowl and press into the tomato shells. If the mixture is too dry, add some tomato pulp that was scooped out of the center of the tomatoes.
3. Place in a shallow baking dish and bake at 350° for 15 minutes or until the tomatoes are soft. They should hold their shape. Serve hot.

Herbed Tomato Rings
Serves 4

Your favorite packaged, seasoned croutons, whirled in the blender provide the magic in this elegantly simple dish.

> ½   *cup seasoned bread crumbs*
> ½   *cup Parmesan cheese, grated*
> ½   *teaspoon garlic salt*
> ¼   *teaspoon pepper*
> ¼   *cup parsley, chopped*
> 3   *tablespoons olive oil*
> 4   *medium tomatoes, peeled and cut in ½-inch slices*

1. Combine bread crumbs, cheese, garlic salt, pepper, and parsley. Moisten with the olive oil. Use just enough to hold mixture together.
2. Place the tomato slices in a greased baking dish and cover with the crumb mixture.
3. Bake in a 400° oven for 5 minutes or place under the broiler until browned. Serve immediately.

Tomatoes Dijon
Serves 6

>   4   tablespoons brown sugar
>   2   tablespoons soy sauce
>   ½   teaspoon salt
>   2   tablespoons vinegar
>   2   tablespoons mustard, Dijon-type
>   4   tablespoons vegetable oil
>   6   firm, medium tomatoes
>   ¼   cup bread crumbs
>   2   tablespoons Parmesan cheese, grated

1. Combine brown sugar, soy sauce, salt, vinegar, mustard, and oil.
2. Cut the top off the tomatoes, and scoop out part of the pulp leaving a shell.
3. Fill the tomato with the sauce.
4. Mix bread crumbs and Parmesan cheese together. Top tomatoes with this mixture.
5. Bake in 350° oven approximately 10 minutes. Then place under the broiler until the bread crumb mixture browns. Serve at once.

Guacamole Tomatoes
Serves 6

>   6   firm, medium tomatoes, peeled and halved
>   salt
>   ¾   cup avocado, mashed
>   2   tablespoons canned green chili peppers, diced
>   1   tablespoon mayonnaise
>   1   tablespoon low-fat yogurt
>   2½ teaspoons onion, finely grated
>   2   tablespoons celery, minced
>   salt and pepper to taste
>   1   tablespoon lemon juice
>   lettuce
>   paprika

1. Scoop out the tomato pulp, and sprinkle inside of tomatoes with salt.

2. Combine the avocado, chili peppers, mayonnaise, yogurt, onion, celery, salt, pepper, and lemon juice and mix thoroughly.
3. Fill the tomatoes with the avocado mixture. Cover and chill thoroughly.
4. Serve chilled on a bed of lettuce and garnish each with a dash of paprika.

Sautéed Green Tomatoes
Serves 6

This is a special treat for those lucky enough to grow their own tomatoes. If you do not have your own supply, look for tomatoes that are barely ripe and very firm.

1 *tablespoon vegetable oil*
2 *tablespoons margarine*
6 *firm, green tomatoes, finely sliced*
½ *teaspoon salt*
½ *teaspoon sugar*
dash of pepper

1. Combine the oil and margarine in a skillet and when the margarine has melted, add the tomatoes and completely coat with the oil mixture. Sprinkle with salt, sugar, and pepper and cook over high heat until the tomatoes are soft. This should require only 3 to 4 minutes of cooking time.
2. Sprinkle with a dash of pepper and serve.

Chili Tomatoes
Makes 12

12 *very small tomatoes*
½ *cup chili sauce*
¼ *cup yogurt*
¼ *cup mayonnaise*
¼ *cup Lappi or Jack cheese, grated*

1. Preheat oven to 375°.
2. Wash and remove tomato stems. Slice in half and set aside.
3. Combine remaining ingredients and put a spoonful on each tomato half. Place on a baking sheet and bake for 10 minutes or until the mixture is slightly browned. Serve hot.

Tomatoes Stuffed with Spinach
Serves 6

A truly special combination, this mixture of spinach and Madeira-flavored mushrooms.

3   *large, firm tomatoes*
salt and pepper
1   *large bunch of spinach, trimmed and washed, or 1 package of frozen spinach, chopped*
2   *tablespoons margarine*
1   *teaspoon lime juice*
salt and pepper to taste
¼   *cup yogurt*
¼   *cup mayonnaise*
¼   *cup mushrooms, sliced*
¼   *cup Madeira wine*

1. Slice tomatoes in halves and remove pulp. Lightly salt and pepper the shells.
2. Prepare and cook the spinach as for Puréed Spinach (see pages 198–99).
3. Place the spinach in a saucepan and add 1 tablespoon margarine. When it has melted, add the lime juice, salt, pepper, yogurt, and mayonnaise. Mix thoroughly and set aside.
4. Melt remaining margarine in a skillet. Add the sliced mushrooms and sauté until soft. Raise heat and cook until moisture has evaporated.
5. Add the mushrooms to the spinach and then add the Madeira. Mix and simmer 3 minutes.
6. Stuff the tomato halves with the spinach and place in a 350° oven for 15 minutes. Serve immediately.

Stuffed Tomatoes à la Schroeder
Serves 6

6   *firm, ripe tomatoes, halved*
salt
½   *cup brown or raw sugar*
4   *tablespoons mustard*

1. Lightly salt tomato halves.

2. Mix the brown sugar and mustard and fill the center of each tomato half.
3. Place in a shallow baking dish and place in a 350° oven for 15 minutes or until the tomatoes are soft. Serve while hot.

Turnips

The turnip has been much maligned. It has often been considered peasant fare, yet holds acclaim from gourmets. This diverse tuber can be traced back to the ancients and is grown all over the globe.

Selection: Choose firm, unwrinkled turnips.
Storage: Remove the green stems and store the bulbs in a cool, dry place.
Nutrition: A good source of minerals and vitamin B complex, moderately low in calories.
Preparation: Turnip greens can be washed, chopped, and steamed and enjoyed as a leafy green vegetable. The roots should be peeled, sliced, and steamed.
Serving: They are good prepared in many ways: boiling, mashing, roasting, frying, and baking all suit turnips. They are also delicious raw as an appetizer.

Scalloped Turnips
Serves 6

Extremely good with roast meats.

2	*cups turnips, peeled and sliced*
1	*cup onion, sliced*
2	*tablespoons flour*
1	*teaspoon salt*
⅛	*teaspoon pepper*
4	*tablespoons margarine*
1	*cup low-fat milk, heated*

1. Toss the turnips and onion with the flour and salt and pepper.
2. Arrange them in layers in a shallow baking dish and dot each layer with the margarine.
3. Cover with the heated milk and bake in a 350° oven until tender and golden brown on top, about 1¼ hours.

Sweet Potatoes and Yams

Sweet potatoes and yams can be used interchangeably. The sweet potato is not related to the Irish potato but is a distinct variety. Yams actually have a sweeter flavor than the sweet potato.

Selection: Choose small, firm tubers.

Storage: Store in a dark, cool place.

Nutrition: They are chock full of vitamin A and minerals and relatively high in calories.

Preparation: Scrub the skin of the yams and sweet potatoes well. Do not peel for baking. Otherwise remove skins with a potato peeler.

Serving: Yams and sweet potatoes are excellent baked, boiled, or mashed. Try peeling and boiling them and then roasting with roast meat or poultry, basting or glazing them with the pan juices. Sweet potatoes adapt well to most white potato recipes.

Candied Yams
Serves 4

This is a must when you are having turkey and all the trimmings.

2 *pounds yams, peeled and sliced*
½ *cup low-fat milk*
3 *tablespoons brown sugar*
2 *tablespoons margarine*
1 *teaspoon cinnamon*
½ *teaspoon ground cloves*
¼ *teaspoon ground ginger*
marshmallows

1. Boil the yams until quite tender, 25 to 30 minutes, then drain thoroughly.
2. Put through a ricer or mash with a potato masher.
3. Add the milk, brown sugar, margarine, and spices. Beat until smooth.
4. Place them in a shallow baking dish and cover them completely with marshmallows.
5. Bake in a 350° oven until the marshmallows melt and brown. Serve hot.

Roast Yams
Serves 6

Consider this simple treatment of yams as a fine complement to roast meats and poultry.

4 medium yams, peeled and cut into 2-inch cubes
3 cups boiling, salted water

1. Place yams in a saucepan and cover with the boiling, salted water and cook until barely tender, about 12 minutes. Remove and drain well.
2. Place in the bottom of the roasting pan during the last 15 minutes of cooking time. Turn on all sides, coating with the roasting juices.
3. Let cook for about 15 minutes or until tender. Turn once or twice to glaze evenly. Serve hot with the roast.

Puréed Sweet Potatoes
Serves 4

   4 medium sweet potatoes
   water to cover
   1 teaspoon salt
   4 tablespoons margarine

1. Wash the potatoes with vegetable brush. Slice in 1½-inch pieces and place in a saucepan. Add water and salt.
2. Bring to a boil and cook at medium heat until tender, 8 to 10 minutes.
3. Drain and remove the skins.
4. Put the cooked potatoes through a ricer or mash and stir in the margarine. Serve hot.

Exotic Sweet Potatoes
Serves 4

   4 medium sweet potatoes
   water to cover
   1 teaspoon salt
   4 tablespoons margarine
   3 tablespoons brown sugar
   3 tablespoons raisins
   ½ cup orange juice
   ½ teaspoon cinnamon

1. Wash the potatoes with vegetable brush, slice in 1½-inch pieces and place in saucepan. Add water to cover and 1 teaspoon salt.
2. Bring to a boil and cook until tender, 8 to 10 minutes.
3. Drain the potatoes and remove the skins.
4. Melt the margarine in a skillet and add the brown sugar, raisins, orange juice, and cinnamon. Stir until the brown sugar dissolves. Add the sweet potatoes and mix well. Serve hot.

15
Greenery

ANYTHING COLD AND crispy can be called a salad but one man's greenery is not necessarily another man's salad. Vegetables, fruits, meats, fish, chicken, rice, and pastas can all form the base for a salad. Take some cold, cooked vegetables, add oil, vinegar, and a judicious amount of salt — and perhaps a little garlic or flavorful herb, toss lightly and you have a salad. Or, carefully arrange an assortment of chilled fresh fruits, sliced oranges, apples, pears, peaches, melon, berries, on a lovely bed of crisp greens and mound with creamy dressing and you have a lovely summer luncheon.

There are no hard and fast rules for salad making. They can be hot or cold, a light and refreshing end to a meal or a hearty entrée. As a rule, a salad is crisper in texture and a bit sharper in flavor and seasonings than other parts of a meal. The type of salad — crisp fresh vegetables, fruits, cooked meats, or rice — determines its place on the menu. Green salads with a tart dressing should be served at the end of a meal, particularly when wine is served. The sharp, pungent flavor of the dressing and the crispness of the greens "cleanse" the taste buds from lingering flavors and leave them ready for the next taste sensation or provide a refreshing end to a meal.

The dressing should complement the ingredients — tartness for vegetables and greens, smoothness for fruits, creaminess for stronger-flavored meats, chicken, or fish. Bottled or commercial dressings are "quickies" to use but your own special dressing can be your individual stamp on a meal.

Flavored vinegars and seasonal herbs add interesting touches to your dressings. The various oils will affect the taste of salad dressings. Peanut oil, while useful in some types of cooking, seems to give an off-taste when used in salads. Corn and safflower oils are somewhat more distinctive than the blander soybean and cottonseed oils. Olive oil has a heavier, fuller flavor but can be overpowering if served with a delicately flavored dish. A mixture of oils can combine and enhance the best flavors of each.

Whatever combination you choose, do not forget to add imagination.

Pickled Apple Salad
Serves 4

⅓ cup white or brown sugar
¼ cup sweet pickle, chopped
¼ cup onion, chopped
¼ cup white vinegar
¼ teaspoon ground ginger
3 cups (2 to 3 medium) apples, finely chopped
4 lettuce leaves
2 tablespoons parsley, chopped, or 1 tablespoon fresh chives, chopped

1. Combine sugar, sweet pickle, onion, vinegar, and ginger.
2. Pour over chopped apples and mix thoroughly.
3. Cover and refrigerate for several hours or overnight.
4. Drain off any collected liquid and serve the drained salad on lettuce leaves with garnish of fresh parsley or sprinkling of chopped chives.

Green Bean Salad
Serves 8

1 cup canned red kidney beans
1 cup canned garbanzo beans or chick peas
1 cup canned green beans
1 cup canned yellow wax beans
1 green pepper, chopped
1 large red onion, cut in thin rings
¼ cup stuffed green olives, sliced
¼ cup wine vinegar
¼ cup salad oil
¼ cup sugar
8 lettuce leaves

1. Thoroughly drain all the beans. Fresh beans may be used but a good quality canned variety will do.
2. Place in a bowl and add the pepper, onion, and olives.
3. Combine the vinegar, oil, and sugar in a covered jar and shake vigorously.
4. Toss with the bean salad and marinate in the refrigerator for at least 6 hours or overnight. Serve on a lettuce leaf.

The following four recipes present an international array of chicken salads. The four treatments are distinctly different and each country adds a unique flavor.

Chinese Chicken Salad
Serves 4

This salad is worth the trouble to find the Chinese noodles, sesame oil, and coriander. The pleasure of eating is matched only by the fun of watching the noodles pop and puff in the hot oil.

1   *frying chicken, skinned, steamed or baked*
¼   *cup flour*
½   *teaspoon Chinese Five Spices, or ⅛ teaspoon each,*
        ground ginger, salt, cinnamon, anise, and cloves
vegetable oil
¼   *cup sesame seeds, toasted*
¼   *cup blanched almonds, chopped*
½   *medium head iceberg lettuce, shredded*
1   *bunch fresh coriander or watercress*
6   *green onions, thinly sliced diagonally*
1½   *tablespoons shredded horseradish*
DRESSING:
½   *teaspoon dry mustard*
1   *teaspoon sugar*
3   *teaspoons soy sauce*
1   *tablespoon lemon juice*
6   *tablespoons sesame oil*

2   *ounces Chinese noodles, rice sticks, or bean threads*

1. Remove all the bones from the chicken and shred the meat. Roll the shredded meat in the flour and spices. Heat 2 tablespoons of the oil in a skillet and quickly stir in the chicken and cook until crispy. Remove and drain on a paper towel.
2. Toast almonds and sesame seeds together on cookie sheet in a 400° oven for 15 minutes or until lightly browned.
3. Place the chicken, shredded lettuce, coriander, sesame seeds, green onions, horseradish, and almonds in a salad bowl and toss.
4. Combine the dressing ingredients and set aside.
5. Heat approximately 1 cup of oil in a skillet and add the noodles or bean threads. The oil must be very hot so that a test noodle puffs up immediately. Add the noodles in small amounts. Press the noodles with a

spoon to make sure they are all cooked and drain thoroughly on a paper towel.

6. Toss the noodles with the other salad ingredients. Warm the dressing slightly, add to salad and toss again. Serve immediately.

Mexican Chicken Salad
Serves 4

> 1 *head of lettuce, iceberg or head variety*
> 3 *large green onions, chopped, including all of the green tops*
> 1 *avocado*
> ½ *cup green olives, pitted*
> 1 *cup chicken, cooked and diced*
> 1 *orange*
> ¼ *cup vegetable oil*
> 2 *tablespoons wine vinegar*
> *juice of ½ lime*
> 1 *teaspoon garlic salt*
> 1 *teaspoon sugar*
> ½ *teaspoon chili powder*
> ¼ *teaspoon salt*
> 3 *tablespoons fresh coriander, minced*

1. Shred the lettuce and place in a salad bowl. Add onions, avocado, olives, and diced chicken. Peel and chop the orange and add to the salad.
2. Combine the remaining ingredients and toss thoroughly. Serve immediately.

Yankee Chicken Salad
Serves 4

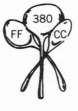

    2   *cups chicken, cooked and diced*
    ½ *cup celery, diced*
    ¼ *cup onion, minced*
    ¼ *cup tart apple, diced*
    ½ *cup Boiled Dressing (see page 259)*
    dash of freshly ground pepper
    ½ *cup Mayonnaise à la Maison (see Saucery), or other*
    1   *tablespoon lemon juice*
    ½ *teaspoon garlic salt*
    1   *teaspoon dry mustard*
    ½ *teaspoon salt*
    4   *lettuce leaves*

1. Combine chicken, celery, onion, and apple in a bowl. Add the Boiled Dressing and toss thoroughly. Chill.
2. Before serving combine remaining ingredients, except for lettuce leaves, and toss with the chicken mixture. Taste for seasoning and serve on a bed of lettuce.

Indian Curried Chicken Salad
Serves 4

    2   *cups chicken, cooked and diced*
    ⅔ *cup cashews, chopped*
    ¼ *cup celery, diced*
    2   *green onions, minced, using all of the green top*
    2   *tablespoons raisins or currants*
    2   *tablespoons Major Grey's chutney, cut in small pieces*
    ⅛ *teaspoon curry powder*
    ¼ *cup mayonnaise*
    ½ *teaspoon salt*
    2   *teaspoons lemon juice*
    4   *lettuce leaves*

1. Combine the chicken, nuts, celery, and onions in a large bowl.
2. Mix together the remaining ingredients, except lettuce, and fold into the chicken salad. Taste for seasoning.
3. Serve on lettuce leaves.

Cole Slaw
Serves 6

1   medium head green cabbage
½ cup onion, diced
½ cup cucumber, diced
½ cup mayonnaise
½ cup Cottage Cream (see Saucery)
salt and pepper to taste

1. Shred the cabbage and toss with the onion and cucumber.
2. Blend the mayonnaise and Cottage Cream and season with salt and pepper. Toss well with the cabbage mixture. Serve cold.

Dilled Cucumber Salad
Serves 6

¼ cup plain low-fat yogurt
¼ cup mayonnaise
1   teaspoon dill weed or seeds
¼ teaspoon salt
3   cucumbers, peeled and sliced

1. Combine yogurt, mayonnaise, dill, and salt. Taste for seasoning.
2. Place the cucumbers in a shallow serving dish and toss thoroughly with the dill sauce. Chill thoroughly and serve.

Cucumber Salad
Serves 6

Excellent as an accompaniment to fish.

2   cucumbers, peeled and thinly sliced
½ teaspoon salt
freshly ground pepper
½ cup vegetable oil
3   tablespoons red wine vinegar
1   teaspoon dill weed or seeds

1. Place the cucumbers in a shallow serving dish.
2. Combine the remaining ingredients in a covered jar and shake vigorously.
3. Pour the salad dressing over the cucumbers and mix completely. Chill for at least 1 hour before serving.

Fruited Slaw
Serves 6

This is cole slaw with a tropical twist.

　4　*cups shredded cabbage, lightly packed (approximately ½ head)*
　½ *cup mayonnaise*
　1　*8-ounce can crushed pineapple, with syrup*
　½ *cup raisins*

1. Place shredded cabbage in a large bowl.
2. Fold in the mayonnaise and add the undrained pineapple and raisins. Mix thoroughly. Serve well chilled.

Spanish Mushroom Salad
Serves 4

The garlic may be increased according to taste and social engagements.

　¾ *pound mushrooms, sliced*
　1　*tomato, peeled, seeded, and chopped*
　½ *cup fresh parsley, minced*
　1 or 2 *cloves garlic*
　1　*teaspoon salt*
　3　*tablespoons red wine vinegar*
　4　*tablespoons olive oil*
　3　*tablespoons vegetable oil*
freshly ground pepper
　4　*lettuce leaves*

1. Toss the mushrooms, tomato, and parsley in a salad bowl.
2. Crush the garlic using a mortar and pestle or small bowl and the back of a spoon. Sprinkle with the salt and mash to a paste. Beat in the vinegar and oils.
3. Toss the dressing over the mushroom mixture and sprinkle with ground pepper.
4. Serve on the lettuce leaves.

Macaroni Salad
Serves 12

　2　*cups small macaroni, elbow or shell*
boiling, salted water

1   *recipe Boiled Dressing (see page 259)*
½   *cup mayonnaise*
1½ *teaspoons salt*
½   *teaspoon ground pepper*
½   *cup pimiento-stuffed olives, chopped*

1. Cook the macaroni in boiling, salted water until tender. Drain, rinse under cold water, and place in a large bowl and pour the Boiled Dressing over the macaroni. Toss well and chill thoroughly.
2. Add the mayonnaise, salt, pepper and olives and mix well. Taste for seasoning and serve well chilled.

Spiced Rice Salad
Serves 6

Curried dishes, barbecues, and roast meats are enhanced by this deliciously different salad.

1   *cup brown rice*
2½ *cups boiling water*
¼   *cup salad oil*
1   *tablespoon lemon juice*
1   *teaspoon wine vinegar*
juice of ½ orange
1   *teaspoon sugar*
¼   *teaspoon cinnamon*
¼   *teaspoon ground cumin*
½   *teaspoon salt*
dash ground pepper
¼   *cup green onions, chopped*
½   *cup nuts, chopped (cashews, almonds, or pistachios)*
¼   *cup Major Grey's chutney, large chopped pieces*
½   *cup raisins*
½   *orange, peeled and chopped*

1. Place the rice in the boiling water and reduce heat to a simmer. Cover and cook for 40 minutes or until fluffy. Do not overcook or the rice will become mushy.
2. Add the rest of the ingredients to the rice and toss thoroughly. Taste for seasoning.
3. Chill thoroughly and serve.

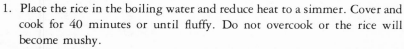

Rice Salad Vinaigrette
Serves 6

This is a winner on a hot day.

¼   *cup salad oil*
1½ *tablespoons garlic-flavored wine vinegar*
3   *cups cooked rice*
1   *teaspoon salt*
¼   *teaspoon pepper*
½   *cup red onion, chopped*
½   *cup green pepper, chopped*
½   *cup cucumber, peeled, seeded, and chopped*
½   *cup frozen peas, uncooked*
3   *tablespoons parsley, chopped*
2   *tomatoes, quartered*
12   *stuffed green olives*

1. Add the salad oil and vinegar to the rice. Season with salt and pepper and toss in the onion. Taste for seasoning. Chill thoroughly.
2. 30 minutes before serving, add the green pepper, cucumber, peas, and parsley. Toss thoroughly and chill.
3. Before serving, garnish with the tomatoes and olives.

Pomegranate Salad
Serves 6

1 *large pomegranate*
2 *oranges, peeled*
1 *pink grapefruit, peeled*
1 *tablespoon lemon juice*
1 *tablespoon lime juice*
1 *tablespoon rosewater*
1 *teaspoon sugar*

1. Remove seeds from the pomegranate by slicing it in quarters and scooping out the seeds. Reserve the seeds and any juice, discard the pulpy parts.
2. Slice the orange and grapefruit in thin crosswise slices. Discard any seeds.
3. Place in a bowl with the pomegranate seeds and toss with the lemon and lime juices, rosewater, and sugar.
4. Serve on a bed of lettuce.

Polynesian Salad
Serves 4

½ cup canned pineapple chunks
1 cup bean sprouts
1 cup shredded lettuce
1 bell pepper, diced
½ cup canned pineapple chunks
1 2-ounce can water chestnuts, drained and sliced
¾ cup mayonnaise
¼ cup pineapple syrup
2 teaspoons soy sauce
1 teaspoon curry powder

1. Drain pineapple chunks and reserve the juice.
2. Combine the bean sprouts, lettuce, bell pepper, pineapple chunks and water chestnuts.
3. Thin the mayonnaise with enough pineapple syrup to make a smooth dressing. Add the soy sauce and curry powder and mix thoroughly.
4. Add the dressing to the salad, toss well and serve.

Fresh Mushroom Salad
Serves 4

1 cup water
1 tablespoon lemon juice
½ pound fresh mushrooms, sliced
¼ cup nondairy creamer
1 tablespoon onion, grated
pinch of sugar
½ teaspoon salt
pepper
4 lettuce leaves

1. Bring water and lemon juice to a boil.
2. Add sliced mushrooms and cover the pan. Reduce heat and simmer gently for 2 to 3 minutes. Remove from heat, drain the mushrooms, and pat them dry with paper towels.
3. Combine creamer, onion, sugar, salt, and pepper.
4. Add the mushrooms and toss lightly in the dressing until they are well coated. Serve on crisp, dry lettuce.

Orange and Onion Salad
Serves 4

> salad greens
> 1   large red onion, thinly sliced
> 3   large oranges, peeled, seeded, and sliced
> ¾ teaspoon salt
> 3   tablespoons salad oil
> 1   tablespoon wine vinegar
> ¼ teaspoon sugar
> freshly ground pepper

1. Place the salad greens in a bowl. Arrange the onions and orange slices on top.
2. Combine remaining ingredients in a bowl and just before serving cover with the dressing. Toss and serve.

Olive Salad
Serves 4

This dish may also be served as an antipasto.

> 2   cups mixed green and black olives, pitted
> ½ cup celery, diced
> ¼ cup vegetable oil
> ¼ cup red wine vinegar
> ¼ cup green pepper, diced
> 1   small red onion, thinly sliced
> 1   teaspoon dried basil
> 1   teaspoon dried oregano

1. Combine all ingredients in a bowl and toss thoroughly.
2. Marinate in the refrigerator for 24 hours, stirring occasionally.

German Potato Salad
Serves 4

What summer buffet is complete without potato salad!

> 2   pounds boiling potatoes, scrubbed and quartered
> salted water to cover
> 1   cup onions, finely chopped
> ⅔ cup chicken stock

⅓ cup vegetable oil
1   tablespoon wine vinegar
2   teaspoons mustard
2   teaspoons salt
1   teaspoon ground pepper
1   tablespoon lemon juice

1. Boil the potatoes in the salted water until *just* tender. Do *not* overcook. Drain, peel, and slice. Chill thoroughly.
2. Combine remaining ingredients in a saucepan and simmer for 5 minutes.
3. Pour the dressing over the chilled potatoes and toss thoroughly. Cool, test for seasoning, and serve.

Potato Salad with Caraway
Serves 4

2½ cups potatoes, cooked and sliced
½   cup onions, finely diced
¼   cup mayonnaise
¼   cup plain yogurt
1   tablespoon wine vinegar
½   teaspoon salt
¼   teaspoon caraway seeds

1. Place the potatoes and onions in a bowl.
2. Combine the remaining ingredients and toss thoroughly with the potato mixture. Serve thoroughly chilled.

basil

Caesar Salad

Serves 4 as salad or 2 as main course

This king of salad can be beautifully reproduced utilizing egg substitute if you wish to forego whole egg.

1   *large head romaine lettuce, thoroughly washed and dried*
½   *clove garlic*
½   *teaspoon salt*
freshly ground pepper
½   *teaspoon mustard*
½   *teaspoon Worcestershire sauce*
1   *tablespoon lemon juice, fresh*
2   *tablespoons olive oil*
1   *egg equivalent*
2   *tablespoons margarine*
½   *cup fresh bread cubes*
4   *tablespoons Parmesan cheese, grated*
3   *anchovy fillets, diced (optional)*

1. Tear the lettuce into ½-inch pieces and refrigerate.
2. Rub a wooden salad bowl lightly with the garlic and reserve the garlic for the croutons.
3. Combine the salt, pepper, mustard, Worcestershire sauce, lemon juice, and olive oil in a small covered container.
4. Place the egg equivalent in a small bowl or ramekin and heat in a saucepan of boiling water for 30 seconds. Remove and blend thoroughly with the dressing ingredients.
5. Melt the margarine in a skillet and add the garlic. Toss the bread cubes over medium heat until they are golden. Place the lettuce and croutons in a salad bowl and toss well with the dressing. Add the cheese, and anchovies if you are using them, and toss again. Serve immediately.

Mushroom and Zucchini Salad with Shallot Dressing

Serves 4

¾   *cup raw zucchini (about 2 medium), unpeeled, thinly sliced*
¾   *cup raw mushrooms, washed and sliced*
⅓   *cup (3 to 6) shallots, thinly sliced or, 4 tablespoons green onions, chopped*
4   *teaspoons Dijon-style mustard*
¼   *cup white wine vinegar*
¼   *cup vegetable oil*
½   *teaspoon salt*

⅛ *teaspoon black pepper*
4 *lettuce leaves*

1. Place zucchini and mushrooms in a bowl.
2. Combine remaining ingredients, except lettuce, in a covered jar and shake vigorously.
3. Pour over vegetables and toss well. Let stand at room temperature for at least 30 minutes.
4. Serve on a lettuce leaf.

Green Salad with Basil Dressing
Serves 6

1 *tablespoon wine vinegar*
3 *tablespoons vegetable oil*
1 *tablespoon fresh basil, minced, or ½ tablespoon dried*
½ *teaspoon salt*
¼ *teaspoon coarsely ground pepper*
mixture of greens, washed and thoroughly dried

1. Combine salad dressing ingredients in a covered jar and shake vigorously.
2. Pour over greens and toss well. Serve immediately.

Tarragon Tuna Salad
Serves 4

This unusual medley is handsomely served on a bed of lettuce leaves surrounded by a garnish of crisp apple slices and spiced peaches. Diced chicken can be substituted for the tuna.

2 *3-ounce cans tuna, drained*
2 *crisp, red apples*
1 *cup celery, diced*
½ *cup Tarragon Dressing (see page 259)*
4 *canned, spiced peaches*
4 *lettuce leaves*

1. Place the drained tuna in a bowl. Core and dice one apple. Add to the tuna with the celery. Mix thoroughly.
2. Add enough dressing to bind the salad.
3. Core and slice the remaining apple. Place a mound of salad on a lettuce leaf and garnish the plate with the apple slices and spiced peaches. Serve chilled.

Spinach Salad
Serves 8

This is the best spinach salad ever made.

DRESSING:
1   *small clove garlic, sliced into 6 pieces*
3   *tablespoons olive oil*
1   *tablespoon corn oil*
¾   *teaspoon oregano*
½   *teaspoon salt*
⅛   *teaspoon coarsely ground pepper*
1   *tablespoon wine vinegar*
1   *tablespoon lemon juice*

SALAD:
1   *large bunch raw spinach, thoroughly washed and dried*
endive, romaine, or other greens if desired
½   *pound raw mushrooms, sliced*
2   *tablespoons Canadian bacon, crisply cooked and chopped*
½   *cup croutons, seasoned*
2   *tablespoons Parmesan cheese, freshly grated*

1. Combine all the dressing ingredients in a covered jar and shake vigorously. Let stand at room temperature for at least ½ hour.
2. Tear the spinach and other greens into a salad bowl. Toss with the mushrooms, Canadian bacon, and croutons.
3. Remove the garlic from the dressing. Shake well and pour over the spinach. Toss well, sprinkle the cheese over the top and serve.

Tuna Salad
Serves 4

This salad also makes a great sandwich spread.

2   *3-ounce cans tuna, drained*
⅓   *cup sweet pickle relish*
3   *tablespoons mayonnaise*
4   *lettuce leaves*

1. Combine all ingredients, except lettuce, in a bowl and blend thoroughly.
2. Serve on lettuce leaves.

Tuna Veronique
Serves 4

A pretty luncheon dish, cool and refreshing with grapes and nuts.

¾ *cup tuna, drained*
1   *cup seedless grapes*
1   *cup celery, finely diced*
¼ *cup green olives, sliced*
¼ *cup mayonnaise*
¼ *cup walnuts or almonds, diced*
4   *lettuce leaves*

1. Place the tuna in a bowl. Add the remaining ingredients, except lettuce, reserving a few nuts for garnish. Blend thoroughly.
2. Divide the tuna salad into equal portions on the lettuce leaves. Sprinkle with the reserved nuts, chill thoroughly, and serve.

Vegetable Salad
Serves 4

2   *cups (about 1 pound) beets, cooked, peeled, and sliced*
1   *red onion, thinly sliced*
1   *cup carrots, julienned and cooked*
½ *cup olive oil*
3   *tablespoons wine vinegar*
½ *teaspoon salt*
ground pepper
Buttermilk Dressing (see page 260)

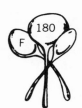

1. Combine vegetables in a bowl.
2. Add oil, vinegar, salt, and pepper and let them stand for 2 hours. Baste frequently.
3. Drain thoroughly and toss with Buttermilk Dressing.

Molded Carrot Salad
Serves 4

    1 package orange gelatin dessert
    2 cups boiling water
    1 small can crushed pineapple
    2 cups fresh carrots, grated
    lettuce (optional)

1. Place the gelatin in a bowl and add the boiling water. Stir until it has completely dissolved and chill until partially set.
2. Add the pineapple, with the juice, and the carrots and mix thoroughly.
3. Chill for at least 4 hours or until completely set.
4. This salad can be made in a decorative mold and served on a bed of lettuce.

Molded Gazpacho Salad
Serves 6

    2   tablespoons unflavored gelatin
    ½   cup cold water
    2½   cups tomato juice
    1   teaspoon sugar
    2   tablespoons wine vinegar
    1   tablespoon lemon juice
    ½   teaspoon salt
    ½   cup onion, diced
    ¾   cup cucumber, peeled and diced
    ½   cup celery, diced
    ½   cup green pepper, diced
    1   clove garlic
    lettuce leaves

1. Soften the gelatin in the cold water.
2. Heat 1 cup of the tomato juice, stir into the gelatin until completely dissolved and add the sugar, remaining tomato juice, vinegar, lemon juice, and salt. Chill until thick and syrupy.
3. Purée the onion, cucumber, celery, green pepper, and garlic in a blender, or finely dice.
4. Fold the vegetable mixture into the gelatin mixture and pour into a lightly oiled ring mold or individual cups. Chill until set.
5. Unmold onto a bed of lettuce by placing the mold briefly into a bowl of warm water and inverting it onto a plate, or place the mold upside down on the serving platter and cover the bottom with a warm, wet dish towel until the salad slips out.

Mincemeat Aspic
Serves 8

2   *envelopes unflavored gelatin*
½   *cup sugar*
2   *tablespoons lemon juice*
2   *tablespoons water*
3   *cups hot cider*
1   *cup red apples, cored and diced*
½   *cup walnuts, chopped*
1   *cup mincemeat*
lettuce leaves

1. Combine the gelatin, sugar, lemon juice, and water in a saucepan. Stir over low heat until the gelatin dissolves.
2. When thoroughly dissolved, being sure there are *no* lumps, add the hot cider. Stir until well mixed and chill in the refrigerator until slightly set.
3. Add the diced, unpeeled apples, walnuts, and mincemeat. Pour into a 6-cup ring or other shape mold. Chill until firm.
4. Unmold by loosening the edges with a knife and inverting the mold over a bed of lettuce leaves. Hold a dish towel under hot water and place over the mold for several seconds or until the gelatin slips out onto the lettuce. Serve immediately.

"Moose" Wood
Serves 6

This "moose," unlike a very large animal, is served as a spectacular, molded salad.

1 *package lime gelatin*
1 *cup boiling water*
1 *cup low-fat cottage cheese*
1 *cup mayonnaise*
½ *cup pecans*

1. Dissolve the lime gelatin in the boiling water. Cool to room temperature.
2. Reserve 7 or 8 pecans for decorations and place the gelatin, cottage cheese, mayonnaise, and remaining pecans in a blender. Whirl until smooth. Or, whip with an electric beater and chop pecans and fold in last.
3. Pour mixture into a salad mold, ring mold, or individual serving dishes. Chill until firm. Unmold mousse to serve and garnish with the reserved pecans.

Dressings

Basic Oil and Vinegar Dressing
Makes ¾ cup

½ *cup salad oil*
3 *tablespoons wine vinegar*
1 *tablespoon of mixed fresh herbs, such as oregano, majoram, basil, and parsley, minced, or ½ tablespoon dried herbs, crushed*
salt and pepper to taste
salad greens

1. The dressing ingredients can be combined in a covered jar and refrigerated. Shake thoroughly and pour over thoroughly **dry** greens. Toss well and serve.
2. An alternative method is to place the greens in a bowl and pour the oil, vinegar, and herbs over them. Toss vigorously and season to taste with salt and pepper.

Boiled Dressing
Makes 2 cups

The perfect dressing for potato, macaroni, and meat salads.

1   *cup onion, finely chopped*
⅔   *cup chicken stock*
⅓   *cup vegetable oil*
1   *tablespoon wine vinegar*
2   *teaspoons mustard*
2   *teaspoons salt*
1   *teaspoon pepper, ground*
1   *tablespoon lemon juice*

1. Combine all ingredients in a saucepan and bring to a boil. Reduce heat and simmer for 5 minutes.
2. Cool to room temperature before using.

Tarragon Dressing
Makes 1 cup

This dressing is very good with chicken or tuna salad or as a sandwich spread.

1   *egg equivalent*
1½   *tablespoons wine vinegar*
1½   *tablespoons lemon juice*
¾   *teaspoon salt*
¾   *teaspoon dry mustard*
¾   *teaspoon sugar*
¼   *teaspoon paprika*
1   *sprig fresh tarragon, or 2 teaspoons tarragon, dried*
¾   *cup salad oil*
1   *tablespoon boiling water*

1. Place all ingredients except the oil and water in a blender. Blend 30 seconds.
2. Add the oil very slowly while the blender is on low speed until the mixture thickens like mayonnaise.
3. Gradually stir in the boiling water, blending thoroughly. Chill. This will keep well, from three to four weeks, in a covered container in the refrigerator.

Buttermilk Dressing
Makes ½ cup

1   *tablespoon vegetable oil*
1   *clove garlic, minced*
1   *teaspoon mustard*
¼   *teaspoon paprika*
¼   *cup buttermilk*
⅛   *cup plain yogurt*
⅛   *cup mayonnaise*
1   *teaspoon salt*

1. Combine ingredients and blend thoroughly. Chill.
2. Serve by pouring over mixed greens.

Ingall's Dressing
Makes 1¼ cups

¾   *cup vegetable oil*
½   *cup wine vinegar*
1½   *teaspoons salt*
¼   *teaspoon pepper*
¼   *teaspoon sugar*
¼   *teaspoon garlic powder*

1. Combine ingredients in a covered jar and shake vigorously.
2. Can be served on greens or cold, cooked vegetables.

Roquefort Dressing
Makes about 1 quart

3   *ounces Roquefort cheese*
2   *cups mayonnaise*
1   *cup Cottage Cream (see Saucery)*
½   *cup buttermilk*
1   *teaspoon wine vinegar*
1   *teaspoon Worcestershire sauce*
1   *level teaspoon garlic salt*

1. Crumble Roquefort cheese in a bowl.

2. Add the mayonnaise, Cottage Cream, and buttermilk and blend well.
3. Add wine vinegar, Worcestershire sauce and garlic salt. Taste for seasoning and chill. Keep in a covered jar in the refrigerator.

Pignolia Dressing
Makes approximately 1 cup

This dressing will keep for 2 weeks in a covered jar in the refrigerator.

¾ cup vegetable oil
¼ cup lemon juice
1 tablespoon red wine vinegar
2 tablespoons pine nuts (pignolias)
1 teaspoon salt
¼ teaspoon dry mustard
¼ cup parsley, chopped
¼ teaspoon garlic salt
¼ teaspoon freshly ground pepper
1 teaspoon basil
1 tablespoon pine nuts

1. Combine all ingredients but the last tablespoon of pine nuts in a blender and whirl until smooth and creamy.
2. Add the remaining pine nuts and mix thoroughly.

White Wine Salad Dressing
Makes enough for a salad for 6

3 tablespoons dry white wine
½ teaspoon dry mustard
1 teaspoon lemon juice
½ teaspoon salt
freshly ground pepper
3 tablespoons olive oil
mixture of salad greens, washed and dried
2 tablespoons white wine

1. Combine the dressing ingredients, white wine through olive oil, in a covered jar and shake well.
2. To serve, pour over washed and thoroughly dried salad greens. Toss well, and sprinkle lightly with two tablespoons of white wine.

Sherried French Dressing
Makes 1¼ cups

   1   *clove garlic, minced*
   2   *green onions, minced*
   1   *teaspoon sugar*
   1   *teaspoon salt*
   1   *tablespoon sherry*
   ¾   *cup vegetable oil*
   ⅓   *cup wine vinegar*
      ground pepper

1. Place the garlic and onions in a jar with a tightly fitting cover.
2. Add the sugar, salt, sherry, oil, and vinegar and shake well. Serve by pouring over greens and sprinkle with ground pepper.

MARJoram

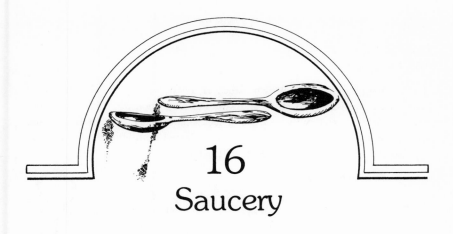

16

Saucery

MACBETH'S WITCHES WERE stirring up trouble, but when your pot boils and bubbles you will be serving smooth delectable coverings for savory meats and toothsome desserts. Saucemaking can be either unbelievably simple as in Sauce Cardinale, or require patience and concentration to produce a perfect sauce such as Hollandaise. Sauces are used to add interest to our meals and are with us in many forms. Wine and mushrooms transform the lowly hamburger to an epicurean delight and Chinese stir-fry dishes would be naked without the finishing touch of soy and stock. Our American contribution is pan gravy which has its own place in the repertoire of sauces.

A few notes for successful sauces. A White Sauce, which is the base for many others, is foolproof if you remember these simple rules. Cook the margarine-flour mixture, called a roux, for at least 2 minutes to thoroughly cook the flour and rid it of a "pasty" taste. Add the liquid warmed, rather than cold if possible, and stir it in off the heat. This will also prevent lumps. Should lumps form, simply force the sauce through a sieve and continue. This basic sauce can be flavored with chicken or beef stock, low-fat milk, wine, Fish Stock, onions, tomatoes, and herbs. Longer cooking thickens a sauce and adding more liquid thins it.

Brown sauces are made in a similar fashion using beef stock. With all flour-based sauces, cook the flour at least 2 minutes, add the liquid, and then bring to a boil. Flour and liquid will not thicken until they have reached the boiling point.

Do not mask a dish with too large a quantity. Serve just enough sauce to flavor it. Keep the number of sauces in a meal to a minimum. If one dish is elaborately sauced, the others should be restrained and simple, if used at all.

Brown Sauce
Makes 1¼ cups

The making of a classic Brown Sauce is a day-long process. It requires homemade, well-flavored stock and hours of slow cooking. There are other shorter methods that will produce an acceptable sauce. When homemade stock is not available, the canned or concentrated bouillon may be flavored for added body. This sauce freezes well.

> *3 tablespoons margarine*
> *3 tablespoons flour*
> *2 cups brown stock, or 2 cups canned or concentrated bouillon*
>   *simmered with ¼ cup vermouth, 1 bay leaf, 1 sprig of thyme,*
>   *6 peppercorns and 1 sprig of parsley for 30 minutes*
> *1 teaspoon tomato paste*

1. Melt the margarine in a saucepan. Add the flour and stir over low heat for at least 2 minutes. This is called a roux. Remove from heat.
2. Heat the stock or bouillon and pour into the roux, stirring constantly. Bring to a boil and reduce the heat. Simmer until reduced to 1½ cups. Stir in the tomato paste. Continue to simmer until it has reduced to 1¼ cups. Serve immediately or store in a tightly sealed container. May be frozen up to 6 months.

White Sauce
Makes 1½ cups

White Sauce is the classic base for many dishes, both simple and grand. An easy cure for a lumpy sauce is to press it through a sieve or whirl in a blender. Prevention is easier though. The following steps will produce a smooth sauce. 1. Cook the flour and margarine mixture over low to medium heat, never high. 2. Add hot liquid rather than cold. Always cook the flour-margarine mixture for at least 2 minutes to remove any floury taste. To make a thicker sauce, cook it for a longer time or increase the flour. For a thinner sauce, add more liquid. Chicken, beef, or Fish Stock, or wine can be substituted for the milk depending on the dish.

> *3   tablespoons margarine*
> *3   tablespoons flour*
> *1½ cups low-fat milk, heated*
> *salt and pepper to taste*

1. Melt the margarine over low heat. Add the flour and stir over low heat for 2 minutes.

2. Remove from the heat and gradually stir in the heated milk. Bring to a boil. Reduce heat and cook for 3 to 5 minutes stirring constantly until it has reached the desired consistency. Season to taste.

Cumberland Sauce
Makes approximately 1¼ cups

Lamb, pork, game, and barbecued meats are all enhanced by this tangy sauce.

>   *juice of 1 orange*
>   *juice of ½ lemon*
>   3   *green onions or shallots, minced*
>   6   *tablespoons red currant jelly*
>   5   *tablespoons port wine*
>   ¼   *teaspoon powdered ginger*
>   ¼   *teaspoon cayenne*
>   ½   *teaspoon dry mustard*

1. Remove the zest (the colored part of the skin) from the orange and lemon with a potato peeler. Do not use white rind, just the thin skin. Cut into thin strips (julienne).
2. Parboil the zest and onions for 2 minutes. Drain well. Add the juice of the orange and half the lemon. Add remaining ingredients and stir over moderate heat until the jelly has melted.
3. Serve the sauce separately.

Mint Sauce for Lamb
Makes 1 cup

An interesting departure from standard mint jelly.

>   ½ *cup mint jelly*
>   ½ *cup Cointreau*
>   *fresh mint, if available*

1. Combine mint jelly and Cointreau in a saucepan and simmer until jelly has melted.
2. Mince 2 or 3 mint leaves and add to sauce.
3. Baste lamb with sauce during cooking and serve remainder in a sauce boat with the lamb.

Gravy
Makes 1½ cups

Gravies should be given the same consideration as fine sauces. Skim *all* but the necessary fat, cook the flour to prevent it from tasting "pasty," and strain for a smooth consistency.

> *pan drippings from roast beef, lamb, or chicken*
> 2   *tablespoons flour*
> 1½ *cups water, stock, or low-fat milk*
> *salt and pepper to taste*

1. Discard all but 2 tablespoons of fat from the drippings. Scrape up the congealed juices, adding a small amount of water if necessary. Over low heat, stir in the flour and cook for at least 2 minutes, stirring continuously.
2. Remove from heat and pour in the liquid while stirring to a smooth consistency. Bring to a boil and reduce heat, simmer and stir until thickened. If too thick, more liquid may be added. Strain if necessary and serve hot. Leftover gravy may be refrigerated. Reheat and thin with liquid before serving. Low-fat milk mixed with half chicken stock is recommended for chicken gravy.

Fish Stock or Court Bouillon
Makes 3 cups

This stock can be frozen and refrozen. Save any fish trimmings or shrimp shells and add them to your stock pot. Use for any recipe calling for Fish Stock, fish fumet, or Court Bouillon.

> 1   *pound fish trimmings, heads, bones, shells, or any combination*
> 2   *cups water*
> 1½ *cups white wine*
> 12   *peppercorns*
> 6   *whole cloves*
> 1   *bay leaf*
> *large sprig of parsley*
> 2   *green onions, chopped (optional)*

1. Place all the ingredients in a saucepan. Bring to a boil, reduce the heat, and simmer gently for 30 minutes. Strain. Use immediately or freeze. It will keep covered in the refrigerator for several days, but freeze it, if you plan to store it for any longer period.

Herbed Fish Sauce

Makes approximately ½ cup

> 3   *tablespoons margarine*
> 3   *tablespoons shallots, minced*
> ¾ *cup red or white dry wine*
> 2   *tablespoons Court Bouillon or clam juice*
> 1   *tablespoon each parsley, chervil, tarragon, and chives, chopped and mixed;*
>   *if dried herbs are used measure ½ tablespoon each*
> *salt and pepper*
> 3   *tablespoons margarine*

1. Melt the margarine in a skillet. Add the shallots and sauté until transparent but not brown.
2. Add the wine and fish stock and boil rapidly until reduced to ½ cup. Add the herbs and season to taste with salt and pepper.
3. Swirl in the remaining margarine and when melted and blended in to the sauce remove from the heat and serve immediately.

Beer Mustard

Makes ¼ cup

An interesting touch with ham, corned beef, or as a sandwich spread.

> 2   *tablespoons dry mustard*
> 2   *teaspoons beer*
> *pinch of salt*

1. Blend mustard and beer to a paste, adding more beer if necessary to make a smooth consistency. Lightly salt and serve.

Golden Mustard Sauce

Makes approximately 1 cup

This tangy sauce is good with ham or fish.

> 3   *tablespoons margarine*
> 3   *tablespoons vegetable oil*
> ½ *cup orange juice, freshly made*
> 2   *tablespoons parsley, chopped*
> 1   *tablespoon chervil, chopped*
> 1   *teaspoon dry mustard*
> 1   *teaspoon orange rind, grated*

1. Melt margarine in small saucepan. Stir in ingredients.
2. Heat until bubbly. Serve hot.

Orange Sauce for Fowl
Makes approximately 1 cup

This sauce defies adjectives. Serve with game hens, duck, or other fowl.

½ *cup sugar*
1 *tablespoon wine vinegar*
¼ *teaspoon cream of tartar*
juice of 2 oranges
¼ *cup orange peel, grated*
¼ *cup Grand Marnier, or to taste*

1. Combine sugar, vinegar, and cream of tartar in a saucepan and stir over low heat until caramelized.
2. Add orange juice and peel and blend well. Remove from heat and add Grand Marnier.
3. Baste fowl with sauce every 30 minutes while cooking.
4. Skim all fat from the cooking juices; blend the juices with the remaining sauce. Serve separately in a sauce boat.

Spiced Plum Sauce
Makes approximately 1¼ cups

The following two sauces are variations on the same theme. The tangy fruit makes an excellent glaze for barbecues and broiling.

1 *cup plum jam*
1 *tablespoon catsup*
1 *tablespoon lemon juice*
2 *teaspoons vinegar*
1 *teaspoon fresh ginger, grated, or ½ teaspoon ground*
¼ *teaspoon Tabasco sauce*
½ *teaspoon aniseed, crushed*
¼ *teaspoon dry mustard*
¼ *teaspoon ground cinnamon*
¼ *teaspoon ground cloves*

1. Melt the plum jam in a saucepan over low heat. Do not let it scorch.
2. Add remaining ingredients and simmer for 15 minutes. Use as a basting sauce for barbecues.

Gingered Plum Sauce
Makes approximately 1 cup

1	*large can purple plums, whole*
1	*medium onion, diced*
2	*tablespoons vegetable oil*
⅓	*cup brown sugar*
¼	*cup tomato-based chili sauce*
1	*teaspoon ginger*
2	*teaspoons lemon juice*

1. Pit the plums and purée them in a blender with the juice.
2. Sauté the onion in the oil until soft but not brown.
3. Add the rest of the ingredients and the plum purée to the onion and simmer for 30 minutes. Brush on meat or poultry while broiling or barbecuing. Serve any remaining sauce in a separate bowl.

Pear Chutney
Makes 3 pints

Canned peaches can be substituted for the pears.

1	*No. 2½-can Bartlett pears*
1½	*cups brown sugar*
2	*cups white vinegar*
½	*cup candied ginger, thinly sliced*
2	*tablespoons mustard seed*
1	*teaspoon ground cloves*
1	*teaspoon salt*
2	*lemons, thinly sliced*
1	*cup raisins or currants*
2½	*cups onion, sliced*
4	*medium tomatoes, peeled and chopped*

1. Drain the pears reserving the liquid. Slice or chop the pears into small pieces.
2. Combine the syrup with the remaining ingredients in a large pot. Boil rapidly for 30 minutes until thick. Do not cover.
3. Add fruit, and heat to boiling once more. Remove from heat immediately, pour into sterilized jars and seal. Refrigerated, it should keep for approximately 1 month.

Fruit Chutney
Makes 1 quart

   1   *cup cider vinegar*
1¼ *cups dark brown sugar*
   1   *tablespoon dark molasses*
1½ *teaspoons salt*
   1   *teaspoon cinnamon*
   1   *teaspoon ground cumin*
  ½ *teaspoon ground coriander*
   2   *teaspoons ground ginger*
   2   *cloves garlic, minced*
   1   *pound green apples, diced*
  ½ *pound dried apricots, diced*
   1   *cup raisins*
  ½ *teaspoon ground cloves*

1. Combine all ingredients in a stainless steel or enamel saucepan. (This is a high acid content relish and you don't want to discolor it in aluminum.)
2. Bring to a boil and simmer until soft, about 1 hour. Stir frequently.
3. Cool and pour into a sterilized covered jar. Refrigerate. It should keep about 1 month.

Pesto
Makes approximately 1½ cups

This is one of those marvelous sauces with myriad uses. Fresh basil must be used so it is a seasonal pleasure unless you decide to reserve some in the freezer. Serve on pasta, boiled potatoes, fresh tomato slices, and hot or cold steamed vegetables.

1½ *cups fresh basil leaves, coarsely chopped, firmly packed*
  1 *teaspoon salt*
dash of freshly ground pepper
  1 *clove garlic*
  2 *tablespoons pine nuts*
  ½ *cup olive oil and ½ cup vegetable oil, combined*
  ½ *cup Parmesan cheese, freshly grated*

1. Place the chopped basil, salt, pepper, garlic, and pine nuts in a blender. Add 3 tablespoons of the oil mixture and whirl until puréed. Gradually pour in the remaining oil until smooth.
2. Mix in the grated cheese and taste for seasoning. Serve. This will keep refrigerated for several days. Whirl before serving if it separates.

Tomato-Leek Sauce
Makes approximately 1¾ cups

Leeks give this sauce its superior flavor. Onions may be substituted, but the results won't be quite the same.

1   *tablespoon margarine*
¾ *cup leeks, minced, white part only*
2   *tablespoons boiling water*
4   *large tomatoes, peeled, seeded, and chopped*
½ *teaspoon sugar*
½ *teaspoon salt*
½ *teaspoon pepper*
   herb bouquet (½ teaspoon thyme, 1 bay leaf, and lots of oregano tied up in parsley sprigs or held in cheesecloth)

1. Melt the margarine in a saucepan and add the leeks. Add 2 tablespoons boiling water and cover. Cook for 20 minutes or until the leeks are soft. Do not let them scorch.
2. Add the remaining ingredients, burying the herb bouquet in the center. Cover and cook 10 minutes.
3. Remove the cover and stir ingredients. Place the cover over two-thirds of the pan and let it simmer for 40 minutes.
4. Whirl the sauce in a blender or force it through a food mill. Serve hot.

Teriyaki Sauce
Makes 1¼ cups

This marinade can be used for beef, chicken, or fish. It can be reused and stores well in a covered jar in the refrigerator. If, however, it has been used for fish do not use it again for meat or fowl.

2   *cloves garlic*
¾ *cup soy sauce*
¼ *cup water*
¼ *cup white wine*
⅛ *teaspoon fresh ginger, grated, or 1 teaspoon ground*
2   *teaspoons sugar*

1. Slice each garlic clove into 6 pieces. Combine all ingredients in a bowl and stir well. Use to marinate meat, fish, or poultry for at least 2 hours and brush frequently while cooking.

Mayonnaise à la Maison
Makes 2 cups

The taste of homemade mayonnaise is in a class by itself. It is effortless with the aid of an electric mixer and well worth the extra time. The flavor can be varied by using seasoned vinegars. Although egg yolks are used, the amount of cholesterol per tablespoon is quite low and need not be generally restricted.

> IMPORTANT: Do not overbeat. Do not add oil too quickly. Have all ingredients at room temperature.

2   *large egg yolks or 6 tablespoons egg equivalent*
1   *teaspoon salt*
dash cayenne pepper
1 to 2 teaspoons vinegar or lemon juice
1   *teaspoon mustard (optional)*
1½   *cups corn oil or ½ cup olive oil and 1 cup vegetable oil*
2   *tablespoons boiling water*

1. Beat egg yolks until thick and pale yellow. Add salt, cayenne, lemon juice, and mustard and beat 1 more minute.
2. Now for the oil. Add ½ teaspoon *only*. Beat until absorbed. Add another ½ teaspoon. Add oil by half teaspoons until ½ cup is absorbed. Dribble the remaining oil in slowly and continuously. Each egg yolk can absorb up to ¾ cup of oil and no more. If too much oil is added, the sauce will curdle. If oil is added too quickly, the egg yolks will not be able to emulsify, and if sauce is whipped instead of beaten slowly, it will separate. If these precautions are noted, the sauce will be successful.
3. When all the oil is absorbed, add 2 tablespoons boiling water. The sauce will then become smoother and turn a pale yellow. Seasoning may also be corrected at this time.
4. If mayonnaise curdles or separates, beat an egg yolk in a separate bowl. Add sauce by spoonfuls and beat until absorbed. This always works.

Sauce Vinaigrette
Makes 1¾ cups

Hot or cold vegetables, salads, and cold fish are elegant when dressed with this classic sauce.

3   *teaspoons Dijon mustard*
salt

freshly ground pepper
3 tablespoons red wine vinegar
1½ cups vegetable oil
1 egg white, lightly beaten
½ cup fresh parsley, chopped
1 tablespoon lemon juice
2 tablespoons dry red wine

1. Place the mustard in a warm bowl. Add the salt and pepper to taste. Beat in the vinegar. Slowly add about ¼ cup of oil, making sure to add it gradually.
2. Add this mixture to beaten egg white. Beat until it is slightly thickened, and beat in ¾ cup of oil, parsley, and lemon juice. Taste for seasoning, beat in the remaining ½ cup oil, and add red wine at the last. Serve immediately.

Hollandaise Sauce
Makes approximately ½ cup

One egg yolk gives a thinner consistency than is usual with Hollandaise, but this remains one of the truly great sauces. The secret is to keep the pan from becoming too hot or the sauce will curdle. This sauce is served warm, not hot.

1 stick margarine, unsalted
1 egg yolk
2 tablespoons lemon juice
salt and pepper

1. Place all ingredients in a **cold** pan. With a small whisk or fork stir the stick of margarine in the pan over *very* low heat. The stirring motion blends the egg yolk and lemon juice and as the margarine melts the sauce will thicken.
2. Remove the pan from the heat from time to time to prevent it from getting too hot. Egg yolks cook instantly and if this sauce gets too hot it will curdle. If the sauce looks as if it is beginning to separate, get grainy, or tiny lumps are forming, immediately remove the pan from the heat and plunge pan into bowl of cold water, stirring vigorously.
3. Stir over low heat until margarine has melted and sauce is smooth and thickened slightly.
4. If not to be served immediately, set aside but lightly stir from time to time or it will curdle in its own heat. If it is necessary to rewarm Hollandaise, place over a bowl of hot water and stir.

Sauce Ravigote
Makes approximately ½ cup

> 1   tablespoon fresh parsley, minced
> 1   tablespoon tarragon, minced
> 1   tablespoon chervil, minced
> 1   tablespoon shallots or green onions, minced
> 1   tablespoon chives, minced
> 8   tablespoons margarine

1. All the herbs and shallots or onion should be minced very finely.
2. Work the herbs and onions into the margarine with a mortar and pestle or small bowl and the back of a spoon.
3. Chill for at least 2 hours.
4. Serve cold on warm green beans, artichokes, or carrots.

Sour Topping
Makes approximately 1 cup

This makes a creamy sour cream-like topping for dips, potatoes, and soups.

> ½   cup plain low-fat yogurt
> ½   cup mayonnaise
> 1   teaspoon lemon juice (optional)

1. Blend the yogurt and mayonnaise thoroughly. Add lemon juice as desired.
2. Store in a covered container and refrigerate. Will keep for several weeks.

Madeira Sauce
Makes approximately 1 cup

Give beef, lamb, or chicken a French touch with this fragrant sauce.

> 3   tablespoons margarine
> ½   pound mushrooms, sliced
> ½   cup nondairy creamer
> 3   tablespoons Madeira wine

1. Melt the margarine in a small skillet.
2. Add the mushrooms and sauté until soft, about 4 to 5 minutes.
3. Add the creamer and stir until blended then, add the Madeira. Stir and simmer for 3 minutes. Serve over broiled beef or lamb or baked chicken.

Sauce Maltaise
Makes approximately ¾ cup

This is a variation on a theme. For an unusual version of Hollandaise, which is excellent on asparagus and fish, add orange juice to the basic Hollandaise. This version uses egg equivalent to show its diversity but it can be made as Hollandaise. Remember to watch the heat carefully.

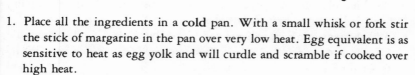

- 1 *stick unsalted margarine*
- 5 *tablespoons egg equivalent*
- 1 *tablespoon lemon juice*
- 2 *tablespoons orange juice*
- *salt and pepper*

1. Place all the ingredients in a **cold** pan. With a small whisk or fork stir the stick of margarine in the pan over very low heat. Egg equivalent is as sensitive to heat as egg yolk and will curdle and scramble if cooked over high heat.
2. Proceed as for Hollandaise. If the sauce is too thin, add ½ tablespoon lemon juice. Taste for seasoning, adding more orange juice if necessary. The acid thickens the sauce so more juice will make it thicker.
3. Serve immediately.
4. If sauce curdles or separates, beat an egg yolk in a separate bowl. Add sauce by spoonfuls and beat until absorbed. This always works.

Cottage Cream
Makes 1 cup

This is a good substitute for sour cream. It can be used in salad dressings, dips, and sauces. It tends to separate when heated but if the sauce is whirled in a blender after heating it will become smooth again.

- 1 *cup cottage cheese*
- 4 *tablespoons buttermilk*
- 1 *tablespoon lemon juice*

1. Place the cottage cheese in a sieve and hold under gently running cold water until all the liquid has been removed. It will be very lumpy.
2. Put the rinsed cottage cheese in a blender. Add the buttermilk and lemon juice. Blend at a low speed until creamy. Taste and chill. This will keep several days in a covered jar in the refrigerator.

Blue Cheese Sauce
Makes 2 cups

Tangy and smooth, this works equally well as a dressing, dip, or cold sauce.

4   *ounces blue cheese*
8   *ounces plain nonfat yogurt*
8   *ounces mayonnaise*
2   *teaspoons red wine vinegar*
⅛   *teaspoon garlic salt*
1   *teaspoon minced mixed fresh herbs, such as parsley, oregano, basil, etc., or*
    ½ teaspoon dried mixed herbs

1. Combine blue cheese, yogurt, and mayonnaise in a blender or mixing bowl and purée or beat until smooth.
2. Add the remaining ingredients and blend thoroughly. Chill thoroughly for at least 4 hours before using. This keeps well in a covered jar in the refrigerator for approximately 10 days.

Apricot Sauce
Makes ⅓ cup

¼   *cup apricot preserves*
2   *tablespoons cold water*
1   *teaspoon sugar*
2   *tablespoons Kirsch (optional)*

1. Combine all ingredients except the Kirsch in a small saucepan. Simmer for 5 minutes.
2. Add Kirsch if desired and simmer 1 minute. May be served hot or cold.
3. This sauce will keep for several weeks in a covered jar in the refrigerator.

Quick Vanilla Sauce
Makes 1 cup

1   *cup vanilla ice milk*
1   *tablespoon cornstarch*
1   *tablespoon water*
½   *teaspoon vanilla*

1. Place the ice milk in a saucepan. Blend the cornstarch and water and add to the ice milk. Bring to a boil, reduce heat, and stir until thickened.
2. Stir in the vanilla and serve warm.

Vanilla Sauce
Makes 1½ cups

½ cup sugar
1 tablespoon cornstarch
¼ teaspoon salt
1 cup boiling water
3 tablespoons margarine
1 teaspoon vanilla
¼ cup nondairy creamer (optional)

1. Combine sugar, cornstarch, and salt in a saucepan. Stir in the boiling water and bring to a boil. Reduce heat and cook until clear and thickened, about 5 minutes.
2. Stir in the margarine and vanilla, then the creamer if used. Serve warm.

Sauce Cardinale
Makes 1 cup

1 package raspberries, frozen
1 teaspoon sugar
1 tablespoon Kirsch (optional)

1. Thaw and drain the berries. Force through a sieve to purée them and extract the seeds.
2. Add sugar and heat until dissolved. Add Kirsch if desired. The remaining sauce may be stored in a covered jar in the refrigerator for several days. The sauce may be served warm or cold.

Whipped Topping
Makes approximately 1½ cups

2 egg whites
2 tablespoons sugar
3 tablespoons nonfat dry milk
3 tablespoons cold water
½ teaspoon vanilla

1. Beat the egg whites until they form stiff peaks. Gradually beat in the sugar until the egg whites are stiff and shiny.
2. Gradually add the dry milk and beat until thoroughly mixed, then add the cold water.
3. Flavor with the vanilla and serve immediately. This does not keep well.

Chocolate Sauce
Makes about ¾ cup

    2   *tablespoons water*
    3   *tablespoons cocoa*
    3   *tablespoons sugar*
    1   *tablespoon Kahlua*
    ½   *cup nondairy creamer*

1. Combine the water and cocoa in a saucepan and stir to form a smooth paste.
2. Add sugar and Kahlua and stir. Bring to a boil.
3. Reduce the heat immediately and simmer for 5 minutes, stirring frequently.
4. Add nondairy creamer and blend thoroughly.
5. Simmer over low heat for 10 minutes, stirring frequently.
6. This may be served hot or cold. Keeps well, up to 10 days, in a covered container in the refrigerator.

Lemon Sauce
Makes approximately 1 cup

    juice of 1 lemon
    ½   *cup brown sugar*
    1   *teaspoon red currant jelly*
    ½   *cup water*
    2   *teaspoons cornstarch*
    1   *teaspoon margarine*

1. Stir lemon juice, sugar and red currant jelly in a saucepan. Heat until the sugar dissolves.
2. Combine the water and cornstarch and add to the sauce. Bring to a boil, reduce heat, and stir until thickened.
3. Stir in margarine and serve on gingerbread or persimmon pudding. Serve immediately.

17
The Finishing Touch

Desserts

UNFORGETTABLE DESSERTS ARE those that put a perfect ending to a meal. An elaborately prepared creation, rich as it is beautiful, will be lost when it has to follow creamed soups and richly sauced fish. But offer instead a bowl of glistening fruit sherbet, cool and tangy after the heaviness of the preceding courses, or a mound of iced lemon meringue surrounded by fresh, perfect strawberries and your finale will be a success. Other occasions demand a masterpiece such as flaming Cherries Jubilee or rich pound cake layered with the incredible Holiday Filling. But in between these rare extravaganzas are the many daily meals, simpler in preparation which are better ended with fresh fruit or a thin slice of Caraway Tea Loaf. Sometimes it may be best to forego dessert entirely, allowing a pleasant meal to linger on the palate uninterrupted by a sweetmeat.

Fruit, plain or in its many disguises, is always a perfect dessert. Put it in breads, tarts, and cakes. Poach it, steam it, purée it, chill it, or pluck it directly from the vine. You need not worry that it will harm your heart and your sweet tooth will be satisfied with its natural sugar.

For a change, make your own ice milk and sherbet. If the seasons are not cooperating, pick your fruit from the grocer's shelf or the jam jar. Water ices can be stirred up any time and be on hand for a quick dessert or refreshing break on a hot day.

Baked goods should be carefully monitored for the hidden cholesterol and saturated fats, but experiment freely with those containing fewer eggs and substituting oil and margarine for butter. Heavily sugared and creamed desserts should be restricted but the wide assortment of fruit treats, sauces, ice milks, and baked goods in this chapter will easily replace them.

Angel Food Cake
Serves 12

This cake has myriad uses. Serve plain, with fresh fruit, Fruit Ambrosia, ice milk, Chocolate Sauce, puréed berries, frosting, or cut in strips and use in place of lady fingers. Note — start with all ingredients at room temperature.

1	cup plus 1 tablespoon cake flour
1½	cups sugar
12	egg whites
½	teaspoon salt
1	teaspoon cream of tartar
1½	teaspoons vanilla

1. Preheat oven to 300°.
2. Sift the flour, measure and then resift 6 times with ¾ cup of the sugar. This step is necessary for a fine texture.
3. Place the egg whites in a mixing bowl and beat at a slow speed until foamy. Add the salt and cream of tartar. Gradually increase the speed and beat until the egg whites are stiff but not dry. They should be glossy and hold stiff peaks. Do not overbeat. While beating, gradually add the remaining sugar, then the vanilla.
4. Sift the flour mixture over the egg whites in 5 portions, folding gently but thoroughly with a wire whisk after each addition.
5. Pour the mixture into a 10-inch ungreased tube pan. Quickly swirl a knife through the batter and lift it higher in the pan. Bake for 60 to 70 minutes or until the cake is golden and springs back when touched.
6. Invert the cake pan over a high necked bottle for 15 minutes, making sure the pan clears the counter and allows air to circulate underneath. Loosen edges with a knife and invert on a cake plate. Rap the bottom sharply and the cake will fall onto the plate. Cool thoroughly and slice.

Burnt Leather Cake
Serves 12

This cake was adapted from a delightful collection of Stanford University Hospital recipes, circa 1920. It was back in the days when Stanford Hospital was in San Francisco and before we worried about cholesterol and saturated fat, so some substitutions have been made.

½	cup brown sugar
¼	teaspoon cream of tartar

1½ cups granulated sugar
½   cup boiling water
½   cup margarine
1   cup water
2   egg yolks, lightly beaten
2½ cups flour
4   teaspoons baking powder
1   teaspoon vanilla
3   egg whites

1. Place the brown sugar and cream of tartar in a saucepan over medium heat until clear and golden brown, making a caramel of the desired color. Do not stir at all.
2. In a separate saucepan, slowly add the granulated sugar to the boiling water. Stir continuously. Cook for 2 minutes and keep hot until ready to use.
3. Add the margarine to the sugar water and beat until smooth and creamy. Add 3 tablespoons of the caramel. Reserve 2 tablespoons caramel for the icing (see following recipe) and store the remainder. (To reuse, heat until softened.) Add the cup of water and egg yolks, and beat well.
4. Sift the flour and baking powder together and add to the creamed mixture in 3 equal portions, beating well after each addition. Beat in the vanilla.
5. Beat the egg whites until stiff but not dry. Gently fold the egg whites into the batter and pour into 2 lightly oiled 9-inch cake pans. Bake in a 350° oven until a knife inserted in the center comes out clean. Invert onto cake racks and cool before frosting.

Icing for Burnt Leather Cake

The original recipe says to cook the sugar and water together until it "hairs." The term "hairs" is unfamiliar but self-explanatory.

1   cup granulated sugar
¼   cup water
2   tablespoons caramel
1   egg white, stiffly beaten
½   teaspoon vanilla

1. Cook the sugar and water together until it hairs, or spins a thread.
2. Stir in the caramel.
3. Beat the egg white until stiff but not dry. Continue beating and pour the syrup into the egg white and add the vanilla.
4. Beat until the mixture is stiff and frost the Burnt Leather Cake (preceding recipe).

Bette's Carrot Cake
Serves 8

This delicious cake was a great hit at a birthday party when it was presented in the shape of Snoopy, the Flying Ace, going after the Red Baron.

3   eggs, *well beaten*
1¼ cups vegetable oil
2   cups sugar
2   cups flour
2   teaspoons cinnamon
2   teaspoons soda
1   teaspoon salt
2   teaspoons vanilla
2   cups carrots, shredded
1   cup walnuts, chopped
1   3-ounce can crushed pineapple, with juice

1. Preheat oven to 350°.
2. Combine eggs, oil, and sugar and beat well. Mix rest of dry ingredients and stir into the egg mixture. Add vanilla, carrots, walnuts, pineapple, and juice. Blend well. Batter will be moist. Pour into 2 9-inch cake pans or a 12-inch rectangular pan.
3. Bake for 50 minutes or until a knife inserted in the center comes out clean.
4. May be served plain or frost with cheese frosting.

Frosting for Bette's Carrot Cake

½ cup margarine
6   ounces Neufchâtel cheese
1   box powdered sugar, sifted
1   teaspoon vanilla
½ cup walnuts, chopped

1. Beat margarine and cheese until creamy. Beat in sugar and vanilla.
2. Frost Bette's Carrot Cake (preceding recipe) and sprinkle with walnuts.

Chocolate Applesauce Cake
Serves 12

2   cups flour
2   teaspoons baking soda

1   *teaspoon salt*
½   *teaspoon cinnamon*
¼   *teaspoon ground cloves*
¼   *teaspoon nutmeg*
½   *teaspoon allspice*
5   *tablespoons cocoa*
1½   *cups sugar*
1   *tablespoon cornstarch*
1½   *cups applesauce*
½   *cup margarine, melted*
1   *cup raisins*
1   *cup walnuts, chopped*

1. Blend all the dry ingredients in a mixing bowl.
2. Stir in the applesauce and melted margarine. Mix just until the dry ingredients are moistened. Fold in the raisins and walnuts.
3. Pour into a lightly oiled Bundt pan or a 9- x 13-inch pan. Bake in a 350° oven for 40 minutes. Cool and slice.

White Cake
Makes two 9-inch layers

1   *cup margarine*
1¾   *cups sugar*
1   *teaspoon vanilla*
3¼   *cups flour*
4   *teaspoons baking powder*
1   *cup low-fat milk*
8   *egg whites*
¼   *teaspoon salt*

1. Beat the margarine and sugar together until light and fluffy. Beat in the vanilla.
2. Sift the flour and baking powder together and add to the creamed mixture, alternating with the milk in 3 equal portions.
3. Beat the egg whites until foamy and add the salt. Gradually increase the speed and continue beating until stiff and glossy. Do not overbeat.
4. Stir ¼ of the beaten egg whites into the batter, then gently fold the remaining egg whites into the batter. Pour into 2 oiled 9-inch layer pans.
5. Bake in a 375° oven for 25 minutes. Cool before frosting.

Chocolate Pound Cake
Serves 12

Rich and chocolaty, and you'll never taste the mashed potatoes.

¼	cup margarine
1¾	cups sugar
1	cup cold mashed potatoes
4	egg equivalents
2¾	cups unsifted flour
3	teaspoons baking powder
1	teaspoon cinnamon
¼	teaspoon cloves
¼	teaspoon allspice
½	cup unsweetened cocoa
½	cup low-fat milk
½	cup dark corn syrup
1	teaspoon vanilla
1	cup nuts, chopped

1. Preheat oven to 350°.
2. Beat the margarine and sugar together until creamy. Beat in the potatoes and egg equivalents.
3. Stir the dry ingredients and spices together. Combine the milk and corn syrup. Add flour and milk mixtures in 3 equal, alternating portions and blend thoroughly after each addition.
4. Stir in the vanilla and nuts and pour into an oiled 10-inch tube or Bundt pan and bake for 1 hour in a 350° oven or until a knife inserted in the center comes out clean.

Chocolate Cheesecake
Serves 8

This wickedly delicious cheesecake is smooth, creamy, and chocolaty all the way through.

Chocolate Graham Cracker Crust
2	egg equivalents
⅔	cup sugar
3½	tablespoons cocoa

1   teaspoon vanilla
3-ounce package Neufchâtel cheese, softened
1   cup low-fat cottage cheese
2   cups commercial sour cream substitute

1. Lightly oil a cheesecake or springform pan and line with the Chocolate Graham Cracker Crust.
2. Blend the egg equivalents, sugar, cocoa, vanilla, and Neufchâtel cheese. When smooth beat in the cottage cheese and commercial sour cream substitute.
3. Pour into the pie crust and smooth the top.
4. Bake in 350° oven for 1 hour and 20 minutes. It should be set around the edges but soft in the center. Chill thoroughly before serving.

Aunt Nell's Fruit Cake
Serves 12

1   cup margarine
1   cup brown sugar
4   egg equivalents
2   cups flour
½   teaspoon salt
2   teaspoons baking powder
¼   teaspoon baking soda
½   teaspoon nutmeg
½   teaspoon cinnamon
½   teaspoon cloves
1   cup glacéed fruit
1½   cups raisins
1   cup nuts, chopped

1. Beat the margarine and sugar together. Add the egg equivalents and beat thoroughly.
2. Sift the flour, salt, baking powder, and spices and add to the egg mixture in 3 equal portions, beating well after each addition.
3. Fold in the glacéed fruit, raisins, and nuts. Pour into a lightly oiled 9-inch loaf pan and bake in a 350° oven for 1 hour or until a knife inserted in the center comes out clean. Invert onto a cake rack and slice when cool.

Pound Cake
Serves 12

Like all pound cakes, this is delicious unadorned. It is superb dressed with fresh fruit, chocolate sauce, or Holiday Filling. The basic recipe can be varied by folding in caraway seeds, nuts, raisins, or diced, candied fruit before pouring into the pan.

1	cup margarine
2½	cups sifted flour
1	teaspoon vanilla
8	egg whites
½	teaspoon salt
¼	teaspoon cream of tartar
1½	cups sugar

1. Preheat the oven to 350°.
2. Beat the margarine until smooth and beat in 1¼ cups of the flour until mixture is light and fluffy. Beat in the vanilla.
3. In a separate bowl, beat the egg whites at a low speed until they are foamy. Add the salt and cream of tartar and beat, gradually increasing the speed, until soft peaks form. Add the sugar in a slow continuous stream, beating continuously. Beat for 5 minutes or until very stiff.
4. Fold ¼ the egg whites into the flour mixture and gently stir to blend. Fold in the rest of the egg whites while sifting the remaining flour over them. Fold gently until well mixed but do not overmix or the egg whites will deflate.
5. Pour into a lightly oiled tube pan or two 9-inch cake pans. Bake for 1 hour or until golden. Turn onto a rack and cool before serving.

Prune Cake
Serves 12

Moist and mouthwatering, even prune haters will love this cake.

1	cup brown sugar, packed
½	cup white sugar
½	cup margarine
2	eggs
⅓	cup low-fat milk
2½	cups sifted flour
2	teaspoons baking powder

½   teaspoon salt
½   teaspoon baking soda
1   teaspoon cinnamon
1   cup walnuts, chopped
1½ cups cooked prunes, drained, pitted, and chopped

1. Beat sugars and margarine together until creamy. Beat in eggs one at a time. Beat in the milk.
2. Sift dry ingredients together and add to the batter in 3 portions, beating well after each addition.
3. Stir in nuts and prunes.
4. Pour into an oiled 12- x 8-inch baking dish and bake at 375° for 30 minutes or until a knife inserted in the middle comes out clean.

Biscotti d'Anice Gurka
Makes approximately 2 dozen

Lovers of licorice will appreciate these delightful Italian cookies.

1   cup sugar
½   cup margarine
2   eggs
1   tablespoon anise extract
1   tablespoon anise seed
2   tablespoons water, or 2 tablespoons Anisette liqueur
2   cups flour, sifted
1½   teaspoons baking powder
2   cups almonds or walnuts, coarsely chopped

1. Beat the sugar and margarine together until smooth. Beat in the eggs, 1 at a time, and add the anise extract, anise seed, water or Anisette and blend thoroughly.
2. Gradually beat in the flour and baking powder and chill the dough for 2 to 3 hours. The dough should be soft and pliable. If the dough is stiff, add 1 to 2 tablespoons of water, 1 tablespoon at a time until smooth.
3. When thoroughly chilled, shape the dough on a floured board to form a flat loaf ½ inch thick, 2 inches wide, and as long as a cookie sheet. Transfer to the cookie sheet and bake for 20 minutes in a 350° oven.
4. Remove from the oven and cool until it can be handled. Cut in diagonal slices about ¾ inch thick. Place the cookies on a cookie sheet, cut sides up and return to a 375° oven for 13 minutes. Serve cooled.

Spice Cake
Serves 12

No eggs and no oil. The result is a moist, spicy loaf.

1½ cups boiling water
1   teaspoon anise seed
1   cup honey
1¼ cups sugar
3   teaspoons baking soda
4⅓ cups sifted flour
¼   teaspoon salt
1   teaspoon cinnamon
½   teaspoon nutmeg
3   tablespoons candied fruit, chopped
1   teaspoon candied ginger, minced (optional)

1. In a mixing bowl pour the boiling water over the anise seed and set aside to steep for 5 minutes.
2. Add the honey and sugar to the anise water and stir until the sugar is dissolved.
3. Sift the baking soda, flour, salt, cinnamon, and nutmeg together and stir into the liquid. Fold in the candied fruit and ginger.
4. Pour the batter into 2 lightly oiled 9-inch loaf pans and bake at 350° for 1 hour. Cool on a cake rack and slice.

Holiday Filling
Serves 12

The flavors in this filling follow the tradition of a holiday season but any celebration would be an excuse for this outstanding cake filling.

1   cup evaporated skim milk
1   cup sugar
¼   cup cornstarch
⅓   cup bourbon
1   cup nuts, chopped
1   cup raisins
1   cup candied cherries, chopped
1   white angel food, or pound cake

1. Combine milk, sugar, and cornstarch in a saucepan. Bring to a boil, reduce heat, and simmer for 3 minutes or until thickened, stirring constantly.

2. Add the bourbon and bring to a boil once more, stirring.
3. Fold in the nuts, raisins, and candied cherries and mix thoroughly.
4. Split the cake into 3 layers.
5. Cover the layers and top with the mixture. Let the cake stand for at least 1 hour before serving.

Almond Meringue Cookies
Makes 1½ dozen

    2 *egg whites*
   ¼ *teaspoon salt*
   ¾ *cup granulated sugar*
   ½ *teaspoon almond flavoring*
   ¾ *cup almonds, blanched and finely chopped*

1. Preheat the oven to 300°.
2. Beat the egg whites until frothy. Add the salt and continue beating until they form stiff peaks.
3. Gradually beat in the sugar, add the flavoring, and fold in the nuts.
4. Drop by teaspoonfuls onto a lightly oiled cookie sheet.
5. Bake at 300° for 45 minutes. Cool before serving.

Brownies
Makes 16 1-inch squares

These chocolaty brownies are luscious enough to satisfy any sweet tooth.

   ⅓ *cup margarine*
   ¾ *cup sugar*
   ½ *cup dark corn syrup*
   2 *teaspoons vanilla*
   1 *egg*
   ½ *cup flour*
   ⅓ *cup unsweetened cocoa*
   ½ *teaspoon salt*
   ½ *cup nuts, chopped*

1. Beat the margarine and sugar together until creamy. Add the corn syrup and vanilla and continue to beat until smooth.
2. Beat in the egg.
3. Blend flour, cocoa, and salt and add to the batter in 3 portions, beating well after each addition. Fold in the nuts.
4. Pour into an oiled 9-inch square pan and bake at 350° for 25 minutes. Cut into 1-inch squares.

Hermits
Makes 2 dozen

These molasses squares are familiar old favorites.

½ cup margarine
½ cup sugar
½ cup molasses or dark corn syrup
1 egg
2 cups sifted flour
½ teaspoon salt
¼ teaspoon baking soda
2 teaspoons baking powder
1 teaspoon cinnamon
¼ teaspoon nutmeg
¼ teaspoon cloves
¼ teaspoon allspice
½ cup raisins
½ cup nuts, chopped
½ cup powdered sugar
4 tablespoons cold water

1. Beat the margarine and sugar together until creamy. Add the molasses and egg and beat until smooth.
2. Sift the dry ingredients and spices together and add to the batter in 3 equal portions, beating well after each addition.
3. Fold in the raisins and nuts. Pour into an oiled 12- x 8-inch baking dish. Bake in a 350° oven for 30 minutes. If desired, glaze while still warm.
4. Blend ½ cup powdered sugar and 4 tablespoons cold water together and paint glaze on warm cookies.

Nutty Crisps
Makes 3 dozen

1 cup soft margarine
½ cup granulated sugar
1½ cups sifted flour
¼ teaspoon salt
2 teaspoons instant coffee, sifted
¾ cup nuts, finely chopped
confectioners' sugar

1. Beat the margarine and sugar together.
2. Add flour, salt, and instant coffee, Mix well.

3. Mix in the chopped nuts and roll into small balls.
4. Place on a lightly oiled baking sheet in small balls and then flatten with a fork dipped in confectioners' sugar.
5. Bake for 20 to 25 minutes in a 350° oven, until the edges are slightly browned.
6. Remove from oven, cool, and serve.

Dorothy's Oatmeal Cookies
Makes 3 dozen

¾ *cup margarine, melted*
1 *cup brown sugar*
3 *cups oatmeal*
1 *cup flour*
½ *teaspoon salt*
¼ *cup boiling water*
½ *cup chopped nuts (optional)*

1. Pour the melted margarine in a bowl and stir in the sugar.
2. Blend the oatmeal, flour, and salt and mix into the margarine and sugar. Stir in the boiling water and nuts.
3. Drop by spoonfuls onto a lightly oiled or sprayed cookie sheet. Bake in a 350° oven for 8 to 9 minutes.

Old Fashioned Peanut Butter Cookies
Makes about 2 dozen

¾ *cup vegetable oil*
½ *cup brown sugar*
½ *cup molasses or dark corn syrup*
¾ *cup peanut butter*
1 *egg*
2 *cups sifted flour*
¼ *teaspoon salt*
¼ *teaspoon baking soda*
2 *teaspoons baking powder*
½ *cup walnuts or peanuts, chopped*

1. Beat the oil and sugar together until smooth. Add molasses and continue to beat. Add the peanut butter, egg, and beat well.
2. Sift the dry ingredients together and add to the batter in 3 equal portions, beating well after each addition. Fold in the nuts.
3. Drop by large spoonfuls on a lightly oiled cookie sheet and bake at 350° for 12 to 15 minutes until golden brown.

Pie Crust
Makes two 9-inch crusts

The test of the Early American Woman's mettle was her pie crust. According to TV commercials, turning out a flaky pie crust is a feat matched only by the ability to make good coffee. To achieve a light flaky pastry you must observe some basic rules. First, water and shortening must be ice cold. Dough must be worked to develop the gluten, giving it stretchability, but don't overdo it or it will become tough. Keep bowls and ingredients well chilled and cool hands by rinsing in cold water and patting dry if they feel warm or the dough will become rubbery. The amount of water used depends upon the type of flour, temperature, and humidity in the air. Add enough so that the dough holds together but don't let it become moist. Now proceed.

3 cups flour
1 teaspoon salt
8 tablespoons chilled margarine
6 to 7 tablespoons ice water

1. Place the flour and salt in a bowl and cut the margarine into small pieces and toss with the flour. With two knives, a pastry cutter or your fingers, quickly work the margarine into the flour until it is the texture of cornmeal. Add the ice water by tablespoonfuls and toss with the flour until you can gather the dough in a ball. It should hold together but not be too sticky. Add more ice water if needed to hold dough together.
2. Place the ball on a floured surface and with the heel of your hand, not the palm for it is too warm, push the dough forward spreading it out in small pieces. Re-form the dough and do this once more. This promotes the formation of gluten which makes the dough flaky when baked. However, do not knead, just push against a hard surface. Re-form into a ball. Press your finger into the ball. If the hole stays open dough can be rolled out in 15 minutes. If it closes it should stand for a longer time. If time permits, let all dough stand overnight preferably in the refrigerator. Unused dough can be frozen. If dough is hard when it is taken out of the refrigerator, beat it with a rolling pin to soften rather than let it warm at room temperature.

Graham Cracker Crust
Makes one 9-inch crust

1½ cups graham cracker crumbs, finely ground
6　tablespoons melted margarine
¼　cup sugar

1   teaspoon cinnamon (optional)
almonds, ground (optional)
ginger snaps crumbs (optional)

1. Grind the graham crackers in a blender or place between 2 sheets of waxed paper and crush with a rolling pin.
2. Melt margarine and combine with crumbs and sugar.
3. Press evenly into a 9-inch pie plate. Fit another pie plate over the top and press it down firmly. This will make an even crust. Crust may be flavored with cinnamon. Ground almonds or ginger snaps may be substituted for part of or combined with, the graham crackers. If they are used, decrease the amount of graham cracker crumbs so that total measures 1½ cups.

Davis Pie
Serves 8

1 9-inch Chocolate Graham Cracker Crust, baked and cooled
3 cups vanilla ice milk, slightly softened
2 cups fresh berries or sliced peaches
2 tablespoons sugar
1 tablespoon Kirsch or orange liqueur (optional)

1. Spread the cooked pie crust with the softened ice milk. Freeze until ready to serve.
2. Toss the fruit with the sugar and liqueur.
3. Just before serving, cover the ice milk pie with the fruit. Slice into wedges and serve.

Chocolate Graham Cracker Crust
Makes 1 crust

This crust can be the underpinning for any creamy type filling.

2 cups graham crackers, finely crushed
¼ cup sugar
2 tablespoons margarine
3 tablespoons vegetable oil
2 tablespoons cocoa

1. Combine the graham crackers and sugar.
2. Melt the margarine in a saucepan and add the oil. Stir in the graham cracker crumbs and cocoa. Blend thoroughly. Spread evenly on a lightly oiled pie pan and add desired filling. May be precooked in a 350° oven for 15 to 20 minutes or until set, if filling is not to be baked.

Buttermilk Pie
Serves 8

Smooth, elegant, and unbelievably good.

1 *9-inch pastry shell*
⅓ *cup margarine*
¾ *cup sugar*
3 *egg equivalents*
⅔ *cup buttermilk*
2 *teaspoons vanilla*

1. Preheat oven to 350°.
2. Beat the margarine and sugar together until smooth.
3. Add the egg equivalents, beat well. Beat the buttermilk and add the vanilla.
4. Pour into the pie shell and bake in the preheated oven for 40 minutes. The filling will puff up and brown, and then deflate while cooking.

Velvet Cheese Pie
Serves 8

This exquisite dessert is reminiscent of cheese cake.

1 *pound ricotta cheese*
2 *egg equivalents*
½ *teaspoon salt*
¾ *cup evaporated skim milk*
½ *cup sugar*
3 *tablespoons cornstarch*
1 *teaspoon lemon juice*
2 *egg whites*
1 *9-inch deep pie shell*

1. Preheat oven to 325°.
2. Combine the cheese, egg equivalents, salt, and about ¼ of the milk and blend thoroughly. Add the rest of the milk and the sugar and beat until creamy.
3. Add the cornstarch and lemon juice and beat thoroughly. Set aside.
4. Beat the egg whites until stiff but not dry. Gently fold into the cheese mixture.
5. Pour the mixture into the prepared pie shell and bake for 1 hour. Cool thoroughly and serve.

Lemon-Lime Chiffon Pie
Serves 6

Tangy and refreshing, this pie keeps well.

> 1   *3-ounce package lemon gelatin dessert*
> ½   *cup sugar*
> 1   *cup boiling water*
> ½   *cup lemon juice*
> ½   *cup lime juice*
> 1   *cup cold water*
> 2   *tablespoons lemon juice*
> 1   *cup nonfat dry milk powder*
> *9-inch baked pie crust*

1. Mix gelatin, sugar, and boiling water in a large bowl. Stir until dissolved.
2. Add the lemon and lime juices and chill till slightly thicker than unbeaten egg whites.
3. Blend 1 cup very cold water, 2 tablespoons lemon juice, and 1 cup nonfat dry milk powder. Beat on high speed about 6 minutes.
4. Beat gelatin mixture separately until *very* foamy, at least 4 to 5 minutes.
5. Blend in the whipped milk. Pile into the pie crust and refrigerate. Serve when firm.

Pineapple Cheese Pie
Serves 8

> 8   *ounces low-fat Neufchâtel cheese*
> 8   *ounces low-fat vanilla yogurt*
> 4   *tablespoons sugar*
> 1   *teaspoon unflavored gelatin*
> 1   *8-ounce can crushed pineapple*
> 1   *Graham Cracker Crust*

1. Blend the cheese, yogurt, and sugar in a blender until smooth.
2. Add the gelatin to 4 ounces of the pineapple juice and heat in a saucepan until dissolved. Add to the blender and beat until smooth.
3. Drain the remaining juice from the pineapple.
4. Pour the cheese mixture into the prepared crust and spoon the pineapple on top. Chill thoroughly before serving.

Apple Tart
Serves 6

    2 *large tart apples, sliced*
    2 *tablespoons lemon juice*
    1 *teaspoon vanilla*
    1 *9-inch pastry shell (see page 292), uncooked*
    2 *tablespoons apricot preserves*
    1 *tablespoon sugar*
    2 *tablespoons water*

1. Preheat oven to 350°.
2. Peel, core, and slice the apples. Place in a flat dish and toss with the lemon juice and vanilla. Let sit for 20 minutes, turning occasionally.
3. Arrange the apple slices in the pastry shell.
4. Combine the preserves, sugar, and water in a saucepan and heat until the sugar dissolves. Brush the apples with the sauce and place in a 350° oven for 1 hour. Brush occasionally with the glaze.
5. Turn the oven to 400° and bake for 15 minutes more and remove from the oven. Let cool before serving.

Pear Tart
Serves 8

    1 *sweet pastry shell*
    1 *tablespoon sugar*
    1 *pound firm pears, peeled, cored and sliced*
    3 *tablespoons sugar*
    1 *tablespoon flour*
    2 *tablespoons melted margarine*
    1 *egg or egg substitute*
    2 *tablespoons rum*

1. Prepare a sweet pastry shell by adding 1 tablespoon of sugar to the basic recipe (see page 292). Or, use a regular pastry shell and double the sugar in the next step.
2. Sprinkle the shell with 1 tablespoon sugar. Arrange the pear slices in the pastry shell.
3. Combine the remaining sugar, flour, melted margarine, egg or egg substitute, and rum. Pour over the pears.
4. Bake 30 to 40 minutes in a 350° oven or until pears are tender. Cool and slice.

Cherries Jubilee
Serves 8

This spectacular dessert is easy to prepare and low in cholesterol if ice milk is used.

2   *tablespoons margarine*
2   *tablespoons sugar*
1   *teaspoon orange rind or zest, grated*
1   *teaspoon lemon rind or zest, grated*
¼   *cup lemon juice*
¼   *cup orange juice*
¼   *cup Kirsch*
3   *cups Bing cherries, pitted and drained*
¼   *cup brandy, warmed*
vanilla ice milk

1. Melt the margarine in a chafing dish and stir in the sugar. Heat until bubbly. Add orange and lemon rind or zest. Simmer until it turns a pale gold color.
2. Stir in the juices and heat until bubbly again. Add the Kirsch and cherries and stir for 1 minute.
3. Warm the brandy. Do not boil. Spoon over the top of the sauce and ignite. Serve over ice milk while flaming.

Fruit Ambrosia
Serves 8

Add any fresh fruit to this ambrosia and serve well chilled.

2   *ripe peaches, peeled and sliced*
1   *cup pineapple cubes*
2   *cups strawberries*
1   *cup seedless grapes*
1   *cup raspberries*
2   *oranges, peeled, seeded, and sliced*
3   *tablespoons sugar*
1   *tablespoon Kirsch or orange liqueur (optional)*

1. Place all the fruit in a bowl and toss with the sugar and liqueur.
2. Chill thoroughly and serve plain or with fruit sherbet or Angel Food Cake.

Apple Crisp
Serves 6

6   tart, green apples, peeled, cored and sliced
¾ cup sugar
¼ teaspoon ground cloves
1   teaspoon cinnamon
⅛ teaspoon ground nutmeg
2   teaspoons lemon juice
¾ cup sifted flour
dash of salt
6   tablespoons margarine, cold
⅓ cup nuts, chopped
ice milk (optional)
nondairy creamer (optional)
Vanilla Sauce (optional)

1. Place the sliced apples in a bowl and toss with ⅓ cup of the sugar, all the cloves, cinnamon, nutmeg, and lemon juice. Arrange in a shallow baking dish.
2. Place the remaining sugar, flour, salt, and margarine in a bowl. Cut the margarine into pieces and with a fork work into the dry ingredients until crumbly. Toss with the nuts.
3. Spread the crumb mixture over the apples and bake in a 350° oven for 45 minutes or until the apples are tender and the crumb topping has lightly browned. Can be served cold or warm with ice milk, nondairy creamer, or Vanilla Sauce (see Saucery).

Banana Peanut Jumble
Serves 4

1   tablespoon vinegar
½ cup water
2   tablespoons cornstarch
¼ cup sugar
1   egg equivalent
3   cold bananas
1   cup salted Spanish peanuts

1. Combine vinegar, water, cornstarch, and sugar in a saucepan. Stir over low heat until it boils and becomes thick and transparent.
2. Add the egg equivalent and stir thoroughly. Chill. It will be quite thick.

3. Slice the bananas in a bowl and mix in the peanuts. Pour dressing over this mixture, stir gently, and serve.

Banana Flambé
Serves 4

> 4 *bananas*
> 1 *tablespoon lime juice*
> 2 *tablespoons margarine*
> ½ *cup brown sugar, sifted*
> ½ *teaspoon cinnamon*
> ½ *teaspoon cloves*
> 1½ *teaspoons orange rind, grated*
> ½ *cup rum, light or medium*

1. Peel and slice the bananas in half lengthwise, sprinkle with lime juice.
2. Melt the margarine in a saucepan and sauté the bananas over low to medium heat for 5 minutes, turning the bananas on each side.
3. Mix the sugar with the spices and sprinkle over the bananas. Cook until the sugar dissolves.
4. Warm the rum and pour over the bananas. Set a match to the rum in the pan (long fireplace matches are good for this) and move the pan around to ignite all the rum. Serve while still flaming.

Hot Spiced Fruit Compote
Serves 4

Just the thing for a chilly morning. This can be prepared in advance and heated just before serving.

> 1 *pound mixed dried fruit (apricots, pears, prunes, apples)*
> 2 *oranges, peeled and seeded*
> 1 *cup raisins*
> 1 *teaspoon cinnamon or a cinnamon stick*
> 3 *whole cloves*
> ¼ *cup sugar*
> 8 *cups water*

1. Cut large pieces of fruit in half. Place fruit, spices, sugar, and water in a large saucepan.
2. Bring to a boil, then reduce heat to a simmer and cook for 1 hour or until fruit is tender.
3. Remove cinnamon stick and cloves. Serve hot.

Peaches Cardinale
Serves 6

> 6   cups water
> 2   cups sugar
> 3   tablespoons vanilla extract or ½-inch piece vanilla bean
> 6   large ripe peaches, peeled, halved, and stoned
> 2   10-ounce packages of frozen raspberries, defrosted and drained
> 2   tablespoons superfine sugar
> 1   tablespoon Kirsch
> ¾   cup vanilla ice milk, softened
> ½   teaspoon vanilla
> Sauce Cardinale (see Saucery)
> ½   cup whole fresh raspberries (optional)

1. Bring the water and sugar to a boil in a large saucepan, stirring until the sugar dissolves. Boil for about 3 minutes and then reduce the heat to a simmer. Add the vanilla or bean.
2. Add the peaches and poach them, uncovered, over very low heat for 10 to 20 minutes or until barely tender. Do not let them become mushy. Remove vanilla bean if used. Refrigerate in the syrup until chilled.
3. Purée the raspberries in a blender and strain or force through a sieve. Heat in a saucepan and add the sugar. Simmer until sugar dissolves and add Kirsch. Cool.
4. Whip the ice milk slightly with the vanilla.
5. Drain the peaches with a slotted spoon and place in serving bowl or champagne glass. Cover with Sauce Cardinale and garnish with ice milk. Garnish with fresh whole raspberries if available.

Pears Helene
Serves 6

The lady Helene, whoever she was, is owed a debt of gratitude for inspiring this superb creation.

> ⅔   cup sugar
> 1   cup water
> ¼   teaspoon cream of tartar
> 1   teaspoon lemon juice
> 6   firm pears, peeled and cored
> Chocolate Sauce (see Saucery)
> vanilla ice milk
> ground almonds

1. Combine sugar, water, cream of tartar, and lemon juice in a saucepan. Bring to a slow boil and reduce heat to moderate.
2. Add pears and poach in syrup until soft, about 20 to 25 minutes. Remove with a slotted spoon and cool. Syrup may be reused for other fruits or used on French toast, pancakes, etc.
3. Warm the Chocolate Sauce.
4. Place a pear on a flattened scoop of ice milk and cover with Chocolate Sauce. Sprinkle with ground almonds and serve.

Pears Poached in Red Wine
Serves 4

    4 *pears, firm and ripe*
    1 *cup water*
    1 *tablespoon lemon juice*
    2 *cups red wine, Bordeaux type (claret)*
    2 *tablespoons lemon juice*
    ¾ *cup sugar*
    1 *stick cinnamon or ½ teaspoon powdered cinnamon*

1. Peel and core the pears and slice in halves. Place in a cup of water mixed with 1 tablespoon lemon juice until ready to poach. This prevents them from discoloring.
2. Bring the wine, lemon juice, sugar, and cinnamon to a boil.
3. Drain the pears and place in the wine syrup. Reduce the heat to a simmer and cook for 10 minutes or until the pears are tender. Do not overcook as they will fall apart as you remove them from the syrup.
4. When done remove with a skimmer or slotted spoon and serve with 2 tablespoons of the syrup. They may be served warm or chilled.

Fennel

Chocolate Pudding
Serves 4

Do not let this boil or you will have chocolate scrambled eggs.

> 3 *egg equivalents*
> ⅓ *cup cocoa*
> ½ *cup sugar*
> 1 *teaspoon vanilla*
> 2 *cups low-fat milk*

1. Combine the egg equivalents, cocoa, sugar, and vanilla in a saucepan and blend until smooth. Stir in the milk.
2. Place over low heat and cook for 5 to 6 minutes until thick and smooth. Stir continuously but **do not** let it come near the boil or the eggs will curdle.
3. Pour into individual dishes and chill thoroughly.

Persimmon Pudding
Serves 6

Many people are unfamiliar with this beautifully colored fruit which can be used only when very ripe. The fruit must be mushy or there will be a bitter taste. When ripe they are divine, whether peeled and eaten right off the tree or prepared in this delicious steamed pudding.

> 1 *cup persimmon pulp, about 3 large fruits*
> 1 *cup brown sugar*
> 1 *cup flour*
> 1 *tablespoon baking soda*
> 1 *teaspoon cinnamon*
> 1 *teaspoon nutmeg*
> 1 *teaspoon ginger*
> 1 *teaspoon vanilla*
> ½ *cup low-fat milk*
> 1 *tablespoon melted margarine*
> ½ *cup walnuts, chopped*
> ½ *cup raisins*
> *boiling water*
> *Lemon Sauce (see Saucery)*

1. Peel the persimmons and mash the pulp. Set aside.
2. Combine the sugar, flour, baking soda, spices, and blend well.

3. Stir in the vanilla and milk and mix thoroughly. Add remaining ingredients and persimmon pulp. Stir until thoroughly mixed.
4. Pour into a lightly oiled pudding mold or small covered casserole. Smooth the top and cover.
5. Set it in a large covered pot on a rack and fill half way with boiling water. Cover pot and steam for 1 hour.
6. Cool slightly, unmold, and serve with Lemon Sauce.

Coffee Ice
Serves 4

Try this light refreshing dessert after a full meal.

> 4 cups strong drip coffee
> 6 tablespoons sugar
> 1 tablespoon rum or coffee liqueur (optional)
> Whipped Topping (see Saucery)

1. Heat the coffee and sugar until the sugar has dissolved. Add the flavoring if desired. Place in an ice tray or cake pan and freeze.
2. Serve in chilled bowls or wide, shallow glasses with Whipped Topping.

Water Ices
Serves 8

A tart fruit ice is a perfect end to a heavy meal or a refreshing break on a hot afternoon.

> 2   cups sugar
> 1½ cups water
> ¼   teaspoon cream of tartar
> ½   cup lime juice, or 1 cup lemon juice
> few drops of food coloring if desired
> 1   egg white (optional)

1. Combine the sugar, water, and cream of tartar in a saucepan and bring to a boil. Reduce heat and simmer for 5 minutes. Stir in the juice and food coloring and freeze in an ice tray.
2. Remove from the tray and beat for 5 minutes and refreeze. Beat one more time, refreeze, and serve in iced sherbet glasses. For a creamier texture, whip one egg white to stiff peaks and fold in before final beating.

Orange Sherbet
Serves 12

The method is the same for iced lemon meringue but the resulting texture is
that of sherbet.

2   *cups sugar*
⅔ *cup water*
½ *teaspoon cream of tartar*
8   *egg whites*
2   *cups fresh orange juice*
orange food coloring (optional)

1. Place the sugar, water, and ¼ teaspoon of the cream of tartar in a
    saucepan and bring to a boil. Reduce heat slightly and when the liquid is
    clear reduce heat and simmer for 5 minutes.
2. Beat the egg whites until foamy at low speed. Add the remaining cream
    of tartar. Gradually increase speed and beat until stiff peaks begin to
    form.
3. Pour the sugar syrup into the egg whites in a slow, steady stream.
    Continue beating for 8 to 10 minutes or until the mixture is very stiff and
    glossy. Beat in the orange juice gradually. Add the food coloring if
    desired. Pour into a shallow dish and freeze until partially set.
4. When partially frozen beat for 5 minutes and refreeze. Beat one more
    time, then freeze until ready to serve.

Plum Ice Milk
Serves 8

Simply delicious and so easy.

2   *large egg whites*
¼ *teaspoon cream of tartar*
¼ *cup sugar*
⅓ *cup light corn syrup*
2   *cups low-fat milk*
10 *ounces plum preserves*
juice of 1 lemon

1. Beat the egg whites until foamy on a low speed. Add the cream of tartar and gradually increase the speed and beat until stiff and glossy. Do not overbeat.
2. While beating, add the sugar gradually, and then add the corn syrup and milk.
3. Beat in the preserves and lemon juice and pour into a shallow dish or tray and freeze. Beat again until smooth and refreeze. Beat once more and when firm, serve.

Iced Lemon Meringue
Serves 12

This light, delicate concoction can be served in a fluffy mound with only a sprig of mint for adornment, or surrounded by big luscious strawberries, chunks of juicy pineapple, a purée of raspberries flavored with Kirsch or freshly picked blueberries.

  2   cups sugar
  ⅔ cup water
  ½ teaspoon cream of tartar
  8   egg whites
  ¾ to 1 cup lemon juice

1. Place the sugar, water, and ¼ teaspoon of the cream of tartar in a saucepan and bring to a boil. Reduce heat slightly and when the liquid is clear, reduce heat and simmer for 5 minutes.
2. Beat the egg whites until foamy at low speed. Add the remaining cream of tartar. Gradually increase speed and beat until stiff peaks begin to form.
3. Pour the sugar syrup into the egg whites in a slow steady stream while beating. Continue beating for 8 to 10 minutes or until meringue is very stiff and glossy. Beat in ½ cup lemon juice, taste, and add more juice until you have the desired tartness. Pour into a shallow dish and freeze until partially set.
4. When partially frozen beat for 5 minutes and refreeze. Beat one more time then freeze until ready to serve.

Rita's Rice Pudding
Serves 6

4   cups low-fat milk
¼   cup raw rice
¼   teaspoon salt
¼   cup sugar
1   teaspoon vanilla
dash nutmeg, grated
½   cup seedless raisins
½   cup nondairy creamer

1. Preheat the oven to 300°.
2. Stir the milk, rice, salt, and sugar in a saucepan over low heat until the milk scalds. Stir in the vanilla and nutmeg.
3. Pour into a shallow baking dish and bake uncovered for 2 hours. Stir every ½ hour and if the pudding seems to cook too quickly, reduce the oven heat.
4. After 2 hours stir in the raisins and nondairy creamer and continue to bake an additional 30 minutes or until the rice is very tender. Serve warm or cold.

18
The Breadbasket

BREAD BAKING IS a touch of reality in a world full of prepackaged, precooked, and sterilized foods. Baking bread is a soul-satisfying experience which arouses the senses. Share the excitement of bread baking with the whole family. Introduce them to the joys of watching the yeast come alive and bubble, the rhythmic kneading of the dough, the suspense of waiting for the dough to rise and finally the incredible aroma wafting through the kitchen as it bakes.

Not all breads demand long periods of kneading, and quick breads require none at all. Some electric mixers are equipped with dough hooks to lighten the job. Remember that yeast is alive, remaining dormant below 80° F. and is killed at temperatures above 110° F. There are several methods of adding yeast to the dough; all work, but some cut down on the steps required. Experiment with different tastes and textures by blending flours. White flour gives the lightest dough, rye the heaviest. Onions, seeds, and herbs can also be added for intriguing tastes.

Some afternoon make your family proud, be the envy of your friends, and do something good for your spirit. Bake your own bread.

Apple Muffins
Serves 6

2   cups sifted all-purpose flour
4   teaspoons double-acting baking powder
6   tablespoons margarine, very cold
¼   cup white sugar
1   teaspoon cinnamon
½   cup applesauce
1   apple, peeled, and grated
¼   cup low-fat milk
1   egg, lightly beaten
2   tablespoons vegetable oil

TOPPING:

¼   cup sugar
2   teaspoons cinnamon
2   tablespoons melted margarine

1. Sift the flour and baking powder into mixing bowl. With 2 knives, pastry cutter, or your fingers, cut in margarine until mixture is well mixed and mealy in texture.
2. Add ¼ cup sugar and cinnamon. Stir in applesauce, grated apple, milk, egg, and oil. Beat well for ½ minute.
3. Lightly oil muffin pans. Fill two-thirds full with batter. Bake at 400° for 20 minutes or until golden. Cool slightly; remove from pans.
4. Make topping: Mix the second ¼ cup sugar and rest of cinnamon. Dip tops of muffins in melted margarine; then in sugar-cinnamon mix.

Ice-Box Bran Muffins
Makes 24 to 30 muffins

2   cups boiling water
2   cups All-Bran
2   eggs, slightly beaten
2   cups buttermilk, cultured type
½   cup vegetable oil
1   cup raisins, or chopped dried fruits (apricots, dates, figs, prunes)
5   teaspoons baking soda
1   teaspoon salt
2   cups unsifted flour
1   cup sugar
3   cups 40% Bran flakes

1. In a large bowl, pour boiling water over bran, stir, let stand until cool. Beat eggs, buttermilk, oil, and raisins together and blend into bran mixture.
2. Mix soda, salt, flour, sugar, and bran flakes together. Stir into wet mixture and lightly blend.
3. Dough can be baked immediately or refrigerated in tightly covered container as long as 2 weeks. Stir batter to evenly distribute fruit before using.
4. Spoon batter into lightly oiled muffin cups, filling two-thirds full. Bake at 350° for 25 to 30 minutes.

Raisin Scones
Serves 10

Bannock, scone, or farl, these Scotch biscuits are delicious by any name. They are best served hot with lots of jam and margarine.

2	*cups flour*
2½	*teaspoons baking powder*
¼	*teaspoon baking soda*
½	*teaspoon salt*
2	*tablespoons sugar*
¼	*cup margarine*
1	*egg*
¾	*cup buttermilk*
1	*egg white*
¾	*cup dates, apricots, nuts or currants (optional)*

1. Preheat the oven to 425°.
2. Combine the flour, baking powder, baking soda, salt, and sugar in a mixing bowl. Do not sift.
3. Add the margarine and cut it into the dry ingredients with a pastry cutter, 2 knives or your fingers until mealy.
4. Lightly beat the egg and add the buttermilk. Mix well and add to the dough. Beat vigorously with a fork until the dough pulls away from the bowl.
5. Turn out on a floured surface and press into a circle, ½ inch thick. Cut into wedges, called farls, or cut circles with a drinking glass. If left whole it is called a bannock. Brush the tops with egg white.
6. Place on a cookie sheet and bake in a preheated oven for 20 minutes.

Variations: Add chopped dates, apricots, nuts, or currants to the batter before baking.

Crumpets
Serves 6

Use open cookie molds or tuna fish cans with tops and bottoms removed to shape these delicious British imports. Be sure to serve them warm.

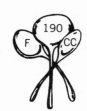

    1 package active dry yeast
    1 teaspoon sugar
    ¼ cup warm water, between 100 and 110°
    ⅓ cup low-fat milk
    1 egg
    1 tablespoon melted margarine
    1 cup flour
    ½ teaspoon salt
    2 tablespoons margarine

1. Combine the yeast, sugar, and water in a bowl and let stand for 5 minutes. Add the milk, egg, margarine and blend well. Add the flour and salt and beat lightly until smooth.
2. Cover and let rise in a warm place for approximately 45 minutes or until the batter has doubled and is foamy.
3. Melt 1 tablespoon margarine in a large heavy-bottomed skillet.
4. Lightly oil the molds and heat them in the skillet. A large skillet will hold approximately 5. When the molds are hot, pour about 3 tablespoons of batter into each mold and let cook for about 7 minutes. When the crumpet is riddled with holes and dry on top remove the mold and turn the crumpets. Brown lightly on the underside and place on a cookie sheet. Use the remaining tablespoon of margarine and cook the rest of the batter.
5. Place the cooked crumpets under the broiler or toast until slightly crisp.

Coffee Can Bread
Serves 8

This is for beginning bread bakers. No kneading is required.

    1 package active dry yeast
    ½ cup warm water, between 85 and 110°
    1 tablespoon sugar
    1 cup evaporated skim milk
    2 tablespoons sugar
    1 teaspoon salt
    ⅛ teaspoon ginger
    2 tablespoons vegetable oil

4   *cups flour (white or half white and half rye or wheat)*
2-pound coffee can, or 2 1-pound cans

1. Combine yeast, water, and sugar and mix well in a small bowl.
2. Combine the milk, sugar, salt, ginger, and vegetable oil and beat well. When the yeast mixture is bubbly, add it to the milk mixture.
3. Add 1 cup of flour at a time and beat well. Dough should be sticky but stand on its own. Add more flour if necessary.
4. Pour into a well-oiled coffee can and let rise in a warm place until it has doubled, approximately 1 hour.
5. Bake in a 350° oven for approximately 1 hour. Do not preheat the oven. This gives a little extra rise to the bread. Bread is done when it sounds hollow when tapped.

Dilly Bread
Serves 12

This is one of the best breads you will ever make.

1   *package active dry yeast*
2   *tablespoons sugar*
¼   *cup warm water*
1   *cup creamed cottage cheese, heated to lukewarm*
2   *tablespoons dry minced onion*
1   *tablespoon margarine*
2   *teaspoons dill seed*
1   *teaspoon salt*
¼   *teaspoon baking soda*
1   *egg, unbeaten*
2½ *cups white flour*
1   *tablespoon softened margarine*
2   *teaspoons coarse salt*

1. Dissolve yeast and sugar in warm water.
2. In a mixing bowl combine cottage cheese, onion, margarine, dill seed, salt, baking soda, egg, and yeast mixture.
3. Add flour gradually to form a stiff dough, beating well after each addition. Cover dough with a warm, wet dish towel and let rise in warm place until doubled in size, about 1½ hours.
4. Punch down and knead the dough for 5 minutes. Place in an oiled loaf or baking pan. Cover and let rise in warm place 30 minutes.
5. Bake at 350° for 40 to 45 minutes until browned. Brush with soft margarine and sprinkle with coarse salt.

Boston Brown Bead
Serves 10

Brown bread is a gift to us from the Puritans. Traditionally, it is served with baked beans but it is good any time and can be varied with dates, nuts, or chopped prunes.

1	*cup cornmeal*
1	*cup rye flour*
1	*cup graham flour*
1½	*teaspoons baking soda*
1	*teaspoon salt*
2	*cups buttermilk*
¾	*cup molasses*
1	*cup chopped fruit, and/or nuts*

1. Combine the dry ingredients in a bowl. Mix the buttermilk, molasses, and fruit and blend thoroughly.
2. Add the liquid to the dry ingredients and stir until moistened.
3. Pour the batter into oiled coffee cans, or steamed pudding molds and cover tightly with foil. Place on a rack in a steamer or roasting pan. Add 1 inch of water and cover the pan. Use foil if a cover is not available. Steam for 2½ to 3 hours or until firm. Do not let the water evaporate during steaming. Add additional water if necessary. Cool before serving.

Corn Bread
Serves 8

A heavy cast-iron skillet will give best results.

½	*cup sifted flour*
2½	*teaspoons double-acting baking powder*
1½	*tablespoons sugar*
¾	*teaspoon salt*
1½	*cups water ground cornmeal, yellow or white*
1	*egg*
3	*tablespoons melted margarine*
¾	*cup low-fat milk*

1. Preheat oven to 425°.
2. Sift the flour, baking powder, sugar, salt, and cornmeal together.
3. Lightly beat the egg and add the melted margarine and milk. Beat thoroughly. Rapidly stir this into the dry ingredients. Blend well.

4. Oil a skillet and heat in the oven until a sprinkle of water dances on top.
5. Pour corn bread batter into the heated skillet and bake in the preheated oven for 25 minutes. Serve hot.

Date Nut Bread
Serves 12

The official testers all gave this one four gold stars.

1½ cups sugar
1   cup vegetable oil
2   eggs
1   teaspoon vanilla extract
2   cups flour, sifted
1   teaspoon baking soda
1   teaspoon cinnamon
½   teaspoon salt
1   cup buttermilk
1   cup nuts, chopped
1   cup dates, pitted and chopped

TOPPING:
¼   cup buttermilk
¼   cup sugar
2   tablespoons margarine
¼   teaspoon baking soda
¼   teaspoon vanilla extract

1. In mixing bowl, beat sugar and oil together. Add eggs one at a time, beating well after each addition. Add vanilla and blend well.
2. Sift flour, soda, cinnamon, and salt together. Add to sugar-egg mixture alternately with buttermilk, ending with flour.
3. Fold in nuts and dates.
4. Bake in a lightly oiled 9-inch square pan for 1 hour at 325°, or until a knife inserted in the middle comes out clean. Frost while warm. It is important to use a large enough pan.
5. Combine all topping ingredients in saucepan and stir over low heat until sugar is dissolved.
6. Continue cooking without stirring until it forms a soft ball when a teaspoonful is dropped into cold water.
7. Poke holes in the cake with a small skewer or knife. Pour icing over the cake slowly until it is absorbed.

Banana Nut Bread
Serves 12

The bananas should not merely be soft or ripe but dark brown, one day away from being tossed out. Then they are perfect for this old favorite.

2   *cups flour*
½   *teaspoon baking powder*
½   *teaspoon baking soda*
½   *teaspoon salt*
¼   *cup margarine*
¾   *cup sugar*
1   *egg, well beaten*
¾   *cup **ripe** bananas, large*
3   *tablespoons buttermilk*
½   *cup nuts, chopped*

1. Sift the flour, baking powder, baking soda, and salt together.
2. Beat the margarine and sugar together until creamy, add the egg and blend thoroughly.
3. Mash the bananas and add to the creamed mixture.
4. Add the dry ingredients alternating with the buttermilk in 3 equal portions, blending thoroughly after each addition. Fold in the nuts.
5. Pour the mixture into a well oiled loaf pan and bake in a 350° oven for approximately 1 hour or until a knife inserted in the center comes out clean.

Carrot Bread
Serves 12

¾   *cup white sugar*
2   *eggs, slightly beaten*
1   *cup vegetable oil*
1   *teaspoon vanilla*
1½ *cups (all-purpose) flour, sifted*
1½ *teaspoons baking soda*
1½ *teaspoons cinnamon*
½   *teaspoon salt*
1½ *cups carrots, grated (about 3 large)*
1½ *cups walnuts, chopped*
½   *cup confectioners' sugar*

1   *tablespoon lemon juice*
1   *teaspoon lemon rind, grated*

1. In large mixing bowl, combine sugar, eggs, oil, and vanilla and beat well.
2. Sift together the flour, baking soda, cinnamon, and salt. Add to sugar mixture.
3. Stir in carrots and nuts. Mix until just blended. **Do not beat.**
4. Turn into lightly oiled and floured 9- x 5- x 3-inch loaf pan. Bake at 350° for 1 hour or until a knife inserted in the center comes out clean.
5. Cool in pan for 10 minutes and turn out onto cake rack. Cool completely.
6. In small bowl combine confectioners' sugar and lemon juice and rind. Stir until smooth. Add a small amount of water if necessary. Drizzle over top and sides of cooled carrot bread.

Gingerbread
Serves 8

1¾   *cups flour*
¼   *teaspoon salt*
½   *teaspoon baking soda*
½   *teaspoon cinnamon*
¾   *teaspoon ginger*
½   *teaspoon allspice*
½   *cup melted margarine*
½   *cup brown sugar*
1   *egg*
½   *cup molasses*
½   *cup plus 2 tablespoons buttermilk*
1   *tablespoon powdered sugar (optional)*
applesauce (optional)

1. Sift the flour, salt, baking soda and spices together.
2. Beat the margarine and brown sugar together until fluffy and add the egg. Beat well and add the molasses. Continue beating for 2 minutes.
3. Add the flour mixture and buttermilk in 3 equal portions, beginning and ending with the flour. Blend thoroughly after each addition.
4. Pour into a lightly oiled 8-inch square pan and bake in a 350° oven for 30 minutes. Cut into squares. Serve warm or cooled. May be sprinkled with powdered sugar or served with freshly made applesauce.

Caraway Tea Loaf
Serves 12

This is a winner for Sunday brunch, afternoon tea, or dessert any time.

½   *cup margarine*
¾   *cup sugar*
2   *egg equivalents*
1½ *cups flour*
1½ *teaspoons baking powder*
1   *teaspoon salt*
½   *cup low-fat milk*
2   *teaspoons caraway seeds*

1. Beat the margarine with the sugar until thick and smooth.
2. Add the egg equivalents and beat well.
3. Sift the flour, baking powder, and salt and add in 3 portions, alternating with the low-fat milk, beating well after each addition. Stir in the caraway seeds.
4. Pour into a lightly oiled or sprayed loaf pan and bake in a 350° oven 45 minutes or until a knife inserted in the center comes out clean.
5. Invert on a cake rack and slice when cool.

Fruit-Flavored Oatmeal Bread
Serves 12

1   *cup raisins or pitted, chopped dates*
¼   *cup margarine*
1   *cup boiling water*
1½   *tablespoons orange or lemon peel, grated (or ½ of each)*
1   *cup orange juice*
2   *eggs, lightly beaten*
2   *cups unsifted flour*
2   *cups rolled oats (regular or quick-cooking)*
⅔   *cup white sugar*
2   *teaspoons baking soda*
2   *teaspoons baking powder*
1   *teaspoon salt*
1   *cup walnuts, chopped*

1. Place raisins or dates in a small bowl with margarine. Add boiling water. Stir until margarine has melted. Cool to room temperature.

2. Stir in orange or lemon peel, juice, and eggs.
3. In large mixing bowl, combine flour, oats, sugar, soda, baking powder, salt, and nuts. Add fruit and water mixture and stir just until well moistened.
4. Pour into lightly oiled and floured 9- x 5-inch loaf pan. Bake in 350° oven for 1 hour and 20 minutes or until a knife inserted in the center comes out clean.
5. Cool in pans 10 minutes; then, turn out on a rack and cool thoroughly before slicing.

Oatmeal Bread
Serves 12

This moist bread is more like a coffee cake.

⅓ cup vegetable oil
¾ cup sugar
1 egg
1¼ cups applesauce
¼ cup low-fat milk
1¼ cups sifted flour
1 teaspoon salt
1 teaspoon baking powder
1 teaspoon baking soda
½ teaspoon cinnamon
¼ teaspoon nutmeg
1 cup quick-cooking oats
½ cup raisins
2 tablespoons brown sugar, firmly packed
1 tablespoon margarine
3 tablespoons pecans, chopped
¼ teaspoon cinnamon

1. Beat the oil and sugar together until creamy and add egg and applesauce, beating well.
2. Sift the flour, salt, baking powder, baking soda, cinnamon, and nutmeg together and add in 3 equal portions alternately with the milk until well blended. Stir in the oats and raisins.
3. Pour the batter into an oiled 9-inch loaf pan. Mix the sugar, margarine, nuts, and cinnamon together and spread on top.
4. Bake for 1 hour at 350° or until a knife inserted in the center comes out clean. Cool and slice in ½-inch slices.

Honey Tea Bread
Serves 12

¼   *cup margarine*
1   *egg*
1   *cup honey*
2½   *cups flour, sifted*
2½   *teaspoons baking powder*
½   *teaspoon baking soda*
½   *teaspoon salt*
¾   *cup low-fat milk*
¾   *·cup nuts (walnuts or pecans), chopped*

1. In large mixing bowl, whip margarine until creamy. Add egg and honey and blend thoroughly.
2. Sift dry ingredients together, twice, and add to the egg mixture alternating with the milk in 3 equal portions. Stir until just mixed together. Fold in chopped nuts.
3. Pour into lightly oiled and floured 9-inch loaf pan. Bake at 325° for 1 hour and 10 minutes, or until a knife inserted in the center comes out clean. Cool in pan on wire rack for 5 minutes. Turn out of pan and cool completely.

Nut Bread
Serves 12

2   *cups flour*
1   *teaspoon baking powder*
1   *teaspoon baking soda*
1   *teaspoon salt*
1   *teaspoon cinnamon*
1   *egg*
1   *cup brown sugar, firmly packed*
4   *tablespoons melted margarine*
1   *cup buttermilk*
2   *cups nuts, walnuts or pecans, chopped*

1. Preheat oven to 350°.
2. Sift the flour, baking powder, baking soda, salt, and cinnamon together.
3. Mix the egg, sugar, margarine, and buttermilk together and stir into the dry ingredients. Fold in the nuts.

4. Pour into an oiled 9-inch loaf pan and bake for 40 minutes or until a knife inserted in the center comes out clean.
5. Cool before slicing.

Zucchini Bread
Serves 24

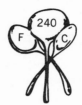

3 eggs
1 cup corn oil
1 cup sugar
3 cups zucchini, grated
1 teaspoon vanilla
3 cups flour
1½ teaspoons baking powder
1 teaspoon baking soda
1½ teaspoons cinnamon
1 teaspoon salt
1 cup walnuts, chopped
1 cup raisins

1. Preheat oven to 350°.
2. Beat the eggs and oil and add the sugar.
3. Add the grated zucchini and mix well.
4. Add the vanilla and stir thoroughly.
5. Sift all the dry ingredients and add to the zucchini mixture one-third at a time, beating thoroughly after each dilution.
6. Add the walnuts and raisins and mix thoroughly.
7. Pour into 2 loaf pans which have been greased with vegetable oil or sprayed with vegetable oil spray.
8. Bake in 350° oven for 1 hour or until a knife inserted in the middle comes out clean.
9. Invert on a rack and slice when cool.

Calories/Cholesterol/Saturated Fat Content Chart

(Vegetables and fruits do not generally have cholesterol or saturated fat except as listed)

Food Item	Measure	Calories	Cholesterol (milligrams)	Saturated Fat* (grams)
Avocado	1 medium	370	0	7
Bacon	2 slices	80	9	2.5
Bacon, Canadian	2 slices	60	20	1
Beef				
Lean cooked	3 ounces	180	75	4
Medium cooked	3 ounces	270	80	10
Bread, white	1 slice	70	0	0
Brownies	1 2-inch square	115	30	2
Butter	1 tablespoon	110	35	7
Cake				
Yellow	1 2-inch slice	180	33	2
Angel Food	1 2-inch slice	110	0	0
Cheese				
Cheddar	1 ounce	115	28	5
Cottage (low-fat)	1 cup	165	12	1
Cream	1 ounce	115	35	6
Mozzarella (low-fat)	1 ounce	75	17	3
Parmesan	1 ounce	108	27	5
Swiss	1 ounce	105	28	4

Chicken				
½ Breast (no skin)	3 ounces	135	70	1
Thigh (no skin)	2 ounces	110	50	1
Drumstick (no skin)	1 ounce	55	25	0.5
Chocolate, sweet	1 ounce	140	0	8
Cocoa	4 tablespoons	130	0	0
Codfish, cooked	3 ounces	105	55	0
Crab	4 ounces	105	110	0
Cream				
Half-and-Half	1 tablespoon	20	6	1
Sour	1 tablespoon	45	8	2
	4 ounces	360	64	16
Eggs				
Whole	1	80	252	2
Yolk	1	65	252	2
White	1	15	0	0
Flounder, cooked	3 ounces	105	55	0.5
Frankfurter	1 (8 per pound)	190	52	7
Halibut, cooked	3 ounces	105	55	0.5
Ice Cream				
Regular (12% fat)	1 cup	275	53	8
Rich (18% fat)	1 cup	340	68	10
Ice Milk	1 cup	100	19	4
Lamb, cooked	3 ounces	270	80	10
Lard	1 tablespoon	115	13	5

Liver				
Beef, cooked	3 ounces	100	370	0
Chicken, cooked	3 ounces	135	635	0
Lobster, ½ broiled	8 ounces	210	205	0
Macaroni/Spaghetti	1 cup	190	0	0
Margarine	1 tablespoon	110	0	2–3
Mayonnaise	1 tablespoon	110	10	2
Milk				
Whole	8 ounces	160	33	5
Low-fat (2%)	8 ounces	140	15	3
Nonfat (1%)	8 ounces	85	2	0
Evaporated				
Whole	8 ounces	345	66	11
Skim	8 ounces	170	4	0
Condensed	8 ounces	980	105	15
Buttermilk	8 ounces	90	8	0
Muffins	1 average	140	24	1
Noodles, whole egg, cooked	1 cup	195	50	1
Nuts				
Peanuts	½ ounce	65	0	1
	½ cup	420	0	8
Walnuts	½ ounce	70	0	0
	½ cup	395	0	2
Soybeans, roasted	½ ounce	20	0	0
Oysters	13–19 medium, 4–6 large, or 1 cup	150	120	0

Food	Serving	Calories	Cholesterol	Saturated Fat
Pancakes	1 4-inch diameter	50	18	0
Peanut Butter	1 tablespoon	95	0	1
Pie, apple	1/6 of 9-inch pie	250	0	5
Pork, cooked	3 ounces	290	75	8
Potatoes	1 cup	130	0	0
Pudding, chocolate (made with whole milk)	1 cup	385	30	7
Salad Dressing				
Mayonnaise	1 tablespoon	110	10	2
Oil & Vinegar; French; and Italian	1 tablespoon	65	0	1
Salmon, cooked	3 ounces	140	40	1.5
Scallops	3 ounces	100	48	1
Sherbet	1 cup	260	7	0
Shrimp	4 ounces; 22 large or 26 small	125	170	0
Soup (canned)				
Cream, prepared with whole milk	1 cup	175	16	3
Cream, prepared with water	1 cup		3–5	1
Cream, prepared with skim milk	1 cup	135	5–7	1
Sweetbreads	3 ounces	160	396	0

Trout	3 ounces	105	55	0
Tuna	3 ounces	170	60	3
Turkey	3 ounces	140	70	1
Veal	3 ounces	135	85	2
Vegetable Oil	1 tablespoon	110	0	3
Vegetable Oils				
Coconut	1 tablespoon	135	0	16
Corn	1 tablespoon	135	0	1
Cottonseed	1 tablespoon	135	0	4
Olive	1 tablespoon	135	0	2
Peanut	1 tablespoon	135	0	3
Safflower	1 tablespoon	135	0	1
Soybean	1 tablespoon	135	0	2
Waffle	1 7-inch diameter	170	90	1
Yogurt, low-fat	8 ounces	120	17	2

*rounded to nearest 0.5 g.

Index

Alcohol, in diet, 26
Antipasto, 74–75
Appetizers:
  Antipasto, 74–75
  Asparagus Foldovers, 66
  Avocado Dip, 64
  Blue Cheese Wonders, 72
  Breaded Vegetable Medley, 80
  Carrots, Marinated, 77
  Celery, Stuffed, 74
  Chicken Wings, Cocktail, 68
  Chicken Wings, Sweet and Sour, 66
  Clams, Deviled, 75
  Cucumbers, Stuffed, 76
  Dill Dip, 64
  Eggplant Caviar, 76
  Eggs in Aspic, 73
  Eggs, Stuffed, 72
  Frito Misto, 82
  Guacamole, 64–65
  Hoummus, 65
  Mushroom Caviar, 78
  Mushroom Pâté, 78
  Mushrooms à la Grecque, 79
  Mushrooms, Stuffed, 81
  Olives, Herbed Antipasto, 77
  Onion Rounds, 70
  Oysters Rockefeller, 68
  Peanut Butter Chutney Spread, 67
  Peppers, Roast, 79
  Pot Stickers, 69
  Quesadillas, 72–73
  Salsa, 65
  Seviche, 70
  Sweet and Sour Meatballs, 71
  Tuna Cream, 67
  Vegetable Dip, 67
Apple(s):
  Baked Carrots and, 184
  Crisp, 298
  Muffins, 308
  Red Cabbage and, 182

Tart, 296
Applesauce Cake, Chocolate, 282–83
Apricot(s):
Sauce, 276
Soup, Cold, 84
Artichoke(s), 159–60
Boiled, 160
Bottoms Stuffed with Spinach, 162
in Chicken Jerusalem, 106–107
Parmesan, 161
Shrimp Stuffed, 161
Asparagus, 158, 162
Benedict, 163
in the Chinese Manner, 163
Foldovers, 66
and Mushrooms Stir-Fry, 166
Newburg, 164
Papillote, 164–65
Parmesan, 165
Piccata, 165
Polanaise, 166
Sole, 131
Vinaigrette, 166–67
Avocado:
Bisque, 88
Dip, 64
Guacamole, 64–65
in Guacamole Tomatoes, 234–35

Banana(s):
Flambé, 299
Nut Bread, 314
Peanut Jumble, 298–99
Beans, Dried, 167
Boston Baked, 168
Chili with, 168
Fava Beans Extraordinaire, 168–69

Garbanzos Elena, 169
Beef, 19, 22, 135–36
Bourguignon, 137
Brittany, 136–37
and Broccoli, Stir-Fried, 140–41
Carbonnade, 138
Cooking Methods, 136
Esterhazy, 138–39
Flank Steak Mary Linda, 141
Flank Steak Teriyaki, 141
Hamburger with Mushroom Sauce, 142
Lasagna, 227
Meat Loaf Meringue, 142
Pot Stickers, 69
Stroganoff, 140
Sweet and Sour Meatballs, 71
Swiss Steak, 144–45
Beer:
Mustard, 267
Sauce for Fish, 122
Soufflé, 120
Beets, 172
Baked, 174
Borscht, 92
Harvard, 174
Minted, 173
Moldau, 173
à l'Orange, 174–75
Bouillabaisse, 119
Breads and Muffins, 26, 307
Apple Muffins, 308
Banana Nut Bread, 314
Boston Brown Bread, 312
Caraway Tea Loaf, 279, 316
Carrot Bread, 314–15
Coffee Can Bread, 310–11
Corn Bread, 312–13
Crumpets, 310
Date Nut Bread, 313

Dilly Bread, 311
Fruit-Flavored Oatmeal Bread,
    316–17
Gingerbread, 315
Honey Tea Bread, 318
Ice-Box Bran Muffins, 308–309
Nut Bread, 318–19
Oatmeal Bread, 317
Raisin Scones, 309
Zucchini Bread, 319
Breakfast Suggestions, 47–52
Broccoli, 157, 158, 175
    Amandine, 176
    Cold, with Warm Hollandaise,
        176–77
    Creamed, 178
    Moutarde, 178–79
    Sauté, 177
    Smetana, 177
    Steamed, 176
Brussels Sprouts, 179
    with Caraway Seeds, 179
    Supreme, 180
Butter, 19, 20, 21, 27
    margarine as substitute for, 19,
        20, 21
Buttermilk, 24
    Dressing, 260
    Pie, 294
    Vegetable Dip, 67

Cabbage, 158, 180
    Colcannon, 181
    Cole Slaw, 245
    Fruited Slaw, 246
    Red Cabbage and Apples, 182
    Royale, 181
    Tarragon, 182
Cakes:
    Angel Food, 280

Aunt Nell's Fruit, 285
Bette's Carrot, 282
Burnt Leather, 280–81
Chocolate Applesauce, 282–83
Chocolate Cheesecake, 284–85
Chocolate Pound, 284
Pound, 286
Prune, 286–87
Spice, 288
White, 283
Calorie Charts, 30–31, 320–24
Carrot(s), 157, 158, 182–83
    Baked, and Apples, 184
    Baked Garlicky, 184
    Bread, 314–15
    Deviled, 183
    Glazed, 183
    Marinated, 77
    and Rutabaga Purée, 228
    Scalloped, and Potatoes, 184
Cauliflower, 185
    Amandine, 186
    Pudding, 187
    with Salsa Verde, 186
Celery, 158, 187
    Braised, 188
    Stuffed, 74
    Vinaigrette, 188–89
Cheese, 24
    in Avocado Dip, 64
    Blue Cheese Sauce, 276
    Blue Cheese Wonders, 72
    Chocolate Cheesecake, 284–85
    Cottage Cream, 275
    Pineapple Cheese Pie, 295
    Quesadillas, 72–73
    Roquefort Dressing, 260–61
Cherries Jubilee, 279, 297
Chicken, 19, 23, 99
    Breast Citron, 105

Breasts with Mushroom Sauce, 106
Cacciatore, 111
Cashew, 101
Chinese Almond, 103
Coq au Vin, 109
Cynthia, 110–11
Hawaiian, 104
Honey-Glazed Barbecued Soy, 105
Jerusalem, 106–107
à la King, 107
Paprikash, 112–13
Roast, with Almond Dressing, 100
Roast, Niçoise, 100–101
Roast, with Spring Vegetables, 102
Salads, 242–44
Sesame, 110
Sherried, and Rice, 112
Soufflé, 108
Tangy, 113
Teriyaki, 104
Wings, Cocktail, 68
Wings, Sweet and Sour, 66
Chili with Beans, 168
Chocolate:
Applesauce Cake, 282–83
Brownies, 289
Cheesecake, 284–85
Graham Cracker Crust, 284–85, 293
Pound Cake, 284
Pudding, 302
Cholesterol, 15–16
Charts, 320–24
Diet Modification, 18–29
Diets, 37–38
Link with Heart Disease, 17–18
Low-Cholesterol Substitutes, 25–26
Serum, Acceptable Levels, 18
Suggested Intake, 39–40
Chutney:
Fruit, 270
Pear, 269
Cioppino, 117
Cookies:
Almond Meringue, 289
Biscotti D'Anice Gurka, 287
Brownies, 289
Dorothy's Oatmeal, 291
Hermits, 290
Nutty Crisps, 290
Old-Fashioned Peanut Butter, 291
Corn, 189
on the Barbecue, 189
Creole, 190
Fritters, 190
Puffs, 191
Cornish Game Hens with Wild Rice Stuffing, 114
Coronary Atherosclerosis, 14–15, 18
Overweight as Factor, 32
Risk Factors, 14, 16–17
Cucumbers, 191
Marinated, 192
Sautéed, 192
Stuffed, 76

Dairy Products, 24
Substitutes, 25–26
Diets:
for Adults, 35–36
for Children, 32–34
Low-Cholesterol, 18–29, 37–38
for Teen-Agers, 34–35

for Weight Reduction, 28–29
Dill Dip, 64
Duck, 23, 99
  with Olives, 115

Eggplant, 192–93
  Caviar, 76
  Imam Bayildi, 194
  Parmesan, 193
  Ratatouille, 194–95
Eggs, 19, 20, 22, 24–25, 28
  in Aspic, 73
  Equivalents, 25
  Fritatta, 211
  Stuffed, 72
  Whole, 19, 20, 22
Endive, 158, 196
  Hearts, Braised, 196
  Par Excellence, 196–97

Fat, Saturated, 20–21, 27, 32
  Charts, 320–24
  Diets, 18–29, 37–38
  Suggested Intake, 39–40
Fillings and Frostings:
  for Bette's Carrot Cake, 282
  for Burnt Leather Cake, 280–81
  Holiday Filling, 279, 288
Fish. *See* Seafood
Fisherman's Stew, 118
Fritatta, 211
Frito Misto, 82
Fruit:
  Ambrosia, 297
  Chutney, 270
  Compote, Hot Spiced, 299
  Flavored Oatmeal Bread, 316–17
  See also individual listings

Green Beans, 169–70

Amandine, 170
Casserole, 170
Herbed, 171
  with Mushrooms, 206
  with Mushrooms and Onions,
    172
Rivigote, 171
Greens, 197
  Mixed, 199
  See also Salads, Spinach
Guacamole, 64–65

Ham Pilaf, 224
Hoummus, 65

Ices, Ice Milks, and Sherbets, 24
  Coffee Ice, 303
  Iced Lemon Meringue, 305
  Orange Sherbet, 304
  Plum Ice Milk, 304–305
  Water Ices, 303
Ideal Weight Tables, 29–30
Imam Bayildi, 194

Kitchen Equipment, 57–61
  Appliances, 61
  Cookware, 59–60
  Cutlery, 60–61
  Gadgets, 57–59
  Utensils, 61
Kohlrabi, 200–201
  au Gratin, 202
  Herbed, 201
  Sunkissed, 201

Lamb, 19, 22, 135
  Boulangère, 151
  Butterflied Barbecued, 152
  Curry, 152–53
  Dilled Boats, 153

Lobscouse, 93
Noisettes of, 151
Rack of, Cumberland, 149
Roast, with Mint Sauce, 148
Shanks, 154
Shish Kabob, 149
Spring, with Vegetables, 150
Leeks, 158, 202
Braised, Persillade, 203
au Gratin, 204
Pickled, 203
Legumes. *See* Beans, Dried
Liver, 22
Lobscouse, 93

Margarine, 19, 20, 21
Mayonnaise à la Maison, 272
Meats, 22–23. *See also* individual
    listings
Menus:
Breakfast, 47–52
Dinner, 40–46
Milk:
Low-fat, 24
Nonfat, 24, 34
Whole, 19
Mincemeat Aspic, 257
Mushroom(s), 204–205
Asparagus and, Stir-Fry, 166
Caviar, 78
à la Grecque, 79
and Green Beans, 206
with Green Beans and Onions,
    172
Monterey, 205
Pâté, 78
Salads, 246, 249, 252–53
Sauce, for Chicken, 106
Sauce, for Hamburger, 142
Sautéed, 205
Stuffed, 81

Trout Stuffed with, 132–33
and Zucchini Casserole, 206

Nondairy Creamers, 25–26

Okra, 207
Diable, 207
Sautéed, 207
Olives:
Antipasto, 74–75
Herbed, Antipasto, 77
Onion(s), 208
Baked, 209
Boiled White, 208–209
Braised with Madeira, 210
Rings, 212
Rounds, 70
Sautéed, 210
Steamed Green, 209
Stir-Fried Peppers and, 216–17
Stuffed, 210–11
Oyster Stew, 118

Parsnips, 212
in Cider, 212–13
Pasta, 220–21
Lasagna, 227
Linguine with Clam Sauce, 226
Spaghetti with Zucchini and
    Tomato Sauce, 226
Peaches Cardinale, 300
Peanut Butter, 26
Chutney Spread, 67
Cookies, 291
Pear(s):
Chutney, 269
Helene, 300–301
Poached, in Red Wine, 301
Tart, 296
Peas, 213
Italian, 214

with Lettuce and Onions, 214
Stir-Fried Snow Peas and Water
    Chestnuts, 215
Peppers, 215–16
    Corn-Stuffed, 216
    in Eggplant Caviar, 76
    in Quesadillas, 72–73
    Roast, 79
    in Salsa, 65
    Stir-Fried, and Onions, 216–17
Pies, Tarts, and Pie Crusts:
    Apple Tart, 296
    Buttermilk Pie, 294
    Chocolate Graham Cracker
        Crust, 292–93
    Davis Pie, 293
    Graham Cracker Crust, 292–93
    Lemon-Lime Chiffon Pie, 295
    Pear Tart, 296
    Pie Crust, 292
    Pineapple Cheese Pie, 295
    Velvet Cheese Pie, 294
Pineapple Cheese Pie, 294
Pork, 19, 22, 135
    Roast, with Prunes, 154–55
    Steaks Jaime, 155
Potato(es), 157, 158, 217
    Colcannon, 181
    Florentine, 218
    Lemon, 220
    Lyonnaise, 218
    Scalloped, 219
    Scalloped Carrots and, 184
    Steamed New, Germaine, 219
    Sunshine, 220
    See also Sweet Potatoes, Yams
Pot Stickers, 69
Poultry. *See* Chicken, Duck, Turkey
Puddings:
    Chocolate, 302
    Persimmon, 302

Rita's Rice, 306

Quesadillas, 72–73

Rice, 220–21
    Grape Pilaf, 224–25
    Ham Pilaf, 224
    Pilau Istanbul, 223
    Provençal, 222
    Pudding, 306
    Risotto, 225
    Sherried Chicken and Steamed,
        222
    Wild Rice and Pecans, 221
    Wild Rice Stuffing, 114
Rutabaga, 227
    Carrot and, Purée, 228
    au Gratin, 228

Salad Dressings, 240
    Basic Oil and Vinegar, 258
    Basil, 253
    Boiled, 259
    Buttermilk, 260
    Ingall's, 260
    Pignolia, 261
    Roquefort, 260–61
    Shallot, 252–53
    Sherried French, 262
    for Spinach Salad, 254
    Tarragon, 259
    White Wine, 261
Salads, 240
    Apple, Pickled, 241
    Caesar, 252
    Chicken, Chinese, 242
    Chicken, Indian Curried, 244
    Chicken, Mexican, 243
    Chicken, Yankee, 244
    Cole Slaw, 245
    Cole Slaw, Fruited, 246

Cucumber, 245
Cucumber, Dilled, 245
Green, with Basil Dressing, 253
Green Bean, 241
Macaroni, 246–47
Molded Carrot, 256
Molded Gazpacho, 256–57
"Moose" Wood, 258
Mushroom, Fresh, 249
Mushroom, Spanish, 246
Mushroom and Zucchini,
    252–53
Olive, 250
Orange and Onion, 250
Polynesian, 249
Pomegranate, 248
Potato, with Caraway Seed, 251
Potato, German, 250–51
Rice, Spiced, 247
Rice, Vinaigrette, 248
Spinach, 254
Tuna, 254
Tuna Tarragon, 253
Tuna Veronique, 255
Vegetable, 255
Salsa, 65
Sauces, 263
Almond, for Trout, 134
Apricot, 276
Beer, for Fish, 122
Blue Cheese, 276
Brown, 264
Cardinale, 277
Cheese, for Baked Zucchini, 232
Chocolate, 278
Clam, for Linguine, 226
Cottage Cream, 275
Cucumber, for Salmon, 124
Cumberland, 265
Fish, Herbed, 267
Fruit Chutney, 270

Gravy, 266
Hollandaise, 273
Lemon, 278
Madeira, 274
Maltaise, 275
Mayonnaise à la Maison, 272
Mint, for Lamb, 265
Mushroom, for Chicken, 106
Mushroom, for Hamburger, 142
Mustard, Beer, 267
Mustard, Golden 267
Orange, for Fowl, 268
Pear Chutney, 269
Pesto, 270
Plum, Gingered, 268–69
Plum, Spiced, 268
Ravigote, 274
Salsa, 65
Salsa Verde, Cauliflower with,
    186
Sour Topping, 274
Teriyaki, 271
Tomato-Leek, 271
Vanilla, 277
Vanilla, Quick, 276
Vinaigrette, 272–73
Whipped Topping, 277
White, 264
Zucchini and Tomato, 226
Seafood, 19, 23–24, 116
in Beer Sauce, 122
Beer Soufflé, 120
Bouillabaisse, 119
Cioppino, 117
Clam Sauce, Linguine with, 226
Clams, Deviled, 75
Fisherman's Stew, 118
Halibut, Broiled in Vermouth,
    121
Halibut, Curried, 122–23
Halibut, Dilled, 123

Halibut, Maltaise, 121
Oyster Stew, 118
Oysters Rockefeller, 68
Red Snapper Aloha, 125
Red Snapper, Baked, 125
Red Snapper, Spinach-Stuffed, 126
Rock Cod with Tartar Meringue, 130–31
Salmon with Cucumber Sauce, 124
Salmon Moutarde, 124
Sea Bass à l'Espagnole, 128
Sea Bass, Plaki, 127
Seviche, 70
Shrimp, Flaming, 128–29
Shrimp Scampi, 127
Shrimp Stuffed Artichokes, 161
Shrimp Tuscany, 130
Sole Apollo, 129
Sole Asparagus, 131
Sole à la Florentine, 132
Sole Meunière, 134
Squid Cutlets, 133
Trout with Almond Sauce, 134
Trout Stuffed with Mushrooms, 132–33
Tuna Cream, 67
Tuna Salad, 254
Tuna Salad Veronique, 255
Tuna Tarragon, 253
Soups and Stocks, 83
Apricot, Cold, 84
Avocado Bisque, 88
Barley, 96
Borscht, 92
Carrot, Curried, 90
Carrot and Leek, 88
Celery, Cream of, 90
Chicken Gumbo, 95
Chicken Soups, 86, 87, 95

Chicken Stock, 87
Chinese, 96–97
Corn Chowder, 97
Court Bouillon, 266
Cucumber, Cold, 84
Far East, 97
Fish Stock, 263, 266
French Onion, 93
Gazpacho, 85
Italian, 92–93
Lobscouse, 93
Minestrone, 94
Mushroom Consommé, 84–85
Mushroom, Cream of, 89
Oriental Goodness, 94–95
Pea, 98
Potato Chowder, 98
Potato, Cream of, 89
Senegalese, 86
Spinach, Cream of, 91
Tomato Bisque, 86–87
Winter Squash Bisque, 90–91
Spinach, 157, 158, 197
Artichokes Stuffed with, 162
Braised, 198
Puréed, 198–99
Salad, 254
Steamed, 198
Timbale, 200
Tomatoes Stuffed with, 236
Squash, 157, 228–29
Baked Winter, 231
Gracie's Baked Acorn, 229
à la Italienne, 231
Sugar, in Diet, 26, 28, 34
Sweet Potatoes, 238
Exotic, 239
Puréed, 239.
See also Yams
Tomato(es), 232
Allison's Favorite, 233

Chili, 235
Dijon, 234
Guacamole, 234–35
Herbed Rings, 233
Ratatouille, 194–95
Sautéed Green, 235
Stuffed, à la Schroeder, 236–37
Stuffed, with Spinach, 236
Turkey, 19, 23, 99
  Marinated Legs, 114
  Roast, 115
Turnips, 157, 237
  Scalloped, 237

Veal, 19, 22, 135
  Goulash, 144
  Marengo, 143
  Piccata, 146
  Quincy, 146–47
  Scallopine Ryan, 145
  Smetana, 147
  Tarragon, 148
Vegetable(s), 22, 156–59
  Breaded Medley, 80
  Carousel, 156, 195

Dip for, 67
  Fritatta, 211
  Frito Misto, 82
  Ratatouille, 156, 194–95
Vegetable Oils, 19, 21, 27

Weight-Reduction Programs,
  28–29, 37–38
Wild Rice:
  and Pecans, 221
  Stuffing, 114

Yams, 238
  Candied, 238
  Roast, 238–39
  See also Sweet Potatoes

Yogurt, 24

Zucchini, 228–29
  Baked, with Cheese Sauce, 232
  Bread, 319
  and Mushroom Casserole, 206
  Spaghetti with Zucchini and
    Tomato Sauce, 226
  Stuffed, el Rundo, 230